HOCKOMOCK
PLACE WHERE THE SPIRITS DWELL

PETER TOWER

Library of Congress Control Number: 2013951937

Designed by John P. Cheek
Cover design by Bruce Waters
Type set in Avenir 85 Heavy/NewBskvll BT

ISBN: 978-0-7643-4515-9
Printed in The United States of America

Published by Schiffer Publishing, Ltd.
4880 Lower Valley Road
Atglen, PA 19310
Phone: (610) 593-1777; Fax: (610) 593-2002
E-mail: Info@schifferbooks.com

For our complete selection of fine books on this and related subjects, please visit our website at www.schifferbooks.com. You may also write for a free catalog.

This book may be purchased from the publisher. Please try your bookstore first.

We are always looking for people to write books on new and related subjects. If you have an idea for a book, please contact us at proposals@schifferbooks.com.

Schiffer Publishing's titles are available at special discounts for bulk purchases for sales promotions or premiums. Special editions, including personalized covers, corporate imprints, and excerpts can be created in large quantities for special needs. For more information, contact the publisher.

THIS BOOK IS FOR ALL THOSE WHO
SAW, SPOKE, AND PAID THE PRICE.

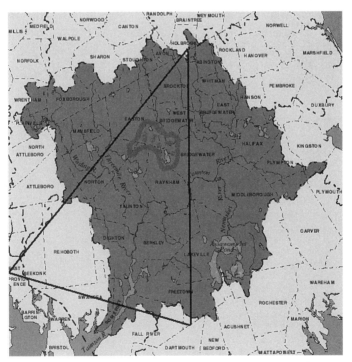

Taunton River Watershed (shaded gray), Bridgewater Triangle, and
Hockomock Swamp.

ACKNOWLEDGMENTS

I gratefully acknowledge the help of the following people: my wife, for her faith in my work and for assuming without complaint the many duties that I neglected while writing this book; my publisher, Peter Schiffer, and my editor, Dinah Roseberry, for making this book a reality; Loren Coleman, for originally bringing the Bridgewater Triangle and many of the events that I explore in this book to the attention of the public; The Old Bridgewater Historical Society, for access to their valuable collections; Kathleen Anderson, for her knowledge of the natural history of the Hockomock, and for inspiring me with her dauntless spirit; Joseph M. DeAndrade, for showing me around the Hockomock and for his personal insight into the area; Father Robert Edson, for spiritual guidance and for introducing me to the genius of Emanuel Swedenborg; Dr. Curtiss Hoffman, Jean-Jacques Rivard, and the staff of the Massachusetts Archaeological Society, for their expertise on Native American culture and the history of the Hockomock region; Jerry Lopes and Steve Sbraccia, for sharing their UFO experience with me; Wayne Southworth, Sr., for teaching me about water; Robert Oldale, for his fine book on Geology: *Cape Cod, Martha's Vineyard & Nantucket, the Geologic Story*; Wayne Legge, for sharing his personal experiences and archaeological finds, and for providing me access to an historical Hockomock "farm"; John Ames III and his wife, Sarah, for graciously sharing their personal recollections and excerpts from the diary of Oliver Ames, Jr.; Marla Taylor of the R. S. Peabody Museum, for helping me research Professor Edmund Burke Delabarre; Ed Hayward, for inspiring me to get out and knock on doors; Walter Mirrione, for putting me in touch with key local people; Attorneys Ed Reservitz and Joseph Krowski, for helping me understand the Commonwealth vs. Kater case; Tom Downey, for trusting me enough to write his story; and last but not least, Stephanie, for helping me to persevere amidst uncertainty by firmly stating:

"*That's* the book *I* want to read."

CONTENTS

HOCKOMOCK Swamp

PREFACE

The Hockomock region has a long, rich history of events involving unexplained phenomena. This book is my attempt to put these events in context, both historically and universally.

Many of the best-known events in this region occurred in the 1970s and early 1980s, which was an extremely active time in the Hockomock, as well as in other hot spots of paranormal activity worldwide. These periods of intense paranormal activity are known as "flaps," and are relatively rare. I have chosen to portray a select few of these events in the latter part of this book: those that I feel are representative of the types of events that have occurred historically in the region and also those that I found to be the most credible instances of their type. Most of these occurrences, such as the Thunderbird sighting, involve paranormal phenomena of a universal nature. Other mysteries featured here, such as those in "Dighton Rock," "Grassy Island," and "Kater IV," are unique to the Hockomock region.

All of the modern events in this book actually happened. Although I have exercised significant poetic license in narrating them, in all cases I have attempted to stay true to the known facts, which I derived either from the firsthand, oral testimony of the witnesses involved or from documented historical sources, such as newspaper articles. In a few places, I have changed the names of witnesses for their privacy.

I have delineated with italics those sections of the book that are historical fiction or purely imaginative, such as the conversations involving Hobbamock and other spirits.

For the most part, I have chosen to omit events involving traditional ghosts, largely because the spirits I consider to be most important to Hockomock's mythology do not conform to Western culture's conception of a ghost as the spirit of a deceased, recognizable human. I also feel that the topic of ghosts has been adequately treated in other works on the area.

Finally, although this book ends with the "flap" of the 1970s to the 1980s, I do not mean to imply that similarly-strange events completely ceased in the Hockomock region after this time or that I do not believe they will someday return in full force. In fact, my hope is that this book will help to establish the idea that the Hockomock is, was, and always will be the "Place Where the Spirits Dwell."

INTRODUCTION

Hockomock: an Algonquian Indian word that has historically been interpreted to mean "place where the spirits dwell." If you break the word down, you get *hock-*, meaning "body," and *-komuck*, meaning "structure" or "enclosure." Therefore, a more literal interpretation of *Hockomock* is "body enclosure" or "place where the bodies are on structures." Regardless of the exact meaning of *Hockomock*, one gets the general idea. Historically, the Hockomock Swamp was a place where the Wampanoag Tribe, the easternmost branch of the Algonquians, buried their dead.

Today, the Hockomock Swamp is a 6,000-acre conservation area used recreationally by hunters, fishermen, canoeists, bikers, birders, scientists, and other, diverse groups. It lays just thirty miles south of the bustling metropolis of Boston, Massachusetts, within the borders of the southeastern Massachusetts towns of West Bridgewater, Bridgewater, Easton, Norton, Raynham, and Taunton. The swamp is the largest remaining wetland in Massachusetts, and one of the largest in all of New England. Thousands of commuters pass the Hockomock in their automobiles each day, but, ironically, intent on the many distractions of modern life, few of them realize that the vast wetland even exists.

The Hockomock Swamp is also the heart of what paranormalists, or those who study the supernatural, call the "Bridgewater Triangle"—a 200-square-mile area world-renowned for unexplained phenomena, including sightings of UFOs and mystery creatures, as well as being the place of many unsolved murders and disappearances. Because these events, as well as other mysteries, occur so often there, the Bridgewater Triangle has become known to paranormalists as the hot spot for paranormal events in all of New England. The apex of the Bridgewater Triangle is the southeastern Massachusetts town of Abington, and the corners below it are the towns of Rehoboth to the southwest and Freetown to the southeast.

The sense in which I have chosen to address the Hockomock, however, is as a region, larger than both the Hockomock Swamp and the Bridgewater Triangle, and one characterized by a similar cultural and natural history. This Hockomock region roughly equates to the forty-three cities and towns that fall within the Taunton River watershed.

The Hockomock Swamp is occasionally referred to as the "Hobbamock Swamp." Although the Indian words *Hockomock* and *Hobbamock* mean completely different things, this variation of the swamp's name occurs for good reason. Hobbamock was the Wampanoag name for the evil god of death and disease. This deity was composed of souls of the human dead. Hobbamock was known to congregate in large numbers in swamps, and in particular, in the Hockomock Swamp.

When the English Pilgrims arrived in Plymouth in 1620, the local Wampanoags worshipped approximately thirty-eight gods, including the Creator, who was known to them as Kiehtan or Cautantowwit. However, their main god—the one to whom they turned the most—was Hobbamock. At the time the Pilgrims landed, the Wampanoag people were living in terror of this evil deity. One reason for this was that Hobbamock continuously frightened them, mostly at night, with apparitions in the form of their most-feared enemies, such as warriors of the Mohawk Tribe or strange mythical creatures.

Early English writers noted that even the brave Wampanoag warriors were so afflicted by these apparitions that they refused to leave their wetus, or huts, to travel after nightfall. Apparently this was the case even in the event of dire necessity, such as when they were under threat of imminent attack. The other reason that the Wampanoag people lived in terror of Hobbamock was related to their priests, or shamans.

Hobbamock's power was brokered by the Indian priests, or shamans, who used the supernatural powers they obtained from this deity in conjunction with medicinal and psychological methods to heal people when they were ill. The shamans also used these powers to inflict death on their own personal enemies and on the enemies of the tribe.

There is sufficient documented evidence from the period to support the belief that by 1620, many shamans in the local tribes were using these powers to hold their people in a state of constant fear and to increase their personal stature in the community. The Wampanoag shamans, also known as "powwows," were highly influential military and political advisors to the sachems, including the great chief of the Wampanoag's, Massasoit. The shamans communed with Hobbamock in the spirit world and brought his guidance to Massasoit, who actively used it to form his decisions when dealing with the newly-arrived English Pilgrims at Plymouth.

The Christian Pilgrims equated Hobbamock with the Devil. This assessment, though not technically accurate, theologically, nonetheless was on the mark in characterizing Hobbamock as an evil deity. By the Wampanoags' own admissions to the Pilgrims, Hobbamock was an evil force, and some Indians even agreed with the Pilgrims' classification of the deity as the Devil. The exact concept of Hobbamock, which evaded William Bradford's Pilgrims, is a slippery one even today, for the idea of a single deity composed of multiple spirits is not well known in monotheistic religions.

The local tribes' emphasis on Hobbamock as their major deity in the early 1600s may not always have been the case. At previous times in their history, like other Indian tribes, such as the Sioux in the American West, the tribes in Massachusetts may well have placed emphasis on the worship of the Creator instead. The Creator was considered by most tribes to be a generally benevolent force, and was often closely associated with the chiefs, or sachems, as opposed to the priests. However, there is little doubt that by 1620 the religious balance of power in the Indian tribes of Massachusetts had shifted to Hobbamock and the shamans.

The fascinating story of the Town of Bridgewater, from its inception as a holy Christian settlement in the wilderness, through its transformations into agricultural, industrial, and finally suburban town, is irrevocably intertwined with both the history of the Hockomock and the fate of the American Indian. In a strange twist of fate, in 1645, Massasoit sold the Hockomock Swamp and the surrounding meadow lands to a group of English settlers from Duxbury, Massachusetts, as part of the purchase of the original Bridgewater "plantation." These settlers, many of whom were the sons and daughters of the Pilgrims at Plymouth, were among the most dedicated Christians in existence at the time.

The Bridgewater Book, written in 1899 (partly from earlier histories), characterizes the early settlement in the following manner:

> It is a significant fact that the first settlers of this town organized a church before they formed a civil government. The religious interests of human life were more important to them than the mere material welfare and comfort of life.

James Keith, the first minister of Bridgewater, was hand-picked for the position by Increase Mather, Cotton Mather's father, and adhered to the same strict Puritan views. It is hard to conceive of a greater religious divide between two groups than the one that must have existed in the 1600s between the devout Christian settlers of Bridgewater and Massasoit's pagan Wampanoags.

In 1675, Massasoit's son, Metacomet, who was known to the English as King Philip, set out to reclaim by military force the land that his father and other sachems sold to the English. In the ensuing conflict, which today is known as the King Philip's War, Metacomet's executive decisions were directly informed by his shamans, as his father's had been before him. Metacomet's War Chief was Tispaquin, a notorious sachem, who was also a shaman. Tispaquin's brutal attacks on the villages of the English settlers were directly influenced by the dreams and visions he received from the evil deity, Hobbamock.

It is a well-known historic fact that King Philip's Wampanoags successfully used the Hockomock Swamp as a base for their military operations. As a wild and nearly impenetrable place known only to the Indians, it was the perfect place from which to launch deadly surprise attacks on bordering English towns. What is less often considered historically is that the Hockomock Swamp, as home to the deity Hobbamock and thus holy ground for the Wampanoag shamans, must also have acted as a major spiritual center for the Wampanoag forces in the war.

There is little doubt that part of the Christian Pilgrims' justification for waging war on the Wampanoags and the other Indians in New England, at least privately, was the fact that the Wampanoags worshipped Hobbamock. Many contemporary accounts of King Philip's War portray it as basically a land-grab by the greedy Puritans, whose agricultural way of life combined with a growing population did necessitate the acquisition of more farmland. In truth, though, the war was as much a religious conflict as it was a practical one based on natural resources. The Pilgrims and the Puritans of the period, as evidenced by volumes of their preserved writings, truly believed that by engaging in war with the local tribes, they were doing their duty as Christians by battling the forces of the Devil.

The brutal and inhuman way in which this conflict was subsequently waged, by both sides, resulted in the deaths of a higher percentage of the local population, both English and Indian, than any other war in America's history. The war nearly annihilated the Indian population and culture in the area, and the tragic fact is that this brief, but bloody, early conflict served as a model to the expanding nation for methods of Indian fighting and treatment in the battles that were to come, including those fought in the American West. Thus, as the physical and perhaps spiritual epicenter of King Philip's War, the Hockomock Swamp and the historic Town of Bridgewater, jointly hold a unique and important place in American history.

"The Hock," as the Hockomock Swamp is known to locals today, is a place of incredible natural beauty. You can find the solace of nature there, just thirty miles south of a major city, especially on one of its several wild streams. The swamp abounds with diverse wildlife and plant species, including rare species, just as it has since the Wisconsin Ice Sheet departed and the land regenerated to its former splendor. There are dense stands of uncommon trees, such as Atlantic White cedars, and rare bog plants, such as colorful orchids, that bring heavenly grace to acres of damp sphagnum moss.

Local hunters say there are deer in the Hock that are tame because they have never seen a man. It is a place where two-and-a-half-foot turtles drift silently under your canoe, and ten-pound largemouth bass are not uncommon. The coyotes in the Hockomock run as big as wolves. It is a place where people can still pick wild cranberries in hidden wet meadows. Perhaps best of all are the roaring streams and vast networks of groundwater that all come together in the end to form the grand Taunton River—the vital waterway that first provided Paleolithic man entry to New England and today serves as the environmental heartbeat and ecological future of the entire Hockomock region.

However, there is a much darker side of the Hockomock…one that acts as a potent counterweight to all of this natural beauty. For the Hock, despite appearances, is still a place of death and disease. Death comes in many forms there, and not least from the mouths of mosquitoes carrying the infamous "Triple E" or Eastern Equine Encephalitis, a deadly, tragic disease that erupted in the 1950s and still has no cure. The Hock is undeniably a place where people disappear, and a place where people go to take their own lives. It is a place where drifters are found dead, shot-gunned in the back or bearing the signs of cruel torture. What's more, strange "apparitions" are still regularly seen in the Hock, some of which seem to differ very little from the "mythical creatures" that were witnessed by the terrorized Wampanoags in the early 1600s.

The many credible people who see legitimate, unexplained phenomena in the Hockomock today, however, are not sympathetically supported by their social group, as were the Wampanoags, or for that matter as were the traditional villagers of rural England, Scotland, or Ireland. Quite the opposite, they are publicly ostracized as lunatics or liars for reporting what they have witnessed. This common practice is not just a great injustice to the witnesses, but also to the rest of us, for it fosters ignorance by allowing us to safely dismiss what may be a vital part of our quest as humans to better understand our world and our place in the cosmos.

By the 1960s, the forces of evil that had followed the Christian Pilgrims to the New World in the form of Old World witches had discovered the Hockomock. Modern cults, reviving the ancient way of the shaman and supplementing it with modern psychedelic drugs, found the Hockomock to be a ready conduit to the spirit world, just as the Wampanoag shamans had found it to be millennia before: the torch-lit ceremonies were summoned from the deep past, the chanting was resumed, and the pentagrams were laid down in the secret recesses of the swamp. Even today, some locals believe that Satanic cults are involved, on some level, with many of the mysterious and often ultra-violent events that occur regularly in the Hockomock region. Whether this is the case or not, the extent of the hidden costs that are imposed on our society by the evil activities of Satanic cults in general is a deeply troubling mystery in its own right.

My own personal journey through the Hockomock was a long, strange, and, at times, very frightening one. Most of the time I welcomed the fear, because one of the reasons I set out to write this book was that I had a strong desire to confront fear, to test myself against it, and to truly *understand* it. I found fear in the Hock—and much more than I had bargained for. What I eventually learned, through both my research and my own experiences, is that fear is a thing of itself, that arises unbidden in even the bravest man. When you are in a truly dangerous situation, there is no question that fear will find you. Fear is a natural defense mechanism that is intended to help preserve your well being. The key to your mission's success, and sometimes to your physical and mental survival, is how well you assess and react to that fear. In other words, everything depends on how you *manage* it.

Personally, I learned much from Charles Lindberg's philosophy of managing fear. This was a philosophy that he developed to manage the fear that he inevitably experienced while setting out on the world's first great airplane voyages. As another means of coping with fear, I learned and adopted many of the practical means by which man has traditionally tried to insure his safety. Ultimately, though, I turned myself over to the Lord Jesus Christ for my main strength and protection.

I consider myself to be as brave as the next man, but I am not ashamed to admit that I was afraid on many occasions while working on this book. Sometimes, unaccountably, I became afraid simply by writing the words you are about to read. As

I studied truly evil people and their ways, I became afraid for the world and for all the good people in it.

I discovered that the war between good and evil is real. It is not something that is found just in the Hockomock, or relegated to the silver screen in fictional productions, such as *Star Wars* or *Ghost Rider*. This war is universal, deadly, and it is being waged continuously, even at this very moment. "Onward Christian soldiers" is not an empty poetic phrase. The thing that makes the Hockomock unique in this context is that, by all accounts, the area is, for some reason, a key battleground in this universal war, and apparently has been throughout history.

I believe there is an underlying spirit to every land, a spirit that helps form the relationship of its inhabitants to it and helps connect them to the spiritual world, and so for me, the Hockomock begs many questions, most notably:

- Can a place be inherently evil? If so, how, and why?
- What are the consequences, to all of us, of a place that is truly evil? Are they the ultra-violent and paranormal events so frequently experienced in the Hockomock region?
- Is it possible for an evil place, like those humans possessed by demons, to be cleansed of its evil?
- Are spirits responsible for many of these mysterious events, as paranormalists currently believe? If so, what kinds of spirits might they be? Could they be our own version of the mischievous and sometimes deadly nature spirits that were so well known to our race in old Europe? Or perhaps the malignant spirits of the evil human dead, as the local Wampanoags historically believed?

The list goes on. These are uncomfortable questions for us at best and questions to which there may ultimately be few answers, but in mankind's eternal quest for truth and understanding they are nonetheless well worth asking.

The Hockomock is a dangerous place on many levels. Those who know it well will tell you: "Don't go in there alone." I foolishly ignored that warning until I learned the hard way. To that wise piece of lore, I will not hesitate to add another, which is: "Don't go in there alone *spiritually*." I say this because I firmly believe that there are forces of evil in the Hockomock that are quite capable of destroying you and that their greatest desire is to do just that.

Now it is time for you to embark on your own journey through the Hockomock. It is a mysterious, dark passage that may forever change the way in which you view the world. In the end, I hope you find, as I did, that it was nonetheless a journey worth taking.

PETER TOWER

PART I: OLD TESTAMENT

GENESIS
23,000 B.C.

Our story begins, as it should, with fear, destruction, and death. For it was then, 25,000 years ago, that the Laurentide Ice Sheet in Canada reached critical mass, its bottom layer morphed to slush, and it began to slide, ever so slowly, towards New England. This moving mountain of ice scraped through the valleys of North America, brutally tearing off the sides of real mountains as it went. The ice tore up bedrock by the ton, cupped it in its lower layers, and carried it along for the ride. It eliminated vast forests, and sent all those creatures that could crawl, run, swim, or fly fleeing south for their lives. The ice then crushed and pulverized everything that remained.

Some 4,000 years later, towering about three-quarters of a mile high, the ice reached the Hockomock. The natural landscape it found may have been much the same as the one that exists today in Southeastern Massachusetts. The relentless wall of ice ground over the magnificent maples, spruce, pines, and oaks like God's bulldozer, reducing them to splinters, and tore deep into the soft, sedimentary bedrock left under the Hock from ancient seas and rivers. It tore the heart out of the land. The ice continued to move south, until finally it was halted by a warmer climate. The ice sheet reached its southern terminus—the area where, today, we find the islands of Nantucket and Martha's Vineyard.

The melting ice probably passed back over the Hockomock on its way north, to the Hudson Bay, sometime around 13,500 years ago. Meltwater flow into the Hockomock area accelerated as the glacier to the north continued to melt, and a very large glacial lake, which we now know as Glacial Lake Taunton, formed. This ancient lake, also sometimes referred to as the Leverett Sea, extended south into the town of Assonet in southern Massachusetts. There, it was likely dammed by rising ground, orphaned ice blocks, and masses of glacial till that were left by the retreating glacier.

Glacial Lake Taunton formed in the extremely ancient, topographical low area we call the Narragansett Basin. This basin was formed millions of years ago when Africa collided with the east coast of North America. The resulting geologic cataclysm is known as the Appalachian Revolution. The collision caused the tectonic plates that form our continent to smash violently together and ramp up into mountain ranges, such as the White Mountains of New Hampshire, or to collapse downward, forming basins or "rift valleys."

An ancient rift valley lays under the Taunton River, the main river that today drains the low-laying Hockomock wetlands. The Narragansett Basin extends south under Narragansett Bay, where the mouth of the Taunton River is now located. This ancient basin helped hold the waters of Lake Taunton. Glacial Lake

Taunton was one of possibly three similar lakes that existed after the Laurentide Ice left the Hockomock area—the others being in the towns of Bridgewater and Brockton—and only one of many left behind by the ice in New England.

Glacial Lake Taunton presided over the Hockomock in all its primal beauty for 300, maybe 400 years. Gigantic ice shards, the size of battleships, slammed about in its waters. The melting mass of ice lingering to the north continued to feed the lake. The land around the lake, if you could call it land at that point, was utterly destroyed. The passing ice sheet had been particularly hard on the soft bedrock of the Hockomock, in some places wrenching out hundreds of feet of it, and on its way back home, the ice had randomly dumped innumerable truckloads of sand, gravel, and boulders. It must have looked like a bomb had gone off. The landscape was barren, with no plants, no animals, and no men. However, what came next was just as bad and just as hostile to life as the ice had been.

As the Laurentide Ice melted back into Canada, the cold air that came off it mixed with the warmer air to the south. This mixing created strong convection currents of wind and the result was an intense and prolonged sandstorm that scoured every inch of Massachusetts's landscape. When the winds finally diminished and things calmed down, the landscape of the Hockomock had changed again.

The sand was deposited two feet thick over the land, and in some places it had formed dunes. The landscape in the Hockomock was now a dunescape, radiating pale yellow under the summer sun and sparkling silver in snow under the winter moon. Square in the middle of it all was the haunting, azure-blue vision of Glacial Lake Taunton.

The lake eventually evolved into a dynamic water body, complete with whitecaps, strong currents that carved steep cliffs on its banks, and sandbars. All that was missing from the primitive scene was life. However, it was not long, as geologic time goes, before life came, and when it did come, it came with a vengeance.

The first to arrive were the Others. They were always first. They came, about 13,000 years ago, just as they had come at least 30 times before following previous glaciations. They came in their true forms of shimmering, silver-blue lights and descended down over the golden dunescape into sparkling blue Lake Taunton. They passed into the lakebed below and formed their kingdom.

The Others came to the Hockomock then for the same reasons that they had come before: to experience the rebirth of Nature and, in doing so, celebrate the Creation. The Others rejoiced in their new kingdom, anticipating the great rebirth they knew was about to take place on the land. In the millennia to come, they would watch with joy as the Creator, Cautantowwit, warmed the land and repopulated it with his tribes of plants and animals.

They would rejoice in thanksgiving, as they had at the blessed time of the Creation when they and the kingdom of their Creator had been one, before the Great Fall.

There was another reason why the Others chose the Hockomock for their home, in addition to its virgin beauty. At the time, America represented the New World, the last frontier of true wilderness on Earth. North America was the last place on Earth where Man did not live.

But unfortunately for the Others, Man, their counterpart in the Physical World, would ultimately be drawn to the place for the very same reasons they had been.

The beautiful, surreal landscape of lake and dune was not meant to last long. Rather, it was only the first act in a famous play. As the melting mass of ice to the north furloughed the land, the earth began to gradually rebound. It rose up, slowly, like blades of grass that had been trampled down by a passing foot. The Hubbard Uplift caused the waters of Glacial Lake Taunton to slosh around and pound its walls of till and ice, to course and rage for release. Several times, the lake's waters temporarily breached its shoreline, escaping in cataclysmic floods that swept away tons of earth and rolled great boulders away like children's marbles.

Finally, as the land continued to spring back, and the currents to course, the inevitable happened. Millions of gallons of frigid, ice-laden water permanently breached the bounds of Lake Taunton and roared away in newborn, whitewater rivers. These chaotic flows quickly found the ancient north-south rifts created by the smashing of tectonic plates, and formed the rivers we know today as the Taunton, the Jones, the Town, the Hockomock, and others. The Taunton River, the largest in the area, formed its course over an ancient river valley from Permian times that had been clogged with glacial till left by the Laurentide Ice.

The great breaching of Glacial Lake Taunton was a cataclysmic event in the Hockomock that changed the landscape of the area yet again. When the flood was over and the roaring waters had subsided, the Hubbard Uplift had successfully banished all but remnants of the magnificent cold-water lake. The single largest body of water that remained was a small, 354-acre pond, located in present-day Bridgewater and Raynham. We know it as Lake Nippenicket, or simply as "the Nip." The waters of this pond would later assume a reddish tinge because of the large quantities of bog iron that lay under it, earning it the native name "Lake of the Red Waters."

Across the former territory of Glacial Lake Taunton were also scattered innumerable small ponds, streams, and vast underground chasms of water that flowed together in mysterious networks. And now, right in the middle of it all, distilled from the pristine, cold waters of glacial lakes was the dark, brooding wetland that would eventually come to be known as the Hockomock Swamp.

When the glacial lakes violently exploded, the Hockomock was born. It is the essence of those lakes, for it was the lakes that left the guts of the swamp behind. Eventually, the glacial lakes had evolved into marginal marine environments, complete with aquatic plants. For hundreds of years, these plants lived, died, and accumulated on the bottom of the lakes. Dead plants turn into peat, a spongy, greenish-brown type of sediment most commonly seen in coastal areas. As a result of this long process, today there is a stupendous amount of peat under the Hockomock Swamp. It is all of forty feet deep in some places.

The parade of life that returned to the devastated Hockomock landscape began with the plants. The species that came first were those that could tolerate the existing cold and wet conditions. The lichens—blue, green, yellow, and orange—began to show up on the rocks that had been so haphazardly dumped by the ice. Pine seedlings came next, raising their tiny bobbing heads bravely towards the blue sky.

The dead orange needles shed by the first pines worked their way into the sandy soil and decomposed, beginning the long process of soil-making. Other trees followed the pines as the soil improved. Wispy hemlocks, towering spruce, and the soft round birches—gray, silver, yellow, and paper—that lightened the dark stands of evergreens.

Next the ants came and built their tunnel systems in the sandy earth. The worms appeared too, eating their way relentlessly through the soil. Both creatures contributing significantly to its formation. In the cold winters, the heavy frosts heaved up rocks, a process which further mixed the strata and improved the quality of the soil.

As the soil formed, the plains of sand greened up with grasses. The classic tundra environment that typically exists on the cold, southern edge of glaciers emerged: vast, park-like grasslands, snow-covered, dotted here and there with a few trees, and blanketed with streams, ponds, and wetlands such as marshes and swamps. And the grandest wetland of all on this newly-formed tundra was the Hockomock.

Soon, the great herds of animals that populated the exposed continental shelf to the south began to move. Many of these herds were made up of massive animals, including mammoth, mastodon, and musk oxen. They edged tentatively into the emerging grasslands of the north, and there they found Paradise. Other mammals came too, such as giant ground sloths, camels, and horses. They came to the great northern grasslands in droves, and the predators, including cave bears, dire wolves, and saber-toothed tigers, followed them. At last, the stage was set for the arrival of one last animal, the two-legged one known as Man.

About 12,000 years ago, far to the northwest of Massachusetts, Paleo Indians who had crossed the 12,000-mile-wide land bridge, known to today's scientists as

"Beringia," were trapped in Canada by a wall of ice. Then the ice melted, creating a corridor that allowed them to continue their epic journey south. They moved with incredible speed and purpose. Within just a few hundred years, these Asiatic hunter-gatherers had reached the far corners of the North American continent, including southeastern Massachusetts.

Like the mammals that arrived before them, these men probably came to the Hockomock region from the south, over the still-exposed continental shelf that extended about 100 miles south of the area before it was submerged by ocean. What these hunters found in the New World might best be described as a big game park. For unlike the rest of the world, it was a place with only animals, and no Men. At the time, as these opportunity-seekers were all too well aware, Asia and Europe were heavily populated with humans.

These Paleo Indians had found a new world, one that was dominated not by Man, but by Animal. And there was only one rule: *kill or be killed.*

And so kill they did. Quite simply, these hunters went on the biggest killing spree the world has ever known. Born without tooth or claw, their only weapons were superior technology. Fire, to panic the herds and to frighten away the monstrous predators at night, and spears, thrown with great power by atlatls, or throwing sticks, and tipped with well-crafted points of flint and chert.

They slaughtered mammoths in pits, using small groups of hunters who jabbed down at them with spears, and drove them off cliffs. The hunters fought the looming cave bears in close-quarter battles in the rocks, and tackled the tigers in frightening, bloody encounters in the tall grass of the swamps. They killed with their delicate, razor-sharp Clovis points, that looked like leafs with a large flake chipped out of either side. They punctured, ripped, hacked, and burned their common enemy, the Animal. They killed for food, for safety, for sport, and for ritual. But in the end, the Paleos killed mostly to establish a safe and dominant role for themselves on the food chain.

The Paleos camped on high points like hills around the wetlands, where they could easily keep tabs on the herd animals below on which they depended. They also preferred to camp on lake shores, so they doubtlessly camped on the shores of Nunkatest, or Lake Nippenicket.

They most likely camped on the shores of the Taunton River as well. The Paleos wore the fur-trimmed hoods of the Eskimo, and finely-made skin clothes trimmed with decorative beads.

They lived in temporary, brush-framed shelters covered in hides, that were big enough to house just one family. In addition to their fluted projectile points, these first people of the Hockomock made many other tools, including axes, adzes, scrapers, awls, and knives. They made these tools from stone, wood, and bone. Due to New England's wet climate, only the stone ones have survived.

The Paleos were very few in number. Probably only a couple hundred of them lived in all of New England. Archaeologists have discovered seven distinct variations of Clovis points in New England, which may mean that roughly seven distinct bands lived in the area. One of these bands, of about thirty souls, lived in the Hockomock area.

The Paleo Indians were highly migratory. They moved in regular patterns over the land, according to where and when they found food. They followed the great herds, and the herds moved often. The Paleos also followed the migratory fish, like alewives, waterfowl, and the seasonal appearances of wild plants. When they moved, they carried their babies on wooden boards strapped to the women's backs, and dragged their heavy belongings, which were very few, on sledges with wooden runners. They buried their dead where they fell. The Paleos scrounged for scarce fuel and cooked on tiny hearths on the tundra. One of these hearths was unearthed in recent times by William Fowler, an archaeologist, on a sand spit that lays roughly a quarter mile from the shoreline of Lake Nippenicket.

The Paleo nomads watched in wonder as the shimmering, colored spheres of the Others dropped down through the mists rising off the Lake of the Red Waters and disappeared into its depths. Whenever the ghostly orbs hove into sight, they clutched fearfully at the carved animal totems of ivory and stone that dangled from their necks. And sometimes, along the edges of the great Hockomock wetland at dusk, they would see processions of little people. They looked like small boys, but peered at them with the faces of men.

They were clothed in a similar fashion to the hunters themselves, and carried tiny spears and atlatls. When the Paleos sought counsel with their shamans, they told them that they had no power over these beings, and that it was best to let the little ones move along on their mysterious journeys undisturbed.

The great war between Man and Animal in the New World continued for roughly two millennia. And then, most suddenly, came the Great Change. Approximately 10,000 years ago the climate warmed, and at the same time, the last of the great herd animals fell crashing to the Earth, twitching and trembling with Paleo spears in their guts. It was over. All of it—the Ice Age, the Age of the Mammals, and the time of the Paleos. The lethal combination of climate change and the relentless persecution of Animal by the hunters had caused a complete environmental shift.

For the first time in history, Man had contributed to an environmental overturn. Most of the mega fauna, like the mammoth, simply became extinct, gone forever from the face of the Earth. Some of these animals fled from New England to the north, only to disappear into the mists of extinction soon after, as the ice sheet continued to melt and the climate to warm.

The vegetation in the Hockomock region began to change, and the tundra began to disappear. New creatures adapted to the warmer climate began to push into the area from the south. The Paleo Indians in New England, with the great herds gone, very nearly died out themselves. But some of them, albeit perhaps very, very few of them, seem to have stayed, adapted, and survived. They were there, just barely, probably around the Taunton River and the Lake of the Red Waters, as a new age dawned on the Hockomock.

The last Ice Age, known as the Pleistocene Epoch, officially ended 10,000 years ago. The age that followed, the Early Archaic, lasted about 2,000 years, from 10,000 to 8,000 years ago.

After the Great Change, the few Paleo families that were left around the Hockomock faded quietly away, like ghosts, into the thickening spruce and birch forests that were overrunning the tundra.

The low topography still held enormous amounts of ice from the glacier, ice that had long ago disappeared from higher ground. Massive ice blocks lay buried by till in some spots, and as the spruce and pine grew in, they shaded the ice, keeping out the warm rays of the sun. Arctic plants and animals—caribou, mastodon, and even the occasional mammoth—that otherwise would have died out, been slaughtered, or fled north, found a miniature arctic environment preserved in the trackless wetland. And they also found a place where it was easy to hide from the Indians.

The Hockomock Swamp retains similar characteristics today, safely harboring locally rare species of plants and animals commonly found only in sub-arctic environments far to the north.

Perhaps the most important ecological feature that came to Southeastern Massachusetts in the Early Archaic was the oak tree. Oaks would not appear to the north until many years later. The oaks brought major change to the region because they produced acorns. The acorns lured the Whitetail deer from the south, as well as turkeys and many other animal species that depended on nuts for food. As the tall, straight oaks spread their canopies wide and quickly shouldered out the softwoods, White-tailed deer became the principal big game animal in the Hockomock. They remain so today.

The Early Archaic hunters adapted to the changes in animal species by abandoning their all-important, leaf-shaped Clovis points in favor of a new design, one with a deeply notched base that archaeologists call *Bifurcated*. Today, the discovery of these notched points clearly identifies an Early Archaic site. In addition, with the thundering herds gone, there was no longer a need for the hunters to frequent high hills, a practice which had allowed them to keep watch for opportunities to strike approaching herds with coordinated groups.

Instead, the men began to hunt alone, or in pairs, because the new species of animals, such as deer, resided in the spruce glens and swamps and were best taken by stealth. Using their throwing sticks and spears, the hunters also took the occasional moose and bear.

They must have learned to rely more on small game as well, such as beaver and squirrels, to supplement their meat supply. The Early Archaic women busied themselves gathering the new species of plants, nuts, and berries that were popping up all around them.

As their hunter-gatherer lifestyles evolved, the Early Archaic peoples of the Hockomock capitalized on ever more resources, both new ones and those that they may have undervalued when the herds provided most of what they needed to live. No longer trailing the herds, their annual movements became more regular than their Paleo ancestors. They moved with the seasons, to set geographic locations which would provide food.

For the people of the Early Archaic in the Northeast, it seems that the Taunton River provided one of the few spots where seasonal resources were rich enough to justify a place where several families could come together into a band. We know this because from 1946-1951, in what is now the southern-most portion of the town of Bridgewater on a ninety-degree bend of the Taunton River, archaeologists excavated a major settlement they call "the Titicut Site" that dates back some 8,600 years.

The inhabitants at Titicut lived in a group of perhaps thirty to forty souls. They built semi-permanent lodges of poles covered by mats and bark. Archaeologists eventually unearthed about 6,000 artifacts and twenty-six burial sites at Titicut. One of the main natural resources for these people must have been migratory fish, like alewives. But archaeologists believe that the site may have been most important to its inhabitants as a "base camp" used to launch hunting and gathering expeditions across southern New England, including to the coastal areas to the south.

Titicut is special in archaeology and human history, and not just to the Hockomock region. There have been so few Early Archaic settlements found by archaeologists in New England that until very recently, most archaeologists believed that there were *no* people residing in the Northeast part of America between 10,000 and 8,000 years ago. Titicut was one of the discoveries that caused them to abandon this theory.

It was probably one of the few places in New England where people lived during this long, quiet age. We also know that people continued to live at Titicut, at various times, all the way up to the point of European contact.

For these ancient inhabitants of the Hockomock, the Early Archaic must have been a time for survival, for learning, and for constant adaptation. And a time, perhaps, of becoming less Animal, less Killer, and more Human than had been their Paleo ancestors. The curse of these people was that they were few, and highly vulnerable in a rapidly changing world. Little did they know that even more rapid change was headed their way.

The Middle Archaic Period lasted from 8,000 to 6,000 years ago and was characterized by a rapid rise in sea levels and temperature. The seas to the south of the Hockomock rose quickly. A good portion of the continental shelf was still above water at this time, however, and there were large populations of people and animals living there. Inland, the rivers, including the Taunton, finished shaping their valleys and settled into the courses they follow today.

As the Atlantic rose and pushed up onto the shelf, more people there starting moving inland.

They migrated into sparsely-populated areas, such as the Hockomock, following the expanding range of the plants and animals that they depended on for food. The people who pushed into the Hockomock from the south merged with the tiny band at Titicut, and they established more semi-permanent villages along the Taunton.

Archaeological sites in the area from the Middle Archaic show that these people also preferred to live on lakes. Many of these sites are located on lake shores, or near wetlands that would have been lakes around 7,000 years ago. Lake sites were probably chosen because lake shores were good spots to find food, such as turtles, frogs, snakes, and small mammals, such as raccoons and muskrats.

The people of the Middle Archaic, sometimes referred to as "Early Indians" today, developed more complex ways of hunting and fishing. These developments, based on the natural resources offered by their particular environment, would eventually allow them to live a highly-specialized lifestyle. Southern New England offered these people a bounty of resources, including rivers, ponds, forests, swamps, and the sea coast.

The population in the Hockomock also expanded during this time period because people started having larger families, possibly to help out with the division of labor. Overall, there were many more people, and more food sources, in the Hockomock in the Middle Archaic than ever before. The people must have rejoiced. The lonely, dark days of the past, drifting like ghosts in the forests, were now behind them.

As their numbers grew, the People began to encounter the Little People with much higher frequency. Sometimes they requested the help of the Indian healers, but mostly they just asked for food. The People learned to give the Little People whatever they wanted, because if they didn't, they would simply take it. And they learned, too, that the little ones disliked being looked at. If you did look at one of them, they would stare back at you with a very odd look. Then they would point at you, or away from you, and then they would disappear.

The People knew that the little ones were spirit beings, for despite appearances, when they were with them, they could sense that they were the Absolute Other. They were as different from, and as devoid of humanity, as anything could possibly be. The People also learned that these beings were the masters of deception. They could shape-shift at will, appearing in the form of any creature they wished. And the People saw that when these apparitions were attacked by the hunters, they always proved invulnerable to their spears, which passed right through them with no apparent effect. And so, hoping to curry their favor, the People began to leave offerings of food for the Little People, in tiny woven baskets hung from the branches of spruce.

The Little People appreciated these favors and the general respect that was paid to them. And they also approved of the way the People lived, in harmony with the land around them. So in return, they led their hunters to the game, the wily, bounding deer, and the crashing moose, that like themselves haunted the depths of the swamps.

The Others also became the guardians of the Indians' graves and the sacred objects that they placed in them. They confused and bewildered those who would tamper with the graves, and sometimes they would scatter fabricated objects about—axe heads, spear points, totems—that were identical to those made by the People, to mislead those who would plunder the sacred resting places of their ancestors.

Along with their numbers, the dead of the People were also now rapidly increasing.

They began to bury their dead in the great swamp they called Hockomock, or "body enclosure." With these mounting numbers of dead, other beings of the Spirit World came to the Hockomock, the spirits of the human dead.

Many of these spirits were not even capable of benevolence, as were the Little People, but instead were truly evil. Collectively, these frightening spirits of the human dead became known to the People as "Hobbamock," or "Cheepi."

The Wampanoags worshipped approximately thirty-seven gods that ranged from major to minor in importance. Their minor gods were embodied by many things in Nature, such as fire, rain, the moon, and woman. However, as, mentioned earlier, they believed in a single creator deity, whom they called Cautantowwit, or Kiehtan. On Earth, Cautantowwit was generally most closely associated with the chiefs, or sachems, but he never appeared to the People in an earthly form.

Hobbamock was the Wampanoag's evil deity of Death and Disease. The spirits that collectively comprised Hobbamock, unlike Cautantowwit, did manifest themselves on earth. Hobbamock appeared to the Wampanoags often, chiefly at night, in the form of terrifying apparitions. These apparitions were typically black.

Some apparitions were of creatures known to the people, such as deer, lions, eagles, or fawns, and especially snakes. Some were of unknown creatures, some were of men—mostly enemies, such as Mohawks—and others were of mythical beasts. These apparitions tended to linger in swamps. By the time the European colonists arrived, the Wampanoags, even their bravest warriors, had stopped going out at night altogether, frightened out of their wits by the appearances of these flapping, dashing, and floating apparitions.

The shamans, who in more recent times became known as "powwows," were the priests of the People. The shamans worshipped Hobbamock, and he gave them the power to heal the people when they were ill, and the power to kill both the enemies of the tribe and their personal enemies, who were mostly other shamans. For their healing work, the shamans always extracted a price of material goods. And they extracted a heavy emotional price as well. The shamans used their power to heal disease and stave off death to increase their personal standing in the tribe, and to hold the Wampanoag people in a permanent state of fear. So entwined was Hobbamock with the shamans that this deity became known to the Wampanoag people as "the Shamans' Helper."

The Wampanoags also offered up their most promising young men to Hobbamock. As a coming of age ritual, they sent them on brutal wilderness sojourns in the dead of winter in the hopes that their ordeal would bring them favor in his eyes. The young men to whom Hobbamock appeared were duly anointed with his dark powers, the most important of which was immunity in battle from tomahawks and spears.

The People later watched with wonder as these braves, called "pnieses," were attacked time and again by enemy combatants with little or no effect. Wampanoag pnieses were fearless, and it was not uncommon for them to give chase to 100 men in battle.

Most times, the enemy fled when they saw them coming, for the pnieses' reputations usually preceded them to the battleground.

There is sufficient evidence in the literature of the 17th century to support the belief that the Wampanoag people knew that the root of Hobbamock's power was evil. But the people were afraid to challenge the shamans because they also knew that the shamans used their undisputed powers, especially the power to heal, strictly at their discretion. And deep down, the People were a pragmatic race as well; they tended to base their actions on what made sense from a practical level. "If Hobbamock brings us disease and death," they reasoned, "why *not* worship him, to curry his favor?"

"As for Cautantowwit," they thought, "well, he will always be on our side, so we had best not spend too much time worshipping him. Simple thanks will do." These religious practices may not have been the case throughout Wampanoag tribal history. And many other American Indian tribes did not place emphasis on the worship of Hobbamock, or they placed emphasis on the Creator deity instead.

But by the time the first European settlers arrived in New England, the Wampanoags clearly placed so much emphasis on the worship of the evil deity Hobbamock that settlers familiar with their religion sometimes described them as "Devil worshippers."

In the Paradisal Age, Man was immortal, and the three Cosmic Zones, Earth, Sky, and Underworld, were one. Man could fly, then, too, under his own power, in order to visit Cautantowwit in person. But Man was too proud, and the day came when Cautantowwit cast him down.

After this Fall of Man, the Creator had removed himself to the highest levels of the Sky, and the People had been left nearly alone. This proved to be a bad thing, for they were attacked and tortured by evil spirits from the Underworld.

Demons, the true enemies of Man, preyed on them, sending them disease and death at will. Finally, Cautantowwit took notice. He realized that if he did not take action, there would soon be no more men. To protect them from the demons, Cautantowwit sent the First Shaman to the People. He gave the First Shaman the knowledge of how to transcend physical reality, to become Dead, to enter the Tunnel and travel to the Sky and the Underworld on behalf of the people. He gave him the ability to become Spirit, to fight the demons. But the days of the shamans using their power of magical flight to travel to the Sky Kingdom did not last.

The People soon abandoned their faith in Cautantowwit as their great hope, as did the other races of Man, in favor of other, more worldly deities that offered immediate returns on their spiritual investment. The People knew that the Creator was powerful, but in the end, he proved to be just too mysterious and too remote, and his actions were unfathomable to them.

In order to continue serving their people, the ancient shamans began spending most of their energy communicating with these other deities that took the place of the Creator in the Peoples' hearts, instead of journeying to the Sky. Increasingly, these shamans focused on communicating with the Ancestors and other spirits of the Human Dead. Collectively, these were the spirits that became known to the People as Hobbamock.

The shamans used the magic they obtained from Hobbamock to heal and otherwise help the People, but in return they demanded a high price from them, one that included both personal rewards for themselves and unquestioned allegiance to their dark masters. And the priests were not always selective about the types of spirits with which they trafficked. In the end, many of the shamans sold out to the very same evil spirits that Cautantowwit had wished them to defend against.

Six thousand years ago, at the start of the period known today as the Late Archaic, the temperature in New England began to rise, once again, and it kept rising. But this time, the rise in temperature was not accompanied by a parallel rise in the sea. This time, the rising of the Atlantic slowed down.

The People traveled to the coast in the summer to harvest shellfish on the new tidal flats that appeared there. In addition to gathering shellfish, the people of the Late Archaic in southern New England fished more as well. One of their most important new tools during this time was the fish weir, a fence-like fish trap made of hundreds of wooden stakes that they hammered into riverbeds.

During the Late Archaic, the people continued to forge a wide variety of their traditional tools from stone, wood, and bone. They made gouges, axes, drills, roughing knives, notchers, plummets, or fishing sinkers, ulus, or semi-lunar knives, mortars and pestles for grinding nuts, and "strike-a-lights" of flint or quartz that they hit against a piece of iron pyrite to make fire. They also made beautiful winged-shaped weights that were part of their atlatls, or throwing sticks, that were as much art as tool.

Sometime during this period, the people in southern New England once again fundamentally changed the shape of their projectile, or spear points. They started making a new, distinctive point that archaeologists call either the Atlantic or the Susquehanna. These points no longer had the deep notch in the base, as had the chosen point style of their ancestors, the bifurcated. Archaeologists know that the people of this time traded heavily with other peoples far to the south because the same broad style of spear points they made were made by peoples to the south, all the way past New York. With trade must also have come other interactions and new ideas. The days of living in small groups, in relative isolation, as their ancestors had, were now gone.

The people of the Late Archaic continued their ancestors' trend towards more permanent settlements. They built large, semi-permanent villages on large lakes, rivers, and streams. These villages contained upwards of 100 people. They lived in surprisingly large, circular-style houses that had a kind of vestibule built in front of the doors to block the wind. These houses were capable of sheltering several families quite comfortably.

In the 1950s, archaeologists excavated a Late Archaic village called "Wapanucket 6" in Middleboro, on the north shore of Lake Assawompsett, that featured seven of these types of homes. Wapanucket is considered to be one of the most important archaeological sites in New England relating to the Late Archaic. Assawompsett is the largest natural lake in Massachusetts, and is the source of the Nemasket River, which flows northward out of the lake. The Nemasket is still noted for the legendary number of alewives that run up it each spring to spawn in the lake, a quality which very likely drew the first people to the site.

We know from Wapanucket and related sites that these people of the Late Archaic cremated their dead, as opposed to burying them in the "flex," or sitting position as did the later Wampanoags. They also buried tools and trade objects with their dead, objects that included special types of stone, copper, and even tropical shells obtained from their new-found trading activities. Other religious rituals of these Late Archaic people probably differed very little from those of their ancient, Paleo ancestors.

The shaman One Eye began to dance around the fire. Overhead, dark clouds drifted across the stars, blotting out their reflections on the wide, glistening waters of Assawompsett. One Eye had great power this night, in this place. The People could feel it. The priest had spent hours in his sweat lodge, reliving his shaman's initiation, celebrating again his acceptance into that ancient and secretive order, building his power. He engaged the people as he pranced. He invited them into the ritual, asked for their participation, their support.

And they gave it to him eagerly, with exclamations of excitement and shouts of approval. For their shaman was about to take them back, back to the Paradisal Age, back to a time when Man was one with the animals, the spirits, and the Gods themselves.

One Eye began to dance harder, to circle the fire faster. He was trying to create heat, to raise his inner body temperature to a very high point, to that point he knew he must reach in order to depart on his magical flight. His red body began to sweat profusely. Then, the shaman started leaping about, pounding his knees and his chest violently, beating himself without mercy, recreating the pain of his initiation. Soon, the people heard the cries of the wolf. Deep snarls, yips, whimpers, moans, and finally, howls, as the tempo of the dance reached a furor.

One Eye was becoming a wolf. He was, to be precise, possessing the spirit of one of his Guardian Spirits, the Red Wolf. The shaman rolled, wagged, grinned, and lolled his tongue at his audience. Then he snapped his jaws at them, and drooled. He began running about on all fours, and the look in his eye changed from Man to Animal. The people urged him on. It was such a realistic performance, so intense, so realistic, that even the most seasoned hunters among them knew that what they now beheld was not Man, but Wolf. There was no doubt in any of their minds that One Eye, the man, had ceased to exist.

The shaman, on all fours, began lunging at the crowd, speaking wolf to them. The people were excited, even joyous, for wolf language was animal language. And animal language was no different from spirit language, the universal language used by spirits of the Earth, the Sky, and the Underworld. One Eye was literally transcending the Great Fall of Man, going back to that age when they too could speak with the animals, something that, deep in their hearts, the People all ached to do. For in the Paradisal Age, there was no difference between Man and Animal. They were One.

The shaman was showing the People that all was not lost.

He was demonstrating to them that he was their link to the spirit world, that he could reclaim, at least partially, their former standing in the Cosmos. And the shaman had become something else as well. Something very important. He was, as in the days of old, their protector from the evil spirits of the Underworld.

One Eye's inner heat had now reached its critical point. The shaman began to test his power, to prove it to the People. The glistening scarlet figure stooped and seized a burning coal from the fire, turned to face his audience, opened his mouth wide, and swallowed it. The crowd gasped. Here was real power that they could see, unlike the vague promises of good things to come made by Cautantowwit. One Eye began muttering unintelligibly, speaking his secret shaman's language that only those of his order knew. Gesturing wildly for a gourd-full of water from the audience, he chanted over it and passed it back to a warrior, whose eyes widened as he tipped it. The People watched in amazement as a solid block of ice slipped out, and then shouted with glee as they passed it around.

One Eye had officially become Dead. What the shaman did next would live long in the oral tradition of the People. It represented a quantum leap in his magical abilities, a feat worthy of the shamans of the distant past, when they were said to be even more powerful than they were at present. One Eye stopped dancing, and stood with his arms outstretched. Then he flew. He rose very quickly, high above the crowd, out of the glow of the fire and into the dark branches of a Tupelo that stood at the edge of the tree line.

The astounded people gasped as they beheld his dark form perched on a branch, and murmurs of wonder rippled through the crowd. Then, as quickly as he had gone, the shaman flew back, to precisely the spot from which he had departed. Later, discussing the incident, the People were undecided whether he had actually flown back or just disappeared from the Tupelo and reappeared at the fire. For it all happened very fast, and it was very dark. But whatever the case, this performance was a triumph for the shaman.

For One Eye had transcended the condition of Man and had become the Dead. The people stood in awe of him then, and felt themselves to be living in the time when all Men could fly. They recalled with the greatest nostalgia their recurring dreams of flight that they had experienced since childhood.

Shortly after landing, One Eye's single eye glazed over and he began to sway violently from side to side. Then he fell abruptly to the grass. The shaman had achieved a state of trance. Now, he and his Guardian Spirit, Red Wolf, would travel to the Underworld to try to determine whether the hunting this winter would be good or bad.

As the shaman lay entranced, White Bear, the tribe's sachem or chief, approached and sat cross-legged in front of him. The sachem stared at his rival with a look of troubled respect, for the shaman's performance had been an impressive one. Then the chief started peppering One Eye with questions that the shaman must answer when he woke from his trance. "Was the deer herd plentiful this year?" "Would the hunters find the game?" "Would they return with meat to stave off the hunger of the people?" When he finished his questioning, White Bear sat back to wait along with the rest of his band.

Now One Eye's Dream Soul left his body, and along with Red Wolf, his companion and guide to the Underworld, he flew out over the Nemasket River. He and his leering canine companion dove into the current and swam down to a spring that gushed up from the riverbed. It was an ancient spring, the same one that One Eye's shaman predecessors had used for millennia before him to descend into the Underworld. Like all regional springs, it also provided an entrance to the vast network of interconnected springs in the Hockomock Swamp. The local shamans often used this watery network to meet their personal rivals in magical flight for the purpose of doing battle. Those combatants that were beaten in these mystical battles returned to the physical world either injured or dead.

The two companions plunged gleefully into the spring, swimming down through it until they entered the immense groundwater chasms of the Hockomock, and then down, down, further into the blackness, until they reached the very bowels of the Earth. There, One Eye felt himself sliding gradually downward at a slight angle, with Red Wolf beside him. He and his Guardian had entered the Tunnel, the universal vehicle shamans had used to transcend physical reality and fly to the Underworld ever since the First Shaman had used it long ago. The Tunnel always appeared slightly different to those who entered it, but its basic features were always the same. It was composed of an unassisted drop downwards, sometimes with obstacles, sometimes without. The Tunnel was usually not too steep or constricting. It always ended with entry to the Underworld.

One Eye and Red Wolf slid down the Tunnel together, through a rushing, subterranean river flanked by dark rock walls, until their progress was blocked by a massive, gray ledge. The two were bumped up against the ledge by the current, and the shaman clung to it while Red wolf attempted to find a way around it. Soon, the wolf yipped for One-eye to follow him. He had located a narrow crack in the ledge that was just wide enough for them to slip through.

Reaching the other side with little difficulty, the pair was immediately swept into rushing whitewater that propelled them rapidly downward. On the narrow, dark banks of this part of the underground river, One Eye could just make out the white skeletons of huge, long-extinct creatures. He beheld the skulls of mammoth and saber-toothed tigers, and some other things that he didn't recognize, that were much larger with enormous teeth. These were the monsters of the dim past.

Suddenly, the underground river banked sharply to their right, and the two travelers were forcibly ejected into a small pool that lay exposed to the glaring light of day. They had reached the Underworld.

They pulled themselves out onto a warm, gray rock on the edge of the pool, where they could see that they had emerged onto a ledge perched high over a far-reaching meadow of tall grass. The meadow was surrounded by a dark spruce forest interspersed with white birch. The place looked just like the landscape at home, but One Eye knew full well, from experience, that it was not.

"Red Wolf" rasped One Eye as he shakily got to his feet, "Go, search. Find the deer." His bedraggled companion shook himself violently, sending water droplets spraying everywhere.

Then, with a sly smile, the wolf scrambled off down the steep incline, and disappeared into the dark grove of spruce below.

One Eye rested in the sunlight on the warm rock ledge, recovering from his watery descent and surveying the pleasing pastoral scene that lay below him. It would be easy to believe that he was still at home, somewhere near the Nemasket River. But after a short while, the shaman sensed something strange about his surroundings. He couldn't put his finger on it, at least not at first. Finally, he realized that the place was utterly deserted.

The landscape around him was still, devoid of animal life, as no such landscape could be in the physical world. He didn't even hear any birds singing. In fact, One Eye soon realized, he couldn't hear anything at all, with the exception of his own breathing and slight movements. It was then that the shaman started to get nervous, and wished that his Guardian would return. But the wolf was nowhere to be seen.

After a very long time, or at least what seemed to him to be a very long time, One Eye saw Red Wolf trot out of the forest onto the meadow. Large and lean, with a reddish tinge to his gray fur, the wolf was sniffing the ground, casting about as if trying to pick up a scent. He then cantered down the tree line for several hundred yards, before abruptly laying down in the grass. Then the wolf appeared to go to sleep.

Dismayed, One Eye cupped his hands to his mouth and shouted in wolf tongue: "My friend! Wake up! Have you found the deer?!" There was no response.

Then the shaman shouted again, and again, his voice echoing across the silent meadow, until at last his Guardian perked up his ears and lifted his ruffed head.

"I am tired now, Man-spirit," said the wolf, "and I must rest. I have found no deer."

"No! No!" bellowed One-eye. "Not Now! You must keep looking for them!"

But the drowsy wolf just laid his head back down on his forepaws and resumed his nap.

One Eye, after shouting several more pleas, finally realized that his companion had failed him. And the shaman had no desire to stay in this place alone. So at last, with great disappointment and reluctance, One Eye dove back into the pool behind him, and descended once again into the Tunnel. It was now pitch dark in the water, and the shaman soon lost his way. But instead of panicking, he remembered the lessons he had been taught at his shaman's initiation. He stopped swimming blindly, and instead just let himself float. Motionless, One Eye felt his body slowly begin to drift upwards. He patiently let himself rise, unobstructed, all the way to the entrance of the Tunnel. His return journey seemed to take much longer than had his descent, but eventually the shaman burst forth from the spring into the cool, rushing waters of the Nemasket River. Then he flew up, and towards the smoke rising from the campfire.

The People sitting patiently around the fire murmured in surprise and anticipation as the shaman suddenly sat up, and muttered unintelligibly. He was very groggy. They waited patiently until he seemed to have come to his senses, at which point White Bear addressed him with great urgency. "Well!? What have you found out, One Eye? Will the hunting be good for us this winter?" One Eye didn't answer right away, and he refused to meet the direct gaze of the sachem. Sensing bad news, White Bear pressed him. "Speak now, Dark One," he said angrily. "The People wish to know whether their bellies will feel the pinch of hunger at the time of the Wolf Moon." One Eye, staring forlornly at the grass, began to speak.

The crowd, hushed, hung onto his every word. "I do not bring good tidings," he said nervously, his voice cracking. White Bear sneered.

"What did your wolf-brother find, frogs?"

"Red Wolf grew tired," retorted the shaman quietly. "He looked long, but he was unable to find the deer."

"Tired?!" roared the chief. "I have known wolves to trail a moose for a week, and your cur grows tired in but an hour? What kind of wolf is he?"

One Eye looked sullen, and fell silent. It was a very tense situation. White Bear was clearly trying to discredit his rival.

The chief leaned forward in the firelight, until his proud, handsome face was only inches from the shaman's. His trembling right hand fell to the bone handle of the war axe on his side. His hand twitched, hard, but he didn't lift it. For in the end, the sachem was afraid to kill the shaman. The truth was that he feared his rival's spirit far more than the man.

One Eye, staring down at the grass, cringed, cowered, and slunk away like one of the band's mangy curs into his lodge at the edge of the clearing. The People began to move away from the fire and into their wetus. For most of them, it would be a fitful, sleepless night, the little that was left of it.

For the most part, life was good in the Hockomock in the Late Archaic. But unbeknownst to the Wampanoags and their New England brethren, their blissful way of life was doomed. The period known as the Woodland, which began 3,000 years ago and extended to the point of European contact, would bring major changes. Sweeping cultural advancements occurring in the Indian tribes to the south would finally reach them. The New England tribes had been slow to adopt these changes, perhaps because their environment provided such a variety of bountiful natural resources that they did not need them.

By the time of European contact around 1500 A.D., the Wampanoags had been using one of these major cultural advancements, fired clay pottery, for more than 2,000 years.

But they had adopted their two most significant cultural changes ever, farming and the bow and arrow, only about 500 years earlier. Now, the arrival of the first European ships in New England meant that the outside world was closing in on them, and it was closing in fast.

The flotilla of dugouts had reached the spot on the Taunton River where it emerges from the Hockomock Swamp and widens drastically on its way south to Narragansett Bay. A few hundred feet off the starboard bow of the lead canoe lay Grassy Island, the place of the Ancestors. Just downstream, where Assonet Neck formed the east bank, lay a great sandstone boulder that was partially exposed by the falling tide. This boulder had long been used by the People to commemorate major events and to leave important messages. They used their stone blades to painstakingly carve rough stick figures of people and animals onto its broad, smooth face.

Red Hawk, the tribe's sachem, was kneeling in the lead canoe, which was paddled by several young warriors. He cut a fine figure in his beaded buckskins, purple wampum, and twin shining black braids pleated with the rich brown fur of otter. Suddenly, the warrior in the bow of Red Hawk's canoe stopped paddling. He held up his hand with an abrupt gesture intended to halt the flotilla, and turned to speak hurriedly to the sachem. Something was sitting on the rock. It didn't take long for the rest of the band to spot it as well.

The people drifted, eying the rock, waiting for directions from Red Hawk. They could see three tiny figures perched there. One was squatting, and the other two sat, dangling their legs towards the water. They occasionally swung their heels rhythmically against the rock in the manner of children. The people were still a ways off, and the light was low on the gray river that day, but they could just make out glimmers and flashes of light—pink, green, and electric blue—around the hands of the squatting figure as they passed with strange rapidity over the face of the boulder.

Red Hawk observed the little figures for a few minutes, and consulted with the other men in his dugout. Then he turned, and signaled for the other canoes to come forward, slowly. When the sachem's canoe was about 100 feet from the rock, he turned again and signaled, this time forking the fingers on his right hand and jabbing them down towards the river.

The People instantly dropped their gaze down towards the water, for they knew then that it was the Little People that occupied the sandstone boulder.

The Little People were dressed in tiny, beautifully-beaded buckskins, and were barefoot. The one that was squatting was significantly bigger than the others, and he wore small strands of purple wampum, which presumably identified him as their leader. It was the big one that had been inscribing some sort of mysterious symbols on the face of the rock. Although the rock lay well out in the current, there was no sign of a boat, and the Little People were dry.

The warriors in Red Hawk's dugout maneuvered it to within twelve feet of the boulder, and held it there in the torrent. The other craft stayed further out on the river.

Continuing to look down at the water, the chief addressed the little figures. "We are very pleased to meet you here, Excellent Ones," he began. "To what do we owe this pleasure?" The sachem was curious, but cautious, for it was very rare to even catch sight of the Little People, and unheard of to find them in such an exposed position.

The larger of the trio looked at Red Hawk in silence for several minutes before he spoke. "You are wise, Red Hawk," he said in a nasally voice, "a real credit to Cautantowwit. But your people have strayed far from the Light." He paused to let his words take effect, and the sachem said nothing. "It has been long since your people have paid us our real dues. And what's more, they have turned their backs on the Creator. Instead, they listen to THAT FOOL!" he continued, his voice becoming shrill as he gestured towards the tribe's shaman, kneeling in one of the trailing canoes.

"That fool knows not from where his power comes, weak as it is," added the little chief. "Hobbamock, the pathetic Man Spirits, trick him into believing that they grant him power."

"But Man Spirits have no power. It only passes through them from the Demons, the true Powers of Darkness, who are far more Evil than even HE can imagine."

Red Hawk was shocked into silence. And not just from what he had heard.

As far as he knew, no one had ever heard one of the Little People speak at such length. They seldom spoke at all. And yet there was even more to come.

"Raise your eyes, Man Chief," said the little figure solemnly. "Look me in the face, Red Hawk, for this will be the last time." The sachem slowly raised his gaze from the river, and looked straight into the black eyes of the little being. They were not the eyes of a Man.

"You have grown many," began the little chief. "You press our strongholds. And you have forgotten your manners. So we will now take our leave of you." Here, the wizened, old-man's face, set on a child's body, softened a bit. "But I bid you good luck, Red Hawk. You and your people will need it."

Still looking into the eyes of the little sachem, Red Hawk felt very afraid. But he forced himself to speak, for he felt that this last statement, at the very least, must be addressed. For it was common knowledge that the Little People knew all things, even those things that have yet to happen. "And why is it, Venerable One, that my people will need luck?" the Sachem asked gravely, dreading the response.

"DO YOU HEAR THAT SONG?" replied the little figure unexpectedly, and with great intensity, as he jabbed his gnarled forefinger into the air. It was then that the People heard the words of a Christian hymn, sung with beautiful, clear voices and joyous hearts, floating over the broad, streaming waters of the Titicut. The people cast bewildered looks about them, but there was no one to be seen.

"Those words are sung by your Conquerors!" shrilled the little sachem. "They worship only the Creator. They have skin the color of the snow, and soon they will come here to take away both your land and your way of life."

Red Hawk felt his heart sink into his stomach. "But why?!" he ventured cautiously. "We too worship Cautantowwit—why will they hate us?"

The little figure cast a very dark look at the sachem. "Many things have transpired of which you know not," he replied after a few moments, with great hesitation. "There has been a Great Change in the Sky Kingdom.

"Cautantowwit grew angry with the lesser beings of his Kingdom, for they grew powerful in his state of removal. In particular, it troubled Him that your shamans fell prey to the lies of the Demons. So some time ago, the Creator sent his only Son, Jesus Christ, to the Earth, in a place far from here, to teach Man the error of his ways. His Son was eventually murdered by Men, but he rose again in triumph, and in doing so forever established dominance over the Kingdom of Evil.

"But in the process, a great being, called Lucifer, the Father of Lies, was cast down by the Creator into the Underworld, along with a host of other great powers that formerly dwelt in the house of the Creator. These beings now reign with great power over the Demons there, and actively seek to destroy Mankind. They stand in opposition to the Creator. Before, by worshipping Hobbamock, your priests merely deprived you of the Light, and cast you and your people into Darkness and Fear. But now, Red Hawk, your shamans have placed your people in mortal danger from the powers of Darkness.

"The Creator, through his Son and his Holy Word, is now reasserting his dominance on Earth. What that means for your kind, Man, his most lowly subjects, fallen from his favor as you are, is exclusive worship. There can be only one God now, and His kingdom is to be reached only through the Son. You must revoke your worship of all the lesser gods, Red Hawk, or your souls will not be allowed to enter the Kingdom of Light. The men with the skin of snow are his chosen disciples, who will carry the new creed around the Earth World.

And as for the other Worlds…." Here the little figure stopped abruptly, nearly biting his tongue, as if he felt he had said too much already.

Red Hawk was now nauseous, for he harbored no doubts that the prophecy of the little chief was accurate. "And what of your race?" he asked. "What will become of your people, the Ancient Ones?" The little sachem dropped his gaze, and Red Hawk watched curiously as a tiny tear tumbled down his wrinkled cheek.

"The Man Spirits with the skin of snow are very many," he replied haltingly. "And they no longer account for us, although we too dwell in Cautantowwit's Kingdom of the Light.

"We have been abandoned by them, and have no recourse. But, we are an Old Race, Red Hawk, very, very, old, and we now grow few. Our time, it seems, has passed. So we go. But we shall miss this place." The little man's moist eyes stared out lovingly over the wild beauty of his surroundings, the river, the tupelo and maple, and he sucked in a deep draught of the salt breeze.

"*Perhaps some day,*" he concluded softly, "*we will return. But that will be long, long, after your time, Man Chief.*"

The two beheld each other then in silence, as Red Hawk tried to digest what he had just heard. It was truly dire news. Then the sachem spoke. "*So the ancient compact, between you and our Ancestors, it is finished?*"

The wizened face of the little chief brightened a bit. "*Not so,*" he replied. "*We will honor our side of the agreement, even though your people did not honor yours. We will leave representatives.*" Nodding upriver towards the blaze of red and orange maple leaves that marked the start of the vast swamp beyond, he went on. "*We will continue to guard the graves of your ancestors. Those who seek to despoil them will be confounded.*"

Red Hawk nodded appreciatively.

"*And here,*" said the little chief, tapping the face of the rock with his finger, "*here I leave you one last, great work of glamour, as a parting favor to your race. We will confuse your new enemies.*"

In response to Red Hawk's quizzical look, the chief replied, "*We have made magic here, marks that will cause their history to elude them. These marks will fracture them, create great strife among them, and destroy the common story that binds them together. This we will do for you, Red Hawk, in honor of the days of old, when our races walked together, in mutual respect, on the shores of Nunkatest, the shining Lake of the Red Waters.*"

Then suddenly, the little figure stood up, pointed directly at Red Hawk, and all three of the little figures vanished.

The chief, astonished and overwhelmed, sat staring at the waves lapping at the tidal boulder for several seconds, before weakly gesturing to his oarsmen to continue downriver. The Indians behind him watched with great concern as their regal leader, tears streaming down his high, bronze cheekbones, slumped motionless into the bottom of his dugout. They could not know that as the swift current of the Taunton whisked him away downstream, Red Hawk was contemplating the end of his people.

That evening, as darkness descended over the Hockomock, the People everywhere stared skyward as long, vertical lines of brilliantly colored spheres, blue, orange, red, and green, dropped down through the gray cloud cover into the waters of Lake Nunkatest, later known as Nippenicket. It was a memorable show, the last great spectacle of The Others. For after that fateful night, the People never laid eyes on the Little People again.

As the years and the centuries rolled by, they ceased even to talk of them. Eventually, the memories of the little ones disappeared, the stories concerning them faded from the oral tradition of the People, and the knowledge of the Little People was lost to them forever.

DIGHTON ROCK
1502 A.D.

One day on the Assonet (Taunton) River, the People saw a wooden house, with men with white skin on it, swimming up the river. These men attacked the People with mighty success, and killed their sachem.

After many moons with no further sign of their attackers, the People looked out over the Titicut one morning to see a Great White Bird swimming up it. Because they associated white birds with bad luck, the People were immediately filled with dread. And what was worse, there were men riding the Bird that had skin the color of the snow. These men came ashore, captured some of the People, and took them back into the belly of the Bird. The Bird then swam upriver, to the place where the Titicut narrows and the Talking Rock with its ancient inscriptions reared its head from the East bank. There, the white men lowered a small boat from the Bird, and rowed ashore. They traveled to a spring that lay just to the northeast of the Talking Rock, and took fresh water from it.

The People fell upon the white men at the spring and slaughtered them. During the fighting, thunder and lightning came from the Bird in the river, and the People that had been captured and held in its belly managed to escape. From this point forward, the People referred to the spring as "White Spring," and to the stream that drains it into the Assonet as "White Man's Brook."

– From the *Indian Legends of the "Wooden House" and the "White Bird"*

Dighton Rock, known to the Wampanoags as the "Talking Rock," is America's oldest and most famous archaeological artifact. In 1916, Professor Edmund Burke Delabarre of Brown University, the Rock's foremost researcher, said that, "No single object of antiquarian interest in America has been so much discussed, probably, as Dighton Rock." For centuries, Dighton Rock has fired the imaginations of millions of people all over the world.

Dighton Rock is now located in a little-known state museum on the banks of the Taunton River in the rural town of Berkeley, Massachusetts. But for thousands of years it lay partially exposed in the shallows of the river, acting as a sort of "natural signpost" for early inhabitants of the region and for European explorers sailing up the Taunton. The massive sandstone boulder inscribed with countless faint lines and mysterious symbols is important to world history because it may offer us unique clues as to who truly first discovered and settled the United States of America. Despite the vast amount of public attention that Dighton Rock has enjoyed in past centuries, however, few people today even realize that it exists.

The Wampanoags called the City of Taunton, which originally included Berkeley, "Cohannet." We know that the Wampanoags were on Assonet Neck, the peninsula adjacent to where Dighton Rock used to lay in the Taunton River, but we have no knowledge of what they used it for. There is little doubt that Assonet Neck was a special place to the Indians, however, because they never sold it to the settlers, despite the sale of all nearby lands and repeated attempts by the settlers to buy it. In 1676, after King Philips War, Assonet Neck was seized by the Colony of New Plymouth.

Early investigations of Dighton Rock by European colonists were largely of a religious nature, and were carried out for the most part by Puritan Ministers. Our first historical record of Dighton Rock is a drawing made by the Reverend John Danforth in 1680. Danforth himself left no written record of the rock, but other writers, notably Professor Isaac Greenwood of Harvard, subsequently brought out the very old and tantalizing "Wooden House" legend that Danforth collected from the area, in addition to his other observations. Danforth apparently believed that part of the famously complex, worn, and puzzling inscription that covers Dighton Rock represents "a Ship without Masts and a mere Wreck cast upon the Shoals," and "an Head of Land possibly a Cape with a Peninsula…Hence a Gulf."

The next character to enter Dighton Rock history is no less a historical figure than Cotton Mather; Puritan minister, Salem witch trial proponent, and at the time America's leading religious figure. In a sermon he gave in 1689, Mather described the artifact as a "Curiosity of New England" on which "are very deeply Engraved, no man alive knows How or When, about half a score Lines, near Ten Foot Long, and a foot and a half broad, filled with strange Characters; which would suggest as odd thoughts about them that were here before us, as there are odd Shapes in that Elaborate Monument…"

We don't know exactly why Cotton Mather was interested in Dighton Rock. That portion of his diary that may have helped us, from January 8, 1687, to May 17, 1690, is missing. But Mather may have been studying the rock to find support for his belief that the Indians were descendents of the Ten Lost Tribes of Israel. The Bible informs us that the people of the ten tribes that populated the northern part of ancient Israel turned their back on the Christian God, and drew his wrath by instead worshipping the pagan god Baal.

These people disappeared from the Biblical account after they were subsequently defeated and banished from the Kingdom of Israel by the Assyrians in 722 B.C. The ultimate fate of these tribes has long been a popular topic of speculation. The theory that the American Indians are descendents of the Ten Lost Tribes, thus "lost" Jews, was commonly adhered to by eminent theologians and scholars in Massachusetts in Cotton Mather's time. This view, which to the Puritans meant that the Indians were in desperate need of conversion to Christianity, may also have been held by John Danforth.

The next significant encounter with our mysterious boulder occurred in 1730, almost 100 years after it was first seen by English colonists. Sometime between January, 1729, and September, 1731, the distinguished Reverend George Berkeley, Dean of Derry, later Bishop of Cloyne, and one of the most eminent of English philosophers, took up residence in Newport, Rhode Island. During one of his many excursions Berkeley visited Dighton Rock.

One account says Berkeley came back convinced that the inscription was "merely the casual corrosion of the rock by the waves of the sea."

Another account, from an obscure paper by Pierre Eugene du Simitiere written around 1780, provides us with the following story. It seems that the Dean of Derry had begun "an Elaborate dissertation" while observing the inscription when he was approached by a local farmer. This farmer might have been Benjamin Jones, who owned the land around Dighton Rock in 1720, and lived there until he died in 1768. Apparently unimpressed by His Eminence, farmer Jones unceremoniously interrupted Berkeley's meditations to inform him that, "that rock had been used formerly by the Indians that resorted hither to Shoot ducks, and dart fish, to wett and Sharpen the points of their arrows and darts on that Stone, which was the cause of the various hollow lines and figures formed thereon."

The belief that local Indians were the authors of Dighton Rock's inscription, which we encounter here for the first time with Dean Berkeley's visit, is one of the most pervasive theories in its history. In fact, despite an almost endless stream of far more exotic and controversial theories regarding the origin of the inscription, this conservative belief has remained popular even to this day.

The last important contributor to what Delabarre would subsequently refer to in his writings as the "Early History" of Dighton Rock was Professor Isaac Greenwood of Harvard College. Greenwood was the first researcher to suggest that the inscription might be of Oriental origin. This idea was destined to become tremendously popular among scholars some fifty to seventy-five years later, near the turn of the 19th century, and it survives even to this day in a variation known as the "Phoenician Theory" of Dighton Rock. The Phoenician Theory is one of the four "official" theories advanced today by the State of Massachusetts, Dighton Rock's current owner.

Edmund Burke Delabarre's "Middle Period" of Dighton Rock history extends from roughly 1744 to 1838. During this time period, scholars the world over advanced theories regarding the origin of the Rock's inscription, ranging from the inscription being inherently indecipherable, to it representing the meaningless scrawl of local Indians, to incredibly elaborate interpretations involving ancient messages of Trojans, Persians, Egyptians, Pelasgian inhabitants of Atlantis, Phoenicians, Tyrians, Jews, Libyans, Roman Catholics, and Chinese. But this period starts with and is dominated by the Phoenician theory, and ends with the advancement of the Norse Theory, which held that Vikings from Greenland inscribed the rock around 1007.

One of the most noteworthy historical figures to tackle the inscription's meaning in this period was Ezra Stiles, Minister at Newport, Rhode Island (1775-1776) and President of Yale College (1778). Stiles was also a recognized authority of the period on "written rocks" like Dighton Rock. Inspired by a copy of a drawing published by Cotton Mather that he had been shown, Stiles visited Dighton Rock and made a drawing by "chalking" the lines, which was the standard practice of the time. He concluded that the inscription was "in Phoenician Letters and 3,000 years old." Stiles wrote to Professor John Winthrop at Harvard, telling him that although he believed the Rock's inscription was "of Great Antiquity," he did not believe it would ever be interpreted.

In 1768, a Harvard Professor of Oriental Languages by the name of Steven Sewall made a life-sized drawing of Dighton Rock. In 1781, Sewall sent a copy of this drawing to M. Court de Gebelin of Paris, France, a celebrated French intellectual. In his letter to Gebelin, Sewall suggests that the inscription on Dighton Rock may be "the work of Phoenicians" or "Chinese or Japanese navigators." That same year, Gebelin published his interpretation of the inscription on Dighton Rock, which he claimed was Phoenician in origin. Gebelin believed that the Phoenicians had "sailed boldly and gloriously" throughout the world in their time, even to America.

Gebelin's Phoenician Theory of American discovery proved influential. It instantly created a lively discussion on the international stage. Many people, including President Ezra Stiles of Yale University, accepted this theory. But many others were critical of Gebelin's theory, even to the point of referring to it as an "explanation repugnant to all history." Despite this criticism of his overall theory, Gebelin's explanation of the origin of the inscription on Dighton Rock remained popular for more than fifty years.

At President Ezra Stile's election speech at Yale in 1783, he delivered a glowing endorsement of Gebelin's Phoenician Theory. In his speech, delivered only a year and a half after Cornwallis surrendered at Yorktown, Stiles predicted the future of America to be "an elevation to glory and honor." Stiles also stated, "Cursed be Canaan;…God shall enlarge Japhet, and Canaan shall be his servant…I rather consider the American Indians as Canaanites of the expulsion of Joshua." Stiles was predicting, on scriptural authority based in the prophecies of the ninth chapter of Genesis, that the American Indians, as descendents of the Canaanites, would become servants of the whites.

Christian extremists would later misrepresent Stile's statements in an attempt to justify the displacement and even extermination of the Indian race, something which Stiles did not speak of or advocate. The Phoenicians, interestingly enough, were Canaanites.

In 1788, James Winthrop, son of John Winthrop, made a life-sized impression of the Rock's inscription. James Winthrop was Librarian at Harvard from 1772 to 1787. George Washington saw this drawing in the Fall of 1789. As the story goes, Dr. John Lathrop was with Washington when he visited Harvard's Museum. Lathrop showed Washington Winthrop's drawing, and told him that there were Oriental characters on the Rock, and that Phoenician Navigators had made them. Washington reportedly smiled and told Lathrop that he "had no doubt that the inscription was made, long ago, by some natives of America." This statement by America's first citizen lent strong support to the ever-present American Indian Theory of the rock.

Other Dighton Rock literature from around this time period indicates that many scholars were now openly despairing that the mysterious inscription would ever be deciphered.

Also in 1789, in a highly confusing set of circumstances, several new drawings of Dighton Rock were produced. The only thing that does appear clear in respect to these new drawings is that President Ezra Stiles of Yale, still not content with his drawings of the inscription, was somehow behind their production. These renditions eventually resulted in one published drawing of the inscription that came to be known as "Dr. Baylies and Mr. Goodwin's Copy, 1790." The ultimate significance of this drawing was that it was published in Rafn's great work of 1837, *Antiquitates Americanae*, which displaced the reigning Phoenician theory of Dighton Rock and altered world history with its claim of a Viking presence in America in the year 1007.

The "Dr. Baylies and Mr. Goodwin's Copy, 1790" drawing was also used by Chingwauk, a well-known Algonquin shaman, in 1839 to provide us with the only detailed American Indian interpretation of the inscription. In his "History of the Indian Tribes of the United States" (1857) Henry Rowe Schoolcraft, the first great chronicler of American Indian life, presents Chingwauk's elaborate interpretation involving Indian exploits as evidence that the native Wampanoags' made the inscription. Delabarre, however, although long a staunch supporter of the Native American theory of Dighton Rock, instead relegates Chingwauk's analysis to the category of "fanciful speculation."

In 1790, for the American Academy of Arts and Sciences, Ezra Stiles wrote his most intense analysis of Dighton Rock ever. In his paper, Stiles discusses once again Phoenicians and the descent of the Indians from the Ten Lost Tribes. This time, however, Stiles actually admits that he might be considered "as carried away into imagination and conjecture." Stiles' paper was not published. However, less speculative parts of it were brought out, and his overall purpose for it, to stir up a general inquiry into written rocks "illustrative of the Antiquities of America" did prove successful. Public interest in the subject increased greatly, in part due to his influence. Professor Delabarre, who never believed Dighton Rock's inscription to be of very great antiquity, later stated that he thought that Stile's ideas were the result of a preconceived belief that the inscription was ancient.

In the early 1800s, a new and fascinating character enters our story. From all available accounts, Samuel Harris, Jr., of Boston, Massachusetts, was a high genius, and possibly the most incredibly profound linguist of all time. Around 1807, Harris studied James Winthrop's drawing of Dighton Rock. He said he saw in it "Hebrew words written in the old Phoenician characters."

We don't know if Samuel believed that this observation supported the Phoenician Theory, or if it linked the Indians to the Ten Lost Tribes, because Samuel Harris was tragically drowned on July 7th, 1810, while still a student at Harvard. Any serious chance for the ultimate acceptance of the Oriental Theory of Dighton Rock probably died with him.

Delabarre analyzed Harris's theory based on the one sheet of paper at Harvard that survives from his comprehensive works, but in the end he decided it was "merely a psychological curiosity." Delabarre does offer us one interesting comment, however. He suggested that Samuel Harris, like Ezra Stiles and the Puritans that came before him, may have believed that Dighton Rock's inscription was proof that the Indians were descendents of the Ten Lost Tribes of Israel.

Perhaps the most astute observer of Dighton Rock ever was Edward Augustus Kendall, an Englishman who traveled through the northern part of the United States in 1807 and 1808. Kendall left us a three-volume account of his journey that includes detailed observations of Dighton Rock, and also a fine sketch of it that he made in oil. In 1917, Delabarre wrote: "In all the history of observation, depiction, and speculation concerning this subject, no one has surpassed and few have equaled this English traveler in freedom from ill-supported imaginings, in accuracy and detail of observation, in saneness of judgment…"

According to Delabarre, in the absence of photography Kendall's drawing was the most accurate one that had been made to date.

His sketch was also significant in that it was the first to begin to expand on the prominent "letters" that are commonly seen on the center of the face of the rock, letters which would later prove so very important to both Rafn's and Delabarre's history-changing theories of American discovery. Kendall, however, offered us no such momentous interpretation of this string of letters. He believed they simply spelled "ORINX."

Kendall's contributions to the subject of Dighton Rock were not limited to an interpretation of the Rock and its inscription. He also collected and recorded local legends from the area of Assonet Neck. Kendall was the one that brought us the legend of the "White Bird," presented at the beginning of this chapter, which is an old Indian tradition from the area that may have a legitimate bearing on the meaning of the inscription. He also recorded, as Danforth had before him, the complementary legend of the "Wooden House" that swam up the Taunton River, which Danforth had said was "gathered from the Tradition of old Indians." The significance of this legend to the history of America becomes clear if we consider that it was probably already very old when Danforth collected it in the late 1600s.

Interestingly, during his research into local legends, Kendall also noted "that a ship's anchor, nearly eaten away by rust, was many years since discovered near this place; and…the still more obscure account of a ship's ribs, which lay and rotted there." Kendall spoke with some locals that believed these accounts were the result of an English ship that had reached the Taunton River very early in the period of European contact. And what's more, these locals believed that the inscription on Dighton Rock was made in relation to this event, which they believed had been either a wreck or the over-wintering of the English ship's crew on Assonet Neck. If these legends have their sources in fact, as many legends do, then taken together with Danforth's interpretation of part of the inscription as depicting an ancient shipwreck, it seems likely that there was pre-Pilgrim contact by Europeans in the locality of Dighton Rock. This event probably included a shipwreck.

Kendall was aware of most of the current theories regarding the origin of the inscription on Dighton Rock. In the end, he apparently decided that all of them were rubbish with the exception of the Native American Theory. Kendall believed the Rock was inscribed by the Indians on "some solemn occasion" to commemorate something. Exactly what that was, he declines to offer. The ultimate importance of this traveling Englishman's contributions to the subject, however, may simply have been his influence on Professor Edmund Burke Delabarre's defining work on the subject in the early 20th century.

Delabarre's "Recent History" of Dighton Rock, starting with his own, final analysis, includes one of the most controversial and significant theories to date. In 1837, Carl Christian Rafn, a Danish Knight, published *Antiquitates Americanae*, an impressive volume which described his "Norse," or Viking Theory of American discovery and settlement.

Rafn (1795-1864) was the scholar who originally brought to public attention the ancient Icelandic Sagas, which describe the epic journeys of Eric the Red, Leif Ericson, and other Vikings to the New World in the 11th century. Rafn subsequently set out to find hard evidence to prove that the Vikings described in the Sagas had reached the shores of the United States of America. Rafn ultimately claimed that the "Vinland" described in the Sagas of the Icelandic Vikings was located on Narragansett Bay, or more specifically, on that part of it known as

Mount Hope Bay, in Rhode Island. He used the inscription on Dighton Rock as the cornerstone of his theory. Finn Magnusen, Rafn's associate, used the "Dr. Baylies and Mr. Goodwin's Copy, 1790" drawing inspired by Ezra Stiles to justify his translation of Dighton Rock's inscription as a record of Norse presence in Rhode Island.

Rafn's theory was widely accepted around the world. "Antiquitates" produced an absolute revolution in thought regarding the discovery of America, for the acceptance of Rafn's theory meant that it was not Columbus who had discovered America, but Icelandic Norse—the Vikings. This theory was finally discredited only in 1937 by Delabarre's work, which established that Rafn's interpretation of Dighton Rock's inscription was based largely on conjecture.

It was only when Professor Delabarre finally, almost a century later, reviewed the two original drawings of Dighton Rock that had been sent to Rafn from Rhode Island by the Rhode Island Historical Society and later published in *Antiquitates Americanae*, that "Rafn's Ruse" was uncovered. Rafn had clearly embellished them. But for the better part of a century after the publication of the book, most educated people in the world probably believed it was a proven fact that the Norse had first discovered America.

The story of Professor Edmund Burke Delabarre is perhaps the most fascinating, and historically significant story to date in the history of the mysterious boulder from Assonet Neck.

Delabarre, to whom we are indebted for researching and writing so much of the history of Dighton Rock, was born in 1863 and hired as an Associate Professor of Psychology at Brown University in Providence, Rhode Island in 1891, and was eventually named Professor Emeritus there in 1932. It appears, however, that the Professor was more interested in Archaeology, and "written rocks" in particular, than Psychology, for the majority of his published works throughout his career related to them.

In 1912, Delabarre bought a summer home on Assonet Neck, about a mile from Dighton Rock. In 1914, he began studying the rock and its history, and he would spend the remainder of his life doing so. The main fruits of the Professor's vast labors on the subject were three papers, published in the "Transactions" of the Colonial Society of Massachusetts in 1916, 1917, and 1919, corresponding to the "Early," "Middle," and "Recent" historical periods of Dighton Rock. Although there have been others to date, Edmund Burke Delabarre produced what has emerged as the definitive study on the history of Dighton Rock.

Ultimately, Delabarre also produced his own theory regarding the meaning of the inscription, one that still stands as one of the most plausible and controversial theories of all.

Delabarre's "official" purpose for studying Dighton Rock, all along, was to discredit Carl Christian Rafn's Norse Theory. Part of the reason he set out to do so was probably because of his belief that Vinland could not have been in Rhode Island. But Delabarre's goal was not that simple. It is likely that he sensed historical injustice as well, and set out to right it purely out of academic integrity. Delabarre also wished to return credit for the inscription to its rightful owners, whom he believed, at least at first, to be solely the American Indians.

Delabarre first achieved his "official" goal of discrediting Rafn's Norse Theory. By doing so, he brought final vindication to the very large crowd of Rafn skeptics that had by now appeared.

The Brown Professor accomplished this goal by comparing the original drawings from the Rhode Island Historical Society with Rafn's versions that he had published in "Antiquitates" and also by leveraging his own knowledge of the inscription. And that personal knowledge was profound. Delabarre doubtlessly spent more hours pouring over Dighton Rock's inscription than anyone has, before or since. Although the Professor did not prove definitively that Vikings never wrote on Dighton Rock, he did expose Rafn's methods as sufficiently shoddy to warrant the dismissal of his version of the Norse Theory of American discovery.

In addition to discrediting "Rafn's Ruse," Delabarre was the first, and perhaps the only, Dighton Rock researcher to fully explore the almost unbelievable ability of the artifact to influence the human thought process. By putting his talents in Psychology, then just a fledgling discipline, into play, Delabarre brought into sharp focus the historic ability of Dighton Rock to act as a kind of Rorschach ("rock shock") test for all who dare study it. Delabarre described this phenomenon as similar to that of a child laying on their back looking up at white clouds in the sky overhead, and seeing there the forms of elephants, faces, or anything else that their imagination dictates.

But by daring to expound openly upon the psychological aspects of Dighton Rock to his far more conservative fellow scientists, Delabarre took serious professional risks. These risks appear to have played out unfavorably, and ultimately resulted in the Professor paying a heavy professional price. His work in this area was by all appearances not taken seriously by them.

Delabarre spent hundreds, maybe even thousands of hours alone with Dighton Rock, staring at its inscription, dwelling deeply on its mystery. Those people close to him may even have questioned whether Delabarre had lost his mind. But if they did fear for the Professor's sanity, they need not have. For the end result of all those hours Delabarre spent obsessing over the Rock turned out to be not madness, but a stroke of genius. Just as the Professor was preparing his final, painfully-researched "Recent History of Dighton Rock" for publication, which he believed would prove once and for all that American Indians had made the inscription, an exceedingly strange and wonderful thing happened.

Delabarre's own words describe it best. "It may well be imagined with what astonishment, on examining the Hathaway photograph for the hundredth time on December 2, 1918, I saw in it clearly and unmistakably the date 1511. No one had ever seen it before, on rock or photograph; yet once seen, its genuine presence on the rock cannot be doubted." The date had always before been viewed as part of a larger drawing on the rock. Delabarre explained his sudden ability to see it as similar to an observer suddenly spotting a smaller, hidden object within a larger picture in a "picture puzzle."

Once he had the date, Delabarre set out to discover what European explorer might have written it. He quickly researched recorded history to determine who might have come up the Taunton River in 1511. One strong possibility was suggested to him by Henry Harrisse's account from 1892, that describes the voyages of the Corte Real brothers from the Portuguese Empire in 1501 and 1502.

After reading Harrisse's account, Delabarre went straight to the "letters" in the middle of the inscription, the same ones that proved so critical to Rafn's Norse theory. There, Delabarre found "CORTE," letters which strongly suggested the name "Corte-Real." Then, above this line, he located an "M." Bingo, he had it.

"Miguel Corte-Real, 1511."

Somewhat to the Professor's chagrin, yet another theory of Dighton Rock had been born, and this time it was of his own making. Delabarre's theory would later come to be known as the "Portuguese Theory" of Dighton Rock. Delabarre included these exciting new discoveries in his soon-to-be published "Recent History of Dighton Rock." Delabarre later also said that he saw a representation of the royal arms of the Portuguese Empire, and a Latin phrase that read:

"V DEI hIC DVX IND."

Delabarre interpreted this phrase as meaning: "By the Will of God, here Chief of the Indians."

The Professor also attempted to assemble evidence for his Portuguese Theory beyond what he said he found in the inscription itself. Delabarre seems to have believed that the Indian Legends of the "Wooden Ship" and the "White Bird" were two different accounts of the same incident, which represented the arrival of Miguel Corte-Real, the Royal Portuguese Explorer, on Assonet Neck. In support of his theory, Delabarre also cited Verrazano's observation from 1524, when the

Florentine explorer, in the employ of the King of France, visited Narragansett Bay for fifteen days and noted that the Indians, probably Wampanoags, had "many plates wrought from copper."

As evidence that Miguel and his men were there, he also pointed to Verrazano's now-famous observation that the Indians of Narragansett Bay were extremely light-skinned, even trending towards white.

Then Delabarre went even further. He suggested that many Wampanoag words could be traced to the Portuguese. One of his examples was the use of "-quin" in chiefs' names, such as "Tispaquin," Philip's brother-in-law and his top general in King Philip's War. Delabarre suggested that "-quin" could have been derived from "Quinas," the Portuguese word for *the royal arms of Portugal*, a type of shield.

Based on this proposed evidence, Delabarre advanced a theory that, in 1502, Miguel Corte-Real had gone in search of his brother, Gaspar—they were both Navigators of the Portuguese Empire. Gaspar had failed to return from a voyage of exploration to Newfoundland the previous year, and had been last seen coasting south. Newfoundland had been discovered previously by their father, also a Navigator of the Empire, who had been in the service of Prince Henry. Henry had founded the famous School of Navigation at Sagres. His community of scholars there, many drawn from the Muslim world, invented the caravel, a revolutionary new kind of sailing ship that tacked. The Prince's Portuguese Navigators used this new technology, together with unrivaled daring and navigational expertise, to discover much of the Western world.

Delabarre initially proposed that Miguel had shipwrecked on the Newfoundland coast, and then made his way south in a small boat, arriving years later at Assonet Neck, where he became chief of the Wampanoags. But later, after he completed his research, Delabarre changed his mind, and instead proposed that Miguel had shipwrecked in 1502, and much closer to Assonet Neck, perhaps on the infamous Nantucket shoals. Delabarre believed that Miguel, perhaps because he was growing old by 1511, or for some other reason, left the inscription on Dighton Rock in a bid to attract the attention of any European ships that ventured up the Taunton River.

Delabarre's Portuguese Theory of Dighton Rock, if it is correct, means that Corte-Real, and probably between twenty-five and fifty crewmen, lived on Assonet Neck for at least the nine-year period between 1502 and 1511 with the Wampanoags.

"Over there!" Miguel said suddenly, "Make for that ledge." The leader of the men paddling the mishoon gestured towards a long, low boulder of grey-brown sandstone that lay near the east bank. The boulder rose about four feet above the flow, stretched

about eleven feet long, and faced the Northwest. As the men approached, they could see many strange engravings on its face, simple pictures, and writing in various scripts that were unknown to them. The designs on it were faint but legible.

"Bring it alongside" ordered Miguel sharply. The men clumsily docked the mishoon against the boulder, even as the flooding current tried to scrape them off. Only by strong-arming the southern end of the slippery rock was Miguel able to hold the dugout fast.

"Miguel," said Carlos, the bowman, "we should follow the shamans. We know not where they go."

"No" replied Miguel curtly. Turning to his men, the nobleman said, in Portuguese: "We shall leave a mark."

Carlos and Diogo exchanged surprised looks. It had been years since any of them had spoken their mother tongue.

"Yes Sir!" exclaimed Carlos, "but that is best done upon our return downriver, is it not?" Then he cast a fearful look upstream. "I do not wish to become lost in the Place Where the Spirits Dwell. We should follow the shamans."

Diogo, shifting his weight nervously in the canoe, chimed in. "We need to keep a close eye on those heathen wretches, Miguel," he muttered darkly. "You know we cannot trust them."

"And that," replied Miguel thoughtfully, "is exactly why we must leave our mark now."

While his men fretted and showed increasing signs of anxiety, in contrast Miguel appeared serene, composed, noble. "The world must know we were here."

"Draw your knife, Carlos" Miguel ordered, now with anger. "Do it now, as I command!"

Carlos swallowed hard and drew his long iron blade, one of his few remaining possessions from Europe.

"You will inscribe your Captain's name, there, in the middle of the ledge," said Miguel.

Carlos remained motionless, kneeling in the bottom of the dugout, staring blankly at the face of the rock.

"Well?!" roared Miguel. "Has it been so long you have forgotten how to write?"

"But I…I…I," stuttered Carlos, "I was never a good writer, Sir. I am a sailor, Sir, only a poor sailor!"

"Then write in Roman," said Miguel scornfully. "The angles will allow you to inscribe the letters easier. Use capital letters—as you remember them on the coins of the Empire."

Miguel's reasoning seemed to motivate the seaman, for in truth, he had been dubious of his ability to scrape curved lines into the rock.

"All right," Carlos muttered, eying the current racing alongside, "hold her steady."
He clenched his knife in his right fist, just as if he was going to plunge it into someone's

chest, and placed his left hand against the wet face of the rock for support as the craft rocked under him. Then he scraped the following text into the rock's gritty face:

MIGVEL
CORTRЄaL

It was a painstakingly slow exercise that took nearly fifteen minutes. Meanwhile, Diogo and Miguel were struggling to hold the canoe steady.

"Now you, Diogo," said Miguel, when Carlos finally finished. "Inscribe the date."

Carlos, his hand shaking slightly, passed the blade to Diogo, who was kneeling in the bow. Diogo inscribed the date as so, a few feet forward of the Captain's name:

1511

Diogo used Arabic numerals, with the "5" in "1511" represented as a capital "S." After carving the date, he looked searchingly at Miguel, who said nothing. "And the Quinas, Miguel?" (Diogo was asking his leader whether he should draw the Portuguese royal shield, which was typically included by Portuguese Navigators in their tell-tale inscriptions. The depiction of the Quinas was intended to honor King Dom Manoel and the Empire.)

"No Quinas," replied Miguel softly. "There will be no mention of Dom Manoel. We are no longer subjects of the Empire. I alone reign here."

Even though he was nine years removed from Portugal, this openly-treasonous statement was enough to cause Carlos to murmur nervously. But Diogo, ever the rebel, merely smiled the sly smile of a pirate. "It is as it should be, Miguel," he offered. "Let's be on our way."

"I am pleased you concur," said Miguel, looking directly at Carlos. "However, our work here is not yet complete. We may not be subjects of the King, but we are still Christians, and I am still a Knight of the Order of Christ. Inscribe the Cruz de Christo," he ordered. (Miguel was referring to the symbol of the cross used by the Order of Christ, that all-powerful Portuguese religious organization that traced its ancestry back to the Crusaders and that at the time controlled Portugal.)

So Diogo raised his blade once again, and just to the left of the date, he drew the following cross, with its distinctive terminal trapezoidal flare at the end of the arms:

✠ 1511

The sailor drew the cross with an elongated base stem, as was sometimes the custom in Portugal. Miguel watched approvingly, then turned to Carlos. "Now draw the cross over my name as well, in honor of our Lord Jesus Christ and the Holy Order."

So Carlos took the knife back and etched the cross, this one with branches of equal length, over his captain's name. "There" he said, when it was complete. "Now let us follow those demons."

If Edmund Burke Delabarre's Portuguese Theory is right, and Miguel Corte-Real was living with the Wampanoags in 1511, this would place the Portuguese nobleman in New England over a century before the English Pilgrims arrived at Plymouth in 1620, and two years before Ponce de Leon discovered Florida in 1513. It would mean that the first European in history known to have set foot in what would eventually become the United States was a Portuguese, and not a Spaniard. The impact of this theory's ultimate acceptance would be limited as far as the history of the United States is concerned, but it would be of great importance to Portugal and the history of the Portuguese Empire.

Professor Delabarre's Portuguese Theory of Dighton Rock sparked major controversy both in America and abroad, because just about everyone, as it turns out, is interested in who first discovered and settled the United States of America. The reaction to this controversial new theory was not entirely positive. This was probably partly because people thought Delabarre took his interpretation of the inscription too far. For many people, Delabarre's claim that he saw the inscription "By the Will of God, here Chief of the Indians" in Latin in association with Miguel Corte-Real's signature cast severe doubt over his entire theory. Delabarre himself never seemed convinced that the Latin inscription was definitely there.

Brown University, for their part, did not officially acknowledge Delabarre's contribution to the subject of Dighton Rock. As might be expected, however, Portugal, the Portuguese people, and Portuguese Americans were significantly more accepting of this new theory. In 1933, the Portuguese Government, who has always considered the lost Corte-Real brothers two of their finest sons, eager to believe that Navigators of the Portuguese Empire had reached America, officially decorated Delabarre for his work.

However, there were major objections to Delabarre's theory, even in Portugal. Professor Edmund Burke Delabarre died in 1945, amid the ongoing controversy regarding his theory of Dighton Rock. Delabarre was probably never completely certain whether Dighton Rock had revealed its true secret to him, or whether it had merely manipulated his unconscious mind as he believed it had done to so many others before him.

After Professor Delabarre passed away, the Portuguese American community took up the cause of the Portuguese Theory. The most recent of these supporters is a Portuguese-born physician named Manuel Luciano DaSilva, a resident of Bristol, Rhode Island. Over the last fifty years, DaSilva has authored many articles and published a book, *Portuguese Pilgrims and Dighton Rock* (1971) in the United

States and Portugal that unabashedly promotes the idea that the Portuguese were both the discoverers and first settlers of the United States. DaSilva was highly instrumental in protecting Dighton Rock. His strenuous efforts in this area contributed directly to the artifact's removal from the Taunton River and the establishment of the current Dighton Rock Museum, thus protecting the artifact from continued weathering by the elements as well as vandalism.

In 1970, Professor George F. W. Young of Harvard University produced a remarkable, scholarly book called *Miguel Corte-Real and the Dighton Writing Rock*. Young's goal was to try and make some sense out of the Corte-Real claims, in an attempt to reverse what he felt was the unjust treatment of them by the academic community. Most historians and archaeologists had by then thrown up their hands. Because the inscription was so devilishly hard to decipher, they either ignored the Portuguese Theory or openly mocked it.

Young examined the validity of the Portuguese Theory using solid scholarship and keen judgment. He discounted all of Delabarre's evidence that he came up with after his initial discoveries of the name and date as either baseless or problematical.

He concludes the entire matter, however, by stating that the signature and the date should be admitted as evidence for the Portuguese Theory. But importantly, Young also concluded that to prove the Portuguese Theory, more evidence is needed, perhaps in the form of a newly discovered old manuscript from the Azores or Portugal, or a new archaeological find, such as Portuguese armor, somewhere in Southeastern Massachusetts.

What is the secret of Dighton Rock? Were Miguel Corte-Real and his Portuguese crew the first settlers of the United States? Who was the first European Christian to greet an American Indian? Was it a blonde Viking from 11th century Greenland, freshly converted to the new faith? Or perhaps some forgotten Englishman, tragically shipwrecked at the turn of the 16th century?

One day, as Young suggested, additional physical evidence may be discovered that lends support to the Portuguese Theory, or even to one of the many other theories of Dighton Rock, and the secret it holds may finally be revealed to us. But for the present, there is one thing of which we can be certain. In 1620, a small, dedicated group of Christian separatists from England arrived in the New World, met the local Indians, and stayed.

COSMIC WAR
1620 A.D.

The song was first heard in the spring of 1617, at the start of the Great Dying. The People all along the Atlantic coast, from Patuxet in the north to Sakonnett in the south, many of them laying sick with fevers in yellowed blankets, gazed weakly skyward in bewilderment. They heard the following words, sung by joyous voices in a foreign tongue.

My soul doth magnify the Lord
My spirit doth rejoice
In God my Savior, and my God
I hear a joyful voice.
Hallelujah, Hallelujah,
Hosanna, Hosanna!

–The "Old Indian Hymn"

This beautiful yet terrifying celestial melody always started off softly, then gradually grew louder, coursing over the harbors, the beaches, and the fields before fading gently away. It was heard many times over the next three years, and was the topic of much speculation.

It had been long now since the Little Chief had warned Red Hawk of the coming of the men with skin the color of snow, and the People did not recall his prophetic words. But the mysterious melody struck great fear into the hearts of the People nonetheless, because a few of them recognized the language as English, the tongue spoken by those men whom in recent years had been fishing off their coast, and who had on several occasions kidnapped and even killed villagers.

Shortly after they first heard the melody, the People suffered a deadly attack by a warlike tribe from the far north. Then many more of the People became sick, and soon they began to die in great numbers. So many of the People were dying that there were too few left with strength enough to bury the dead. The People prayed to Cautantowwit to stop the dying, but he was silent. They asked the shamans to implore Hobbamock to stop it, but the shamans told the People that Hobbamock had informed them that this plague was sent by Cautantowwit, and as a result, there was little he could do to help them.

The plague eviscerated the village of Patuxet on Massachusetts Bay, which lay on the site of modern-day Plymouth, as surely as a scalpel. This was the home of the Patuxet tribe of the Pokanokets, as the People were then referred to by outsiders. All that was left of the village were piles of skulls and bones. Heaps of them lay upon the hills that looked out on the sparkling waters of Massachusetts Bay and beside the deserted fields of waving Indian corn, now ravaged by crows and raccoons.

In August, 1620, a wretched band of English Separatists set forth from the Netherlands on a journey to the New World. They had fled government oppression in England earlier, in 1607/1608, in order to worship God in their own fashion. They were poor, ill-prepared, sorely vexed by non-Separatist passengers, and according to all accounts, including their own, totally incapable of settling a new continent. But their God filled them with his Holy Spirit, took away their fears, and gave them immense strength.

Wracked by storms and disease, they suffered a terrible voyage across the Atlantic on their ship, the Mayflower. Many of the passengers and most of the crew died. But against all odds, on November 9th, 1620, they arrived off Provincetown, Massachusetts, at the tip of Cape Cod.

The first thing the Pilgrims on board did was fall to their knees on the shore, and thank God for bringing them safely to the New World. Here, they believed, free from oppression, they were destined to build a holy community of Saints with which to honor Him. It was near Provincetown, at today's First Encounter Beach, that the Pilgrims first met the People. The Nauset Tribe was already hostile to Europeans, having recently suffered depredations by them.

The Nausets attacked the Pilgrims, but did not manage to harm any of them. The Pilgrims quickly realized that barren sand dunes, full of hostile natives, was no place to settle. So they set sail and ended up off Patuxet. When they saw the heaps of bones, the deserted fields, and the acres of cleared land that reminded them so much of their past home in England, they believed that God had prepared the place for them, and they promptly settled the town that they called Plymouth.

Massasoit, the "Great Chief" of the Pokanokets, from his capitol at Sowams, at the mouth of the Taunton River on Narragansett Bay in modern day Bristol and Warren, Rhode Island, observed the movements of the Pilgrims closely through his scouts. Massasoit noticed that for the first time, the whites had brought their women and children. In addition, these newcomers did not trade, as their predecessors had— they kept to themselves. He knew that they had come to stay. As leader of a once-powerful people now laid low by the plague, and one that had experienced firsthand the worst tendencies of the whites, Massasoit was deeply concerned.

The Great Chief wasted no time praying to Cautantowwit, for he had little faith in the Creator. Instead, he went straight to his shamans. He told them to go into their stronghold in the Hockomock, consult with Hobbamock on the matter of the settlers at Patuxet, and come out with a recommendation on how to deal with them. So the shamans removed themselves into the dark recesses of the swamp, donned their masks, and danced themselves into a trance state, just as the powerful shamans of old had in the days of their Paleo ancestors.

The shamans swept away on their magical flights down through the cold springs of the Hockomock, and further still, into the darkness of the Underworld, and there they communed with Hobbamock in all of his dread forms.

The shamans begged Hobbamock to aid them in destroying the whites. But instead, to their great disappointment, he warned them not to attack. When the shamans emerged from the Hockomock three days later, they went to see Massasoit at Sowams. Massasoit asked them what course of actions Hobbamock had recommended.

The shamans told him that now was not the time to kill off the whites, although that time may come. And what else had they learned? queried Massasoit angrily, for he was hungry for concrete information with which he could form a strategy. Hobbamock had told them, the shamans said, that he would aid them, and bring them victory if a battle did come. And there was more.

Hobbamock had sent a personal message to the chief, offering him protection in the event of war. He had told the shamans that Massasoit would die by no English hand. The shamans had brought Massasoit a clear, if unsatisfying message from the Underworld, and one which he was compelled to accept. There would be no hasty action against the settlers at Plymouth.

The Pokanoket shamans, mortally disappointed with Massasoit's verdict to spare Plymouth, later begged Massasoit to let them curse the newcomers. At first the Great Chief refused, then he consented to their request, mostly to appease them but also because he wanted to assess the affect of their powers against the whites. So the shamans gathered in their dark haunts in the Hockomock, communed with Hobbamock, and sent their Guardian spirits, or familiars, to do their dirty work at Plymouth. Then they sat back and waited. And waited some more.

When the chief demanded to know why their curses were not working, the shamans told him it would take more time. But eventually, through word from Massasoit's scouts, it became obvious to everyone that nothing momentous had occurred at Plymouth. As a result of this exercise, Massasoit became even more concerned about Plymouth than he had been before, and the shamans were secretly deeply shaken. Never before had their combined powers proven so impotent. From that day forward, the shamans knew just how difficult it would be for them to fend off the whites and their powerful faith.

That first winter of 1620-1621, the Pilgrims were dying in droves. This had to do with disease and exposure, and nothing to do with the shamans' curse. The fledgling colony at Plymouth was in real danger of being destroyed by the Pokanokets. Massasoit did indeed forfeit a great opportunity, for at that time the Pilgrims could probably have raised only about twenty fighting men had they been attacked. The winter was unusually mild for the region, one factor which probably helped the English survive.

Another reason they survived was that an Indian named Tisqauntum, or Squanto for short, abruptly appeared in Plymouth offering to help them. Squanto had been one of the Indians violently plucked from his homeland by the whites a few years earlier, and taken to Europe. When he eventually returned to his village of Patuxet, everyone was dead from the plague. Squanto was the one person at the time who knew the language and ways of both the whites and the Indians. As an interpreter between them, he could easily influence the interactions between the two groups. Squanto was a natural politician, who probably had dreams of ruling the Pokanokets in Massasoit's stead.

When Squanto went to Plymouth and offered his assistance, the Pilgrims, poised on the edge of disaster, were delighted. Massasoit, for his part, probably distrusted Squanto from the start, but he had little choice but to engage his services because he desperately needed intelligence about the newcomers, and there was no one else to whom he could turn. Squanto ensnared Massasoit.

He played on the Chief's greatest fears by telling him the English had the ability to inflict the plague on the Pokanokets. Then he tactfully pointed out that an alliance between Massasoit and the English could shift the political balance of power in the region back to the Pokanokets, who were now greatly reduced in power by the plague.

Squanto had chosen his words well. Massasoit knew that the Narragansetts, his enemies to the south, were probably planning on conquering him. And he was rightly terrified of more plague. And so, in his moment of weakness, directly influenced by Squanto, Massasoit not only did not crush the English, but he actually chose to ally with them. This decision was not a popular one with all his subjects, particularly so with Corbitant, the powerful sachem of the Pocassets. Corbitant had advocated for destroying the English at once. He would later plot against Massasoit, probably with Squanto's support. But Massasoit remained firmly in control.

It was Squanto who made the first introduction between the Pilgrims and Massasoit. Interestingly, Edward Winslow, one of the religious leaders of the Colony, later noted that Squanto "did not translate [his words of peace] well." From the very beginning, Squanto used his position to keep the Indians from massacring the whites, and also to his own advantage. Many Indians distrusted and hated Squanto for these reasons, but he always had the ear of Massasoit. And what's more, Squanto somehow managed to become a trusted advisor and friend to Governor Bradford of the Plymouth Colony. After Squanto's death, which may have been the result of an Indian plot to poison him, Bradford wrote that the interpreter was "a special instrument sent of God for their good beyond their expectations."

Massasoit also sent a Pokanoket pniese, ironically named Hobbamock, to the Pilgrims' aid as an insurance policy for Squanto. By all accounts, Hobbamock cut a fine figure, and seems to have been a powerful individual of character. Hobbamock, who, as a pniese, was part of Massasoit's inner circle of advisors, ultimately became a close friend of Miles Standish, the military leader of the Colony. The two were both warriors by trade.

While helping the Pilgrims, Hobbamock, like Squanto, was out for his own gains, and was generally despised by his own people as a traitor. All evidence points to the fact that Squanto and Hobbamock, despite their apparently similar roles, actually hated each other, and each actively worked to undermine the other's efforts to aid the Pilgrims.

While the threat of massacre by the Pokanokets was momentarily averted, there soon proved to be other serious threats to the tiny group of Pilgrims as well. Soon after they settled Plymouth, Thomas Weston, one of their financial backers, frustrated with their seeming inability to produce dividends on his investment, arranged for another colony to be established in America.

This colony, called Wessagussett, was located at modern-day Weymouth, Massachusetts. Established right next to a Massachusetts Indian village, Weston's colony was composed of all men, who were roughnecks devoid of the Christian faith. Weston's faithless men floundered, despite the plentiful natural resources of their coastal surroundings. The men soon started abusing the local Indians by stealing their food and attempting to seduce their squaws. Then they started to starve, and the Indians turned on them.

The colony begged Plymouth for help. While offering advice and encouragement to Weston's men at Wessagussett, Plymouth learned that the Massachusetts were so angered by their behavior that they were planning to massacre all the whites, including those at Plymouth, with a regional force of warriors.

Miles Standish, Plymouth's military leader, convinced Bradford and the other cautious leaders of the colony that he should be allowed to resolve the issue with force. Standish had his own reasons for arguing for this use of force. One of the Massachusetts Indians who was instigating the attack on Wessagussett and the other whites, a pniese named Wituwamatt, had personally insulted Standish in a prior encounter. The pniese had contemptuously called Standish, who was a short man, "a midget." Standish, always quick to anger and violence, had not forgotten the slight, and was eager for revenge.

In 1623, with Plymouth's blessing, Standish, taking his friend Hobbamock, the Pokanoket pniese, as his translator and just a handful of men, sailed straight for Wessagussett. He arrived to find the colony in shambles, with many of the Englishmen living as slaves to the Indians. The Massachusetts were immediately suspicious of his motives, so Standish was careful. He decided to set a trap.

Standish invited Wituwamatt, his hated adversary, and another Massachusetts pniese to a feast of roast pork at a house in the village, knowing full well that this meat was a delicacy to the Indians. The warriors came, partly because they were hungry, and they brought women and children with them. At the appointed hour, Standish opened the door of the house, watched with satisfaction as the Indians filed in, closed the door, and turned to them, smiling. Then, as he had planned, the door was locked from the outside.

Standish had never felt so alive, so ready. His senses were incredibly heightened. When the plank thudded into place against the outside of the door, to him it sounded like a thunderclap. The personal scent of the Indian closest to him, Wituwamatt, smelled as strong as body odor, even though the pniese had purified himself with a sweat bath before his arrival. Standish could feel the blood moving through every inch of his veins, hear his own heart thumping.

But strangely, he could hear nothing around him. The background noises of the busy room were strangely muted; he could not hear the deep tones of the men as they extended strained greetings, the shrill outbursts of the infants, or the murmurings of the squaws attempting to hush them. He existed, momentarily, in an alternate state, independent of space and time.

Then suddenly, a great surge of energy electrified Standish's small frame. As the closest observers gasped and fell back, he went up on his toes, then left the ground completely as he strained to reach the large knife hanging from a cord around Wituwamett's thick, brown neck. The warrior stood six-feet-four-inches tall, while Standish's own crown was a foot lower.

Standish grabbed the cord with such power that he wrenched the Indian's broad, shocked face down close to his own, and then, despite the fact that the cord was made of fresh, strong buckskin, snapped it easily. As the cord broke, the animated Englishman's teeth tore into the ear of the pniese, and with a wrench of his neck, amputated it. Wituwamett just stood there for a few seconds, his countenance a mixture of amazement and outrage, one hand clamped onto the side of his head, with crimson blood spurting out between his fingers. Then Standish spat his ear at him and started screaming unintelligibly.

The pniese finally reacted by going for Standish's throat, but it was too late. The Pilgrim Captain was already stabbing him, repeatedly, with his own blade. By now the room was chaos. Standish's men had attacked the other Massachusetts pniese, and were stabbing him as well. People were slipping, sliding, and falling down in all the blood. The Indian women and children were frantic, wailing, and trying to push their way in a mass out the door, but it would not yield.

To the observers in the room, Standish seemed to be experiencing a sort of epileptic fit. His small, compact body was convulsing, and contorting in unlikely directions. His stabbing arm was ratcheting back and forth at incredible speed as he stabbed the pniese over and over again. Standish stabbed Wituwamett in the chest, the stomach, the shoulders, the back, the head, stabbed him so many times that when it was all over, the warrior's body was unrecognizable to his own people.

The strangest thing about the conflict, at least to the English observers, was that when it came time for the two pnieses to die, they didn't. Covered in blood, their bodies perforated with stab wounds and gushing out intestines, the Massachusetts pnieses at no time cried out. And for quite some time, it appeared that the stabbing was having no effect on them, to the great wonder of the English. This did not surprise the Indian witnesses, however, for they were well aware that their pnieses never died in battle.

But this time, in the end, they did die. When they finally dragged Standish off Wituwamett, the Indian lay still. Standish was still stabbing his lifeless body, gasping and sputtering obscenities, interspersed with grins and manic outbursts of laughter. Hobbamock steadied Standish on his feet, tried to calm him down, and helped him get cleaned up. Then, pausing to take a good look at the butchered remains of the powerful Massachusetts pniese, he turned to the little Captain and smiled broadly. "Not bad for a midget," he said, then clapped his English friend approvingly on the back.

After Miles Standish killed Wituwamett, the threat to the Pilgrims evaporated. The roughnecks at Wessagussett sailed away to Maine, never to return. When the Indians in the region heard of the incident, they were terrified.

It wasn't so much because of the brutal nature of the killings. The Indians were afraid because it had been pnieses that were killed, and pnieses were supposed to be invulnerable in battle. Men like Wituwamett, and Hobbamock, for that matter, regularly performed acts such as running directly into enemy fire, without any fear of being struck down.

Here was yet more proof, thought the Indians, that their power, drawn from Hobbamock, was useless against the whites and their God. In addition, the Indians were simply shocked by the whole affair. They hadn't thought the English had it in them. The People from all over the region were so affected that they fled from their villages in panic and hid in the swamps. In the Hockomock and elsewhere, mysterious illnesses took them, and they began to die. In addition, because they left their villages, their crops failed, and starvation caused more of them to perish.

The Indians weren't the only ones horrified by the events at Wessagussett. The Pilgrims faced severe criticism for Standish's behavior from some Englishmen as well. Their own Pastor, John Robinson, who had been left sick back in Europe, was distressed.

He wrote Governor Bradford condemning the attack, and criticized Plymouth for not converting more Indians to Christianity, as opposed to killing them. Robinson, who had always been the voice of moderation to his followers, was not replaced in Plymouth in the first years. With Robinson in Leiden, where he stayed until his death in 1625, it was practically guaranteed that the hardliners like Standish would have their say in Plymouth.

Shortly after the incident at Wessagussett, the great sachems of the People mysteriously began to die, one after the other. These included Aspinet, of the Nausets, and the Iyanough, the sachem of Cummaquid, which is now Barnstable on Cape Cod. Iyanough was universally recognized on both sides of the conflict as a great leader. Before Iyanough died, he said, "...the God of the English was offended with [the Indians], and would destroy them in his anger."

In the end, some of the Pokanokets tried to appease Plymouth by sending them a canoe full of gifts. But the craft mysteriously overturned, went to the bottom, and three Indians died.

After that, most of the Indians in the region gave up. Only Massasoit and his Wampanoags turned out to be winners. After Wessagussett, the great sachem was able to capitalize on his alliance with the English to reinstate the power of his tribe. The new power structure created by this first Indian-white alliance brought political stability back to the region.

In 1623, the Pilgrims imported chickens and goats to the Colony, and cattle followed shortly after. This was a momentous move. These domestic beasts were intensely hated by the People, for they destroyed the land. Pigs let loose by colonists destroyed the shellfish beds where they were left to root. And worst of all, the cattle and horses, left free to roam, ransacked and trampled the Indian cornfields. These domestic animals would prove to be a major source of friction between the whites and the Indians far into the future. To the Indian, perhaps more than anything else, including the colonists' hated houses, domestic farm animals were a symbol of the colonists' desecration of their sacred land. It was not long before these animals became, for that reason, a favorite target of destruction for the Indians.

In 1630, 1,500 English came to settle the city of Boston, just to the north of Plymouth, and more came to the State of Connecticut to the south. The Boston settlers formed a large, rival Puritan Colony called the Massachusetts Bay Colony that challenged Plymouth's own tiny enclave. The Massachusetts Bay Colony was geographically situated in a much more advantageous spot, with a deep harbor, as opposed to the shallow one at Plymouth. The Pilgrims were no longer the only European settlers on the scene.

Plymouth immediately began to fall into the shadow of Massachusetts Bay. Despite their vigorous efforts to generate capital to pay off the debt they owed to their backers, they were unable to do so. They experienced a long string of business reversals—commercial ships sinking and duping by villainous business partners, to name a few—that were so unbelievable that they were seemingly sent by God to keep them poor.

One of the Pilgrim's few profitable enterprises was breeding large numbers of cattle and hogs to sell to the Puritans in Boston. The Pilgrims were not able to pay off their debt until much later, in 1648, and then only by selling off the only valuable possession they had—the land they had purchased from the Indians. To their great credit, this land, with very few exceptions, had been purchased fairly from the Wampanoags at market price.

In addition to declining politically and struggling commercially, the Colony that William Bradford and his Pilgrim shipmates on the *Mayflower* had hoped would become a holy community of Saints was rotting spiritually. Bradford seemed to have seen clearly what was coming. By 1650, the people of Plymouth were failing morally in the eyes of their Lord, and Bradford was keenly aware of it. They were becoming land hungry. They were not disciplining their children strictly enough, they were not dressing simply enough, they were not drinking moderately enough, and there were even incidences of bestiality and sodomy.

Bradford believed that God would exact a toll on the Pilgrims for these failures. And what's more, he believed that the Indians, many of whom, despite his best efforts, were now armed with guns, would be the Lord's means of carrying out this punishment.

Governor Bradford's belief that the Wampanoags would be God's instruments of punishment represented standard Puritan beliefs. The Puritans believed strongly that the Lord allowed evil to be inflicted on them by Satan's instruments as retribution for their failing to live a moral life. They also believed that after Adam and Eve's fall in the Garden of Eden, Satan was allowed by God to inhabit the "Wilderness," or Nature. Thus, they believed that any native peoples that inhabited nature were, as a result, Satan's children.

A supreme irony of the Puritan-Indian conflict was that although this general belief about native peoples was essentially unfounded, in southeastern Massachusetts, the Puritans may have actually found exactly what they assumed to be true everywhere. For while not all American Indians placed emphasis on the worship of the evil deity Hobbamock, or even worshipped this deity at all, at the time of the Pilgrims' arrival, Massasoit's Wampanoag shamans, and hence his people, clearly did.

The Lord called William Bradford to him in 1657, and Plymouth lost their great spiritual leader. Before he died, Bradford told his people that God had come to him and assured him that he held a special place in Heaven for him. Bradford was greatly comforted by this communication, and he died in peace. But Bradford, by the time he died, also must have realized that his Pilgrims had been naïve, and perhaps vain as well, to dare to believe that their destiny was to establish a Holy community in the New World. God had surely had his reasons for planting the Pilgrims in America, but those reasons were known to Him alone.

As opposed to becoming a holy community of saints, Plymouth was starting to disintegrate. Bradford had suffered the loss of his first wife shortly after the *Mayflower* arrived in the New World, and before his death, he would see his best men leave his side as well.

Miles Standish and John Alden, leaders of the colony who were also his friends, left to settle the town of Duxbury just to the north. Other key figures left Bradford as well, and not for God's reasons, but for land. Edward Winslow, the Pilgrim most trusted by Massasoit, who had once saved the chief's life when he was ill, left America altogether. He returned to England, and never came back.

The Puritans of the Massachusetts Bay Colony in Boston felt more strongly about converting the Indians to Christianity than did the Pilgrims in Plymouth, and they started doing just that shortly after their arrival. The Puritans also believed it was their duty to teach the local Indians, who had no written language, how to read and write. In the 1650s, John Eliot created several "Praying Towns" of Christian Indians. Eliot somehow even managed to complete the daunting task of translating the Bible into the Massachusetts language.

These efforts to convert the Indians, however, proved only marginally successful.

During the coming war, every single Praying Town would yield warriors to fight with Philip against the colonists. Many of the Indians that converted to Christianity later renounced their Faith, or through their actions, made it obvious to all that they had converted for purely pragmatic reasons. The Indians of Cape Cod, such as the Mashpees, proved to be a notable exception. The fact that many of them were Christians allowed their tribes to survive the war.

Why didn't more of the Indians convert to Christianity? One reason was that the Pilgrims did not actively try to convert the Indians. And truth be told, as their morality declined after the early years, Puritans in general may not have set the best Christian example. But the Wampanoag shamans were the primary cause of the failure of more Indians to adopt the faith. From the very start, when the shamans tried to curse Plymouth, they used their power over the Wampanoag people to actively fight against Christianity, and to preserve Hobbamock's influence over them.

The shamans were successful despite the fact that many of the Wampanoag people had doubtlessly witnessed the apparent power of Christianity over the shamans and Hobbamock on many occasions, and thus must have at least considered converting. And many of them were probably fed up with being manipulated and held in constant fear.

Massasoit and his sachems were the other main reason more Indians didn't convert. Massasoit was the Wampanoag's supreme leader for almost all the years leading up to the war, and his people knew that he harbored a deep distrust, even hatred, of the Christian religion. There were several reasons for this attitude. Massasoit and his sachems were heavily influenced by the shamans, who were in league with Hobbamock. And Massasoit's inner council of advisors was composed of pnieses, warriors who believed that very lives had been protected in battle by Hobbamock since they were young men.

In addition, the political power and the livelihoods of the sachems were directly threatened by Puritans like John Eliot, who were actively trying to convert their subjects and move them away into Praying Towns, because these subjects were important sources of tribute payments to them. This recruitment of their subjects enraged the sachems, and caused them to actively discourage conversion to Christianity.

One notable exception to the Pilgrim's overall lack of interest in converting Indians to Christianity was Edward Winslow. Winslow studied the religion of the Wampanoags, and was probably the first among them to understand that Cautantowwit was, as the Creator, God. He also learned that the People had turned their backs on Cautantowwit, and instead worshipped Hobbamock, mostly out of fear of death, disease, and the shamans. In the 17th century, death was a primary motivating factor in life, for both the Wampanoags and the Pilgrims. Death was much more important than it is today, because there was so much more of it around.

Death was a daily visitor to people's lives at that time, and they needed a powerful means of coping with it.

Hobbamock was the God of Death and disease, as well as healing, and the shamans brokered his power. As a result, to cross the shamans meant nothing less than risking death.

Winslow knew that the Wampanoags were worshipping some form of evil, which he assumed to be the same as the Christian Devil, as did the other Puritans. The Puritans made this assumption simply because they had no parallel concept in their religion for Hobbamock, the Wampanoags' name for the evil deity comprised of the spirits of the human dead. The Puritans drew the best analogy they could. In a similar vein, the Indians had no concept in their religion of the Devil, or any single master of the Underworld.

But the Indians knew, without a doubt, that Hobbamock was an evil force. They told the Puritans as much on many occasions. Some Indians even agreed with the Puritan characterization of Hobbamock as the Devil, probably feeling that the characterization was "close enough" to the truth. Winslow also was the first to discover that when an English Christian was present among the shamans,

Hobbamock would neither appear nor do their bidding. This fact was supported by the shamans' own testimonies. Hobbamock, it seemed, was totally impotent in the face of the Christian Lord.

Winslow, unlike most of his fellow Christians at Plymouth, believed it was the Pilgrim's moral duty to actively convert the Indians to Christianity. He developed an Indian-centric proposal for use in conversion, based on parallels drawn between Cautantowwit and God and Hobbamock and the Devil. But Winslow, inadvertently, may have been his own worst enemy. For once Winslow knew that the Wampanoags were worshipping an evil force, the Plymouth Elders knew. And once they knew that, their worst fears were confirmed.

These natives were no innocent heathens in the Wilderness, bereft of the word of Jesus, as the critics of the Pilgrims claimed. No, these natives were true worshipers of Satan. After the Elders at Plymouth learned about the Indians' relationship with Hobbamock, if conversion efforts had ever had a chance, they were now doomed. Winslow's proposals were ignored.

In addition, after Winslow's initial revelation, future Puritan missionaries knew the truth about the People, and acted in a predictable fashion.

The Wampanoags believed that Hobbamock himself attempted to foil their conversion to Christianity. Winthrop, in 1825, offers the following curious record:

> About this time (1637) the Indians, which were in our families, were much frightened with Hobbamock (as they call the devil) appearing to them in divers [sic] shapes, and persuading them to forsake the English, and not to come at the assemblies, nor to learn to read.

The hope of the Puritans was that if the Indians learned to read the Bible and heard the words of truth spoken at their assemblies, they would see the Light of God.

Other, similar afflictions experienced by the Indians during this time period were described by Mayhew in 1727 as follows:

> There was this Year 1643 a very strange Disease among the *Indians*, they ran up and down as if delirious, til they could run no longer; they would make their Faces as black as a Coal, and snatch up any Weapon, as tho they would do Mischief with it, and speak great swelling Words, but yet they did no Harm. Many of these *Indians* were by the *English* seen in this Condition. Now this, and all other Calamities which the *Indians* were under, they generally then attributed to the Departure of some of them from their own Heathenish ways and Customs.

With so many of their priests and chiefs, and seemingly even the gods against them, what chance did the typical Wampanoag of the first half of the 17th century really have to convert to Christianity, even if presented with the opportunity?

In 1650, for the first time, the English colonists of the New World moved inland. The Pilgrims established a Holy Settlement just northwest of their New Jerusalem in Plymouth.

The settlement that would later become known as Bridgewater was the first interior settlement of the Old Colony. The land for the settlement, then known as a "plantation," was granted by the Plymouth court to settlers from the town of Duxbury in 1645. Plymouth made the grant to compensate Duxbury for the loss of valuable grazing land that had been the result of the incorporation of part of the town into Marshfield in 1640/1641.

The land included in this court grant was later purchased on March 23, 1649, by Miles Standish, Constant Southworth, and Samuel Nash, directly from Ossamequin, also known as Massasoit. The land included in the purchase extended seven miles in each direction from an old Indian herring weir on the Satucket River, and encompassed more land than had been granted to the purchasers by Plymouth. The center of the land purchase at the weir was never adopted as the official Town Center, a position that lay in flux for quite some time.

The settlers of Bridgewater later, in 1658, asked Plymouth to officially grant them an additional area of land to their west, that they believed had been included in the land purchase from Massasoit, but that had not been included in Plymouth's 1645 land grant. In Edward Cushing Mitchell's *History of Bridgewater, Massachusetts* he writes:

> In 1658, the town petitioned the court for a grant of a large and valuable tract of swamp and meadow lands, called by the Indians *Hockomock*, lying on the west side of the town towards Taunton (now Easton and Raynham)...

It seems that the Plymouth court was uncertain whether the settlers' 1649 purchase from the Indians had included these additional lands. The key issue appears to have been whether the land in the purchase extended *six* or *seven* miles west from the unofficial town center, or far enough west to encompass the newly requested lands.

As a result of this uncertainty, the Plymouth court, in 1662, issued a deposition for Constant Southworth and Samuel Nash, who testified that the original purchase deed signed by Ossamequin read that the lands purchased by them extended *seven* miles west of the town center. The original purchasers may have bought more land from Ossamequin than had been originally granted to them by Plymouth with the intent of requesting subsequent grants, or perhaps to allow them flexibility in establishing the best placement for their "official" town center, a task they had not yet accomplished.

The testimony of Southworth and Nash apparently convinced Plymouth that Bridgewater owned the land in question. Mitchell writes:

> The same (land request) was afterwards granted, and confirmed to them as follows:…

The key part of the Plymouth court's confirmation of Bridgewater's request reads:

> 1662. In answer to a petition preferred to the court by Bridgewater it is agreed, that the meadow land lying northward and westward from the *Centre* within the *seven* miles is granted them.

Ownership of the Hockomock, or the "Place Where the Spirits Dwell," had officially passed from the Indians to the English colonists.

The plantation that is now Bridgewater lays squarely in the heart of the Hockomock, in the ancestral land of Chickataubet, who was one of the greatest sachems in the entire region when the Pilgrims first landed. It is in an area known to the colonists as Satucket, a spelling derived from the earlier English spelling "Saughtuckquett." The latter is a Wampanoag place name that according to one, general interpretation means "Place Where the Rivers Meet." A literal translation of the variant spelling "Saughtucket" is "outlet of a pond," which would have referenced the outlet of the Satucket River at Robbins Pond, a 125-acre lake in the southeastern portion of the town, in present-day East Bridgewater. The more complete Wampanoag "Massasaukituckut," meaning "Land at the Great Outlet," was what the Indians probably called the entire region included in the original Plymouth land grant.

The original plantation purchase was made on an ancient, rocky hill called Sachem's Rock, known to the Wampanoags as "Wonnocooto," on the banks of a peaceful stretch of the Satucket River. The plantation was level, with no hills, which made it desirable for farming. It also had many streams and rivers, the land along the banks of which was highly productive for crops. Judging by the large number of Indian artifacts found along its rivers, these areas had been those most heavily frequented by the local Wampanoags. The first colonists settled in what is now the town of West Bridgewater on the north and south banks of the Town River, which they then called the "Nunkatest" River. The Town River flows from

Lake Nippenicket, that last remnant of the ancient Glacial Lake Taunton. The lake was sometimes referred to by the colonists as "Unkatest." The Wampanoag word "Nippe" means "water."

The Town River drains the Hockomock Swamp. It meets the Hockomock River, the Matfield River, and the Satucket River to form the headwaters of the Taunton River, which then winds leisurely towards the southwest until it empties, wide and strong, into Mount Hope Bay. The first settlers began farming the highly-productive Town River land in six-acre, adjacent plots in order to allow for group defense against the Indians. At first, they called their new settlement Nunkatest, after the river. "Nunckatateset" in Wampanoag probably means "At the Place of the Bend of the River."

Upon incorporation in 1656, the inhabitants of the plantation officially dubbed their town Bridgewater, a name that had been in use at least as early as 1654. Today, no one knows for sure whether the town was named after the English town with the same name, as was nearby Taunton. In fact, some histories go so far as to say that the settlers named it Bridgewater "for no apparent reason." However, the townspeople themselves believe that it probably was named after the town in England, where some of its first inhabitants came from.

They state as much in their official town history, noting that prominent citizens of the English town included Mitchells, Hoopers, Bryants, and Allens, all familiar names in the history of their New England town.

If this is truly the case, then the name Bridgewater may have been a particularly apt choice. Bridgewater, in Somerset, southwestern England, split by the river Parret, played a very special role in English history. It was King Alfred's special country, that storied Christian leader who saved England from the invading pagan Danes when it was on the very brink of becoming a Danish kingdom. The "isle" of Athelney, which lay six miles to the south of Bridgewater in the marshes, now drained, was where Alfred successfully hid from the Vikings in the year 878, immediately before he launched his great campaign and ultimate victory.

King Arthur, who with the help of his Christian Knights of the Round Table battled the pagan Angles and Saxon invaders some 400 years earlier, is said to be buried in Glastonbury, just 12 miles east of Bridgewater, which would have made Bridgewater his chosen country as well.

The people who formed the Bridgewater of the New World were exceptionally religious Christians. Some of these proprietors were sons of the Plymouth Pilgrims. Their names included Alden, Southworth, Willis, Merrick, Nash, Eaton, Simmons, Ames, Godfrey, and Snow. Many were "second comers" from England, who had arrived after the first three ships, among whom were an additional group of Pilgrims from Leiden, who had arrived at Plymouth in 1629 and 1630.

These founders of the new Holy City in the Wilderness dedicated themselves completely to the worship of Jesus Christ and the Lord God. And as a result, some believe that the Lord infused them with his Holy Spirit, made them exceptionally strong, and granted them his protection. It is an inescapable and strange irony that the New World Bridgewater, like its Old World counterpart, was destined to play a key role in successfully defending a Christian civilization against powerful pagan foes.

It was another strange irony when, in 1662, Bridgewater was granted by Plymouth, the additional "valuable swamp and meadowland" to the town's west that the Indians referred to as "Hockomock." This grant meant that perhaps the holiest of Christians now owned the "Place Where the Spirits Dwell," the ancient abode of Hobbamock, the Wampanoag evil deity composed of the spirits of the human dead. By 1672, the town had extended its limits south to the most ancient resting place of the People, the banks of the Taunton River. They displaced the last of the People that dwelled there, from the village called Titicut, that had formerly been granted to them by Plymouth as a last refuge.

Titicut had formerly been the favorite resort of Chickataubet, the great sachem. Curiously, Chickataubet was a Massachusetts sachem, not a Wampanoag. It appears that the Massachusetts sachem, whose lands ranged to the north, was asserting control over this area at the time. Chickataubet's territory had also included Lake Nippenicket. His son and successor, Wampatuck, had originally granted Titicut, which comprised three miles of land on each side of the Taunton, to the Indians living there some time before 1644.

In 1660, Massasoit, the Great Sachem of the Wampanoags, died of the plague. It was just three years after William Bradford passed away. Before Massasoit died, he made a point to take his sons, Wamsutta, later known as Alexander, and Metacomet, later known as King Philip, from Sowams to the nearby home of his English friend, John Brown. There, the chief asked them to always look out for Brown's family. Before he died, Massasoit mysteriously faded from the political scene, and went to live among his ancient allies, the Nipmucks, in central Massachusetts. There, he worked to strengthen the old ties that had historically held that tribe together with his. These ties would ultimately prove critical to his son Philip's survival in the war to come.

By the 1660s, after both Bradford and Massasoit passed, Plymouth Colony was a different place. The spiritual slide had continued. Church membership both there and in Massachusetts Bay had dropped significantly. The children of the Pilgrims had become materialistic. They wanted land more than religion. They had fallen into disfavor with their God, and they were keenly aware of it.

Another, fundamental change had taken place in the Plymouth Colony as well. The Pilgrims were no longer weak, no longer dependent on the Indians for survival. In fact, the children of the Pilgrims now looked upon the Indians as an obstacle on their quest for land on which to settle.

This new Puritan generation had also grown up hearing horror stories about the Pequot War, a conflict with the Indians in Connecticut that had ended in a shaky peace in 1638.

Things had changed dramatically for the Wampanoags as well. Massasoit, the friend of the English, was gone. His sons, who would inherit his title as Great Sachem, felt only hostility towards the Pilgrims, whom they felt were stealing their land, which was their inheritance and birthright. Wamsutta, Massasoit's first-born son, immediately started acting aggressively towards the English after becoming sachem of the Wampanoags. He sold land to Rhode Island, openly breaking the treaty his people had always had with Plymouth to sell land exclusively to them. He may also have been conspiring with the Narragansetts to attack Plymouth. Whatever the case truly was, rumors to that effect reached Plymouth.

Plymouth ordered Josiah Winslow, Edward Winslow's son, to get Wamsutta and bring him to Plymouth. Tragically, Wamsutta died on the journey back, with the circumstances of his death unclear. Ironically, the son of Massasoit had died in the hands of the son of the man whom had once saved the life of his father. Wamsutta's suspicious death in 1662, the same year Plymouth granted the Hockomock to Bridgewater, accelerated the region's pace towards war.

After Wamsutta's death, his younger brother Metacomet assumed the role of sachem. Philip was a firebrand: proud, haughty, and angry. The Wampanoags looked to him for redemption from the ever-encroaching whites. With Philip at the helm, it seemed only a matter of time before war broke out.

But Philip proved cunning as well; he immediately started telling the Puritans at Plymouth what they wanted to hear. Peace would be maintained, he told them. Meanwhile, between 1665 and 1675, he made seventy-five land transactions to the whites, probably to fund his war chest while secretly plotting war.

The Wampanoags' faith in Philip soon proved to be in vain. It was not long before he displayed his true colors. In 1665, Philip journeyed to Nantucket, part of his inherited kingdom, to discipline an Indian who had broken a taboo by speaking Massasoit's name too soon after his death. When the English there unexpectedly backed the Indian transgressor, Philip fled the island. This political blunder probably helped cost him the support of the substantial Indian population on the island during the impending war, just ten years away.

As his secretary, Philip engaged an Indian named Sassamon, a "Praying Indian" who had been educated at Harvard. Like Squanto and the pniese Hobbamock before him, Sassamon was an interpreter. Also like them, he was sometimes a self-serving opportunist known to twist correspondences for his own benefit. For example, in 1667, Philip asked Sassamon to write his will. Later, the sachem discovered that the Praying Indian had written a document that left everything Philip owned to himself. Understandably, this incident enraged Philip, and caused him to hate Christians even more than he already did.

Meanwhile, Plymouth increased the pressure on Philip. They told him that he was now their subject, and as such must pay them annual tribute. In 1672, probably to raise funds for war, Philip sold off all the remaining land of his tribe around his headquarters at Mount Hope. He was also successful in cobbling together an alliance between his Wampanoags and the Narragansetts, the Nipmucks, the Nemaskets, and the Pocasetts in a plan to attack the white settlers.

In early 1675, Sassamon told Josiah Winslow, who had also attended Harvard, that Philip was planning an attack. Sassamon lived on land next to Assawompsett Pond in modern day Lakeville.

The land had been given to him by Tispaquin, Philip's brother-in-law, who was married to his sister and Massasoit's daughter, Amie. Tispaquin was the notorious and bloodthirsty "Black Sachem" of the Assawompsetts, and probably the Nemaskets as well. These two tribes lived in territory today included in the towns of Lakeville and Middleboro, and areas of Freetown (East), Acushnet, and Rochester.

Tispaquin was a very rare and extremely powerful individual among the Indians, for he was both a powerful sachem and a shaman. These two roles typically did not mix. But when they did, as in the case of Passaconaway, the celebrated sachem of the Pawtuckets at the mouth of the Merrimack River just to the north of Puritan territory who could "make water burn, and rocks move," they produced a leader of tremendous and unique powers.

Tispaquin, who was said by some to have "possessed in abundance the most savage traits of the Indian race," was probably personally responsible for most of the massacres of whites in the Old Colony in King Philip's War with which Philip is generally credited. Tispaquin's military decisions in this war were directly influenced by his intimate relationship with Hobbamock.

Sassamon, who had betrayed his people, was beaten to death shortly after he communicated Philip's plans to Winslow. His body was found under the ice of Assawompsett Pond. Plymouth ordered a trial, and ended up executing a counselor of Philip's, Tobias, Tobias's son, and another Indian, with little evidence. The executions left Philip with little choice but to go to war, even though it was probably a year in advance of his timetable. The Hockomock Swamp, home to Hobbamock, Tispaquin's source of spiritual power, and crisscrossed by trails known only to the Indians, became Philip's base of operations, from where his warriors would launch devastating surprise attacks on the colonists.

One of the first things Philip did was gather his shamans together and ask them for advice. They powwowed together in the recesses of the Hockomock, and the god of Death sent them back with a mysterious message.

"Do not draw first blood," the shamans told to Philip at Mount Hope, "and you will be victorious." The warriors set themselves to dancing the war dance at Mount Hope. For three weeks they danced, while the shamans hid themselves away and prayed to the Spirit of Death. Then, on Sunday, June 20th, 1675, the war unfolded. The warriors began harassing the residents of Swanzea, but in accordance with Philip's orders, they did not kill. It was there that the Indian's first employed fire, Hobbamock's most ancient ally. The flames they set burned two English houses to the ground.

To the north in Boston, at the Massachusetts Bay Colony, Governor Winslow could see that God was unhappy with the Puritans. So before going to the aid of Plymouth, he declared June 24th to be "a day of fasting and humiliation" in order to atone for the Colony's sins. On the night of June 26th, 1675, a total eclipse of the moon came to New England. Everyone agreed that it was an ominous sign. Soldiers later said that they had seen the scalp of an Indian in the black spot in the moon's center.

When the hostilities broke out, Benjamin Church was asked by William Bradford, Governor William Bradford's son, to lead some troops against the Indians. The younger Bradford was second in command of the combined Puritan forces. Church was the grandson of the Warrens, who had arrived in Plymouth on the *Mayflower*. He was married to the daughter of Constant Southworth, who was Governor William Bradford's stepson.

Ben Church, however, at heart was more frontiersman and soldier than Puritan. In this regard, as well as in the military role he provided for Plymouth, he was similar to Miles Standish. Church was the first settler of Sakonnet, now Little Compton, Rhode Island. He had befriended the Indians in Sakonnet, and they came to trust him. The English Puritans throughout the region, including the Massachusetts Bay Colony, Plymouth, and Rhode Island, quickly joined forces against the Indians. This decisive act seemed to have caught the Indians by surprise.

Church later made an attempt, as a friend of the Pocassets, to convince Plymouth that they and other tribes could be convinced not to join Philip. But the Elders of Plymouth, including his father-in-law, Constant Southworth, chose to ignore him, and they allowed the war to escalate.

The English Puritans sent their combined force to a garrison in Swanzea to counter Philip's harassment, where they engaged perhaps 500 Indians that had staged at Mount Hope. When they reached Swanzea, the Puritans found pages of Bibles scattered all over. The Indians had torn them to pieces to express their hatred of Christianity.

At Swanzea, it quickly became apparent that Benjamin Church was invested with the same strange powers formerly wielded by Miles Standish. After the

English troops gathered at the garrison, Church and a small group of volunteers ventured out to engage the enemy. The Indians, from hiding, quickly mowed them down. The survivors retreated to the garrison, but Church stayed behind, alone. There, he exposed himself to enemy fire. To the astonishment of all observers, Church didn't get a scratch.

In Church's second encounter with the Indians, these curious powers emerged to an astonishing degree. In July of 1675, Philip's Indians, trapped by the Puritans on the Mount Hope Peninsula, escaped across Mount Hope Bay to the Pocasset Swamp to the east. Church and his men pursued them ahead of the main force, and eventually came face-to-face with an enormous force of enemy warriors. For several hours, Church's men somehow held off a force of 300 Indians before escaping, in stages, in a small boat. As the last of his men shoved off from the shore, Church realized that he had forgotten his hat and sword at the last position they had abandoned during their retreat.

Church rose up and walked, alone, across an open field that lay directly in front of the watching Indians to retrieve his belongings. Hundreds of Indians, the same ones that the colonists held in great esteem for their marksmanship, fired on Church. But none of the bullets came any closer than the one that grazed his hair.

Church casually picked up his belongings, walked back to the boat, and shoved off, unhurt. Church later stated that this incident at Pocasset proved "the glory of God and his protecting Providence." During another one of his early encounters, Church told his men that God directed the enemy's bullets, and that He was on their side. His men soon came to believe him. Church, like Standish before him, was no Puritan. But nonetheless, like Standish, Church did believe that he was empowered and protected by the Puritan Lord.

Later Church, along with a Major Cudworth and their men, chased Philip's force into the Pocasset Swamp. There they found it impossible to engage the enemy, who, camouflaged with ferns and other plants, disappeared. In the meantime, the sachem Totoson attacked Dartmouth, so Church and the others left to go to the aid of the town. Philip and his followers, together with Weetamoo and her warriors, forged their way seven miles north through the Pocasset Swamp, up to Dighton at the spot where the Taunton River narrows.

Somewhere in the vicinity of Dighton Rock, near the edge of the Hockomock, the Indians built crude rafts, and escaped in the night across the waters of the Titicut. The next morning, several hundred Indian men, women, and children left the bank of the river, heading west. But English and Mohegan Indian forces pursued Philip and devastated his force. Weetamoo and her people, not surprisingly, deserted him. Weetamoo was Philip's sister-in-law, for she had been married to his brother Wamsutta, or Alexander. But Weetamoo was also the daughter of Corbitant, the powerful Pocasset sachem who had so vigorously opposed Massasoit's plan to ally with the whites at Plymouth, and plotted to overthrow him.

Due to a tactical blunder by the English, however, Philip managed to escape to Nipmuc territory with only forty remaining men. Philip found support among the Nipmucs, probably because of his father's prescient work years earlier to strengthen ties with them. Philip also broke up a massive wampum coat he owned, and handed pieces of it out to the Nipmuc sachems. In the end, he was able to gain their support, which allowed him to continue the war.

In July 1675, the Black Sachem Tispaquin destroyed the town of Middleboro, which lay squarely in his native territory. And in August, with Philip far away and things quiet around Plymouth, Benjamin Church went to Duxbury to see his wife, where he had moved her from Sakonnet for protection.

Meanwhile, the war spread to the Connecticut River Valley of Massachusetts, New Hampshire, and Maine. On August 2, 1675, the Nipmucks attacked Brookfield, in western Massachusetts, which heralded a state-wide attack in Massachusetts. They were about to burn down the garrison there, which was packed with desperate Christians, when a heavy rain shower suddenly erupted from the heavens, and extinguished the fire. English reinforcements then arrived, and the Nipmucs were pushed back.

Later in August, both Lancaster and Deerfield were attacked, and more colonists died. Four days after Deerfield, a powerful hurricane smashed into the New England coast. The Wampanoag shamans, who had implored Hobbamock to send a great storm to shatter their enemies, publicly took credit for the event. The shamans had even predicted that "the English would die like trees blown down in the woods." The Indians next successfully ambushed the English at Northfield.

On September 17th, Boston held a "Day of Public Humiliation." Colonists were told to refrain from pride in their dress and to avoid taverns. The following day, fifty-seven English evacuees from Deerfield were slaughtered by the Indians. Samuel Mosely, a giant and brutal Dutch privateer who was playing an increasingly important role in the war, arrived with his men expecting to save the day, but instead, he and his men were nearly annihilated. Increase Mather later wrote that the Indians were "boastful" about this event. The plight of the English Puritans now seemed grim indeed.

On October 5th, the Massachusetts town of Springfield was nearly burned to the ground. This attack, in particular, caused the English to assume a much harder stance towards the Indians.

The settlers of Springfield had always maintained good relations with the local natives, and now they had turned on them without mercy. The conclusion that the colonists drew from this incident at the time was that Indians were truly the children of the Devil.

If there ever had been compassion shown to the Indian race before the burning of Springfield, afterwards it became scarce. The Praying Indians, whom many colonists distrusted, were all rounded up and shipped out to Deer Island, in Boston Harbor, where many of them died of exposure. Selling captured Indians into slavery in the West Indies to fund the war became standard practice.

October of 1675 just kept getting worse for the Puritans. White settlers from Western Massachusetts, made into refugees by the Indians, flocked into Boston. The settlers up in the isolated villages of Maine were being butchered. It got so bad for the colonists that the Boston authorities seriously considered physically barricading in the immediate Colony, and forfeiting all lands around it to the Indians.

Philip became an almost mythical figure to the whites, as they imagined him to be striking everywhere, looting and rampaging at will. Later, it became apparent that nothing could have been farther from the truth. Philip, who many saw as the match that ignited the war, actually played a relatively minor role in the conflict. Many Indians in New England probably detested Philip for getting them involved in a brutal war that many thought unnecessary. And few actually followed him. There was even an unsuccessful assassination attempt on Philip's life in Western Massachusetts, by an Indian.

All this time, the powerful Narragansetts had stayed out of the war. If they had joined Philip earlier, the English would probably have been destroyed. The Narragansetts were harboring hostile members of the Pokanoket and Pocasset tribes, however, including Weetamoo.

When they refused to give them up, in late October of 1675, the United Colonies of Plymouth, Massachusetts, and Connecticut attacked them. This attack was led by General Josiah Winslow, and with him, as his "trusted aide," was Benjamin Church.

Church was acting as a military advisor to the United Colonies in this role, and with him rode his strong belief that the Christian God directed his actions. In this sense, he was playing a parallel role to Tispaquin and the Indian pnieses, who, guided by Hobbamock, were leading the Indian offenses. And in the background, Puritan Ministers such as Increase Mather were constantly advising the political leaders of the Colonies on God's behalf, much as the Indian shamans were advising the sachems.

Winslow and Church assembled approximately 1,000 men, and staged them throughout New England in preparation for the attack on the Narragansetts. Although he was an advisor and had a few Indian battles under his belt, Church, up to this point, was considered a minor player in the war. Samuel Mosely, with his roughneck band of ex-pirates, had taken center stage.

On December 2nd, a "Day of Prayer" was held by Puritans across New England. According to Increase Mather, the English were all in the churches praying to "the

Lord, the God of Armies" for success in the coming battle with the Narragansetts. Winslow and Church moved south on December 8th against a formidable enemy.

Then, an Indian named Peter betrayed the Narragansetts. Peter told the English that the Indians were hiding in the Great Swamp, a swamp that lays to the southwest of Narragansett Bay in modern-day Kingston, Rhode Island. Because the Indians had burned the garrison from which the English had planned to launch their attack, 1,000 men were forced to sleep out in an open field on the night of December 15th.

That night, as if to test them, a great blizzard and freezing temperatures came. The next morning, a Sunday, the frostbitten English rose and went into the swamp after the Indians.

There had been unusually cold temperatures that December, so fortuitously for them, instead of facing the wet morass they might have expected, the men were able to move across the frozen terrain. Finally, on a five-acre island in the swamp, the English confronted a goal worthy of their heroic effort, a true monstrosity. In silence, they stared upwards at an enormous heathen fort. It had a high palisade, blockhouses, a sixteen-foot wall of brush and clay around it, and a frozen moat at the entrance. Inside were approximately 500 huts—and there were thousands of Indians.

The English stormed the one low spot in the palisade, which may have been created purposefully by the Narragansetts as a trap, for inside the walls it was heavily manned by warriors. The first English who made it in died. Then Mosely charged in with his men, but they made little headway. During this charge, Mosely, in a feat that rivaled Church's walk through the field, was personally fired upon at close range by at least fifty Narragansetts, but the giant Dutchman emerged from the fort unscathed.

Next, Church volunteered to go into the fort with his men, and other English followed them. Soon, 300 to 400 English were battling the Narragansetts inside the fort, with some of them shooting each other in the chaos. Eventually, the Indians began running out of gunpowder. Some of them left the monstrous structure and went into the woods around it, and started trying to fire down into it from outside. Church and his men pursued them, killed a group of Indians, and then went back into the melee in the fort, where something exceedingly rare happened. Church was shot, through the thigh, by a Narragansett. He tried to get his men to keep fighting, but they retreated, taking him with them. By this time, the English had managed to gain control of the heathen fort. And it is here that a very curious chain of events occurred, in the battle that would later be referred to by historians as the "Great Swamp Fight."

With the heathen fort firmly in English control, Josiah Winslow ordered it to be burned; complete with wigwams, stockpiled provisions, and Narragansett men, women, and children.

But Benjamin Church stepped in, and argued that the burning, already being carried out inside, should be stopped. He based his opinion on his belief that the English needed the food and shelter that the fort could provide them to get through that night.

It seems that Church had convinced Winslow to reverse his decision, when Mosely appeared out of nowhere. The giant pirate seized the bridle of Winslow's horse, as the commander was headed to the fort to give the order to stop the flames, and stopped him short. Mosely argued forcefully that the plan was "not safe," and refused to take his hands off the bridle.

At this critical juncture, Church, bleeding heavily from his wound, began to quickly fade, and was apparently unable to remain in the discussion. Suddenly a mysterious, unknown doctor appeared on the scene, and adamantly backed Mosely on the grounds that the English wounded needed to be removed to a town immediately. If they stayed the night, the unknown doctor predicted, many of them would be dead by morning. Fatefully, Winslow again reversed his decision.

On December 19, 1675, the great swamp fort went up in flames, and all the Indians inside perished. The English began a hell march of sixteen miles to the nearest garrison, at Wickford, a march on which many of their wounded died. It seems the doctor had been wrong. For the first three miles of their march, the burning Fort of Death lit up the Wilderness around them. The war claimed many souls on that day, from both sides. The Narragansetts lost 350-600 people, who were either shot or burned to death. The English suffered more than 200 dead or wounded.

In late January 1676, a great thaw came to New England, and the snow melted. The 4,000 remaining Narragansetts, including 1,800 warriors, knowing they could not be tracked without snow, fled north to Nipmuck territory. Winslow, together with Church, who had by now recovered from his wound, marched after them in an attempt to destroy them once and for all. But the English effort turned into a disaster. Winslow turned back, and the Narragansetts, like Philip had before them, made it safely to the Nipmucks.

Philip was now in New York. In February, 1676, he attempted to orchestrate a triumphant return to New England by forging an alliance with the French and their northern Indian allies. He apparently was successful, obtained massive numbers of reinforcements, and was preparing to launch a devastating attack on New England's Puritans when disaster struck. Philip himself was attacked by the local Indians, the powerful Mohawks, a tribe that everyone feared. His force was destroyed.

Increase Mather later claimed that Philip had brought this disaster on himself by attacking a group of Mohawks and then blaming the English, in an attempt to pull that tribe into his corner. But he was found out, said Mather, and the plan backfired with terrible consequences. Philip's reputation among the Indians, already poor, suffered greatly from this incident in New York. Increasingly, they viewed him as simply a coward and a bungler, someone who had started the war, but couldn't finish it.

On February 10th, the Nipmucks and other tribes attacked Lancaster, Massachusetts. Mary Rowlandson, the Minister's wife and a prominent member of the community, was shot in her side as she fled her burning home, which had been converted into a garrison to shelter about fifty townspeople. The bullet passed through Mary and into the belly of her six-year-old daughter, Sarah. As English troops arrived on the scene, the Indians seized Mary and her daughter, whom she was holding in her arms, and fled.

Mary, who possessed a fine eye for observation and great courage, would subsequently pen one of the most moving captivity narratives ever written. A faithful Puritan and woman of fine character, Mary Rowlandson firmly believed that God had sent her into captivity as a means of punishing her for her sins, and her account consistently reflects this belief. Mary also clearly believed that the events of the war, which she witnessed firsthand over the coming months, were closely orchestrated by the Lord.

The Indians took white prisoners as hostages with the intent of trading them back to the English for money, a practice that they typically used to fund their war chest, just as the English did by selling their captives into slavery. After she was first taken captive, Mary was marched for several days without food. The Indians refused to give her injured daughter, Sarah, food, water, or medical attention. The little girl eventually died in Mary's arms. Mary slept alongside her dead child, out in the woods, the night that she died. Rowlandson subsequently became the slave of Weetamoo, the Pocasset sachem, who was now traveling with the Nipmucs on the warpath.

Weetamoo had married a Narragansett sachem and nephew of the former, great sachem of the Narragansetts, Minatonomo. Her husband's name was Quinnapen, a name that some Portuguese American supporters of the Portuguese Theory of Dighton Rock might trace to the Portuguese "quinas," or royal coat of arms. Weetamoo proved to be a cruel mistress, and she seldom allowed Mary to see her son or daughter who were close by, also traveling in captivity with the Indians.

On February 22nd, the town of Medfield was raided by a combined force of Nipmucs and Narragansetts. They burned fifty houses, and killed a dozen settlers. When the Indians returned triumphantly to camp, one of them gave Rowlandson a Bible. When she opened it, she immediately read the following line, from Deuteronomy, Chapter 30: "though we were scattered from one end of the earth to the other, yet the Lord would gather us together, and turn all those curses upon our enemies." These words turned out to be prophetic.

Mary Rowlandson's poignant account of her brutal treatment by the Indians is quite hard to read, and because it was widely read in Colonial times, it seems reasonable to assume that it negatively impacted the treatment of all conquered Indians following the war. Mary's account is also important because it includes the only known eyewitness account by an English observer of an Indian appeal to Hobbamock in wartime.

After Medfield was attacked, 2,000 Nipmucks and Narragansetts moved north to meet the remnants of Philip's crushed band, to plan for a spring offensive against the whites.

Mary, her children, and the other English captives had to endure a brutal, forced march, during which Mary was beaten, turned out of lodges into the cold at night, and deprived of food. She later wrote that God answered her prayers by giving her the strength to endure.

The Indians were trailed at this time by a large English army. They came to a great river, and successfully completed a dangerous crossing on rafts. Major Thomas Savage, in hot pursuit, reached the river just as the Indians crossed. But for some reason, with his quarry within reach, Savage decided not to go after them. Rowlandson's interpretation of this failure was that "God did not give them courage or activity to go after us…we were not ready for so great a mercy as victory and deliverance." As a result, Mary's captivity dragged on. The Indians she was traveling with met Philip at Northfield, and she met him on several occasions.

Shortly after Medfield, Weymouth was raided, and in early March, the Nipmucs attacked Groton. On March 9th, Philip met with Canonchet, the young, powerful sachem of the Narragansetts. Canonchet was the son of Minatonomo, the former great sachem of the Narragansetts. Canonchet greatly overshadowed Philip politically, and as perhaps their greatest leader in the conflict, he was an inspiration to all Indians. Canonchet offered to bring the war back east, to Plymouth, for Philip.

Back there, to the east, hatred of the Indians had reached new heights among the Puritans. Mosely and his pirates were pushing for the outright extermination of the Praying Indians. Many English, including Mary Rowlandson, although not willing to embrace these tactics, distrusted the Praying Indians and felt they only added to the great dangers the settlers faced. At about this time, Benjamin Church was approached by Puritan leaders and offered a conventional military command. Church turned it down, and instead proposed he be allowed to lead a mixed force of 200 English and 100 friendly Indians against the enemy. They would wipe them out. Plymouth refused. It was too expensive, and by now, they didn't trust any Indians.

Soon after, Church told the Plymouth elders that he was leaving the Colony immediately. He was taking his pregnant wife and son to Aquidneck Island in Mount Hope Bay, back near his homestead in Sakonnet, for safety. Everyone told Church to take them to Clark's garrison in Plymouth instead. Church ignored them, and went straight to Aquidneck. Just a few days later, he and his family got word that the Indians had attacked Clark's garrison and burned it. Eleven English, including women and children, had been slaughtered there.

In addition to attacking Plymouth, the Indians now launched devastating attacks on other towns in Massachusetts, the Connecticut River Valley, Maine, and for the first time, Connecticut. Captain Pierce, the man chosen by Plymouth to command in Church's stead, was ambushed by 1,000 Indians in Rehoboth, Massachusetts and massacred.

Two days later, Canonchet, the young Narragansett leader, led an attack on Rehoboth and burned the town. On March 29th, Canonchet and his warriors attacked Providence, Rhode Island, and burned it. The inhabitants had abandoned the town before the attack, but Roger Williams had remained behind. Williams, the great leader of the Quakers, historically had never sided with Plymouth against the Indians. Now an old man, he went out to meet the Indians alone.

Williams reprimanded them for their acts of savagery against the English. The Indians, who liked Williams, told him that "they were in a strange way." At Providence, one of their sachems pointed out to Roger Williams that the English were clearly losing, so God must be on the Indians' side. By April 1676, it surely looked as if the Indians would make good on their original promise to "drive the English to the edge of the sea." To make things even worse for the English, a deadly flu swept through New England, killing many of them, including soldiers. The Puritans continued to pray to the Lord God for deliverance from their enemies.

On April 9th, Captain George Denison's troops from Connecticut unexpectedly captured Canonchet, the Narragansett sachem, with help from friendly Indians.

The great leader apparently slipped on a rock in a river while being pursued, and soaked his gun, rendering it useless. Canonchet then experienced a strange and complete loss of bodily strength. He gave himself up without a fight. Canonchet was later executed by a firing squad of Pequot Indians, and his body was butchered and burned by Indians, including Pequots, Mohegans, and Niantics. The loss of Canonchet was a great blow to the combined Indian force in the war.

In mid-April, Mary Rowlandson was taken to Wachusett Mountain to rendezvous with a large contingent of Indians camped there. The Indians had received a letter from the English, requesting peace talks and the release of hostages. The Indians declined the peace talks but agreed to negotiate ransom offers for the hostages. By this time, they were running out of food. They knew they would starve soon, if they didn't get the English to declare peace, but they believed they needed more leverage before beginning talks. As a result, they started to plan an attack on the town of Sudbury.

It was before the great battle of Sudbury that Mary Rowlandson witnessed the direct appeal to Hobbamock for victory by three of her Indian captors. One of them, the man in her account that kneels on the deerskin, she describes as a "Powaw," or shaman. The following is what Rowlandson witnessed, in her own words.

> There was one that kneeled upon a Deer-skin, with the company round him in a ring who kneeled, and striking upon the ground with their hands, and with sticks, and muttering or humming with their mouths; besides him who kneeled in the ring, there also stood one with a Gun in his hand: Then he on the Deer-skin made a speech, and all manifested assent to it: and so they did many times together. Then they bade him with the Gun go out of the ring, which he did, but when he was out, they called him in again; but he seemed to make a stand, then they called him the more earnestly, till he returned again: Then they all sang.
>
> Then they gave him two Guns, in either hand one: And so he on the Deer-skin began again; and at the end of every sentence in his speaking, they all assented, humming or muttering with their mouthes [sic], and striking upon the ground with their hands.
>
> Then they bade him with the two Guns go out of the ring again: which he did, a little way. Then they called him in again, but he made a stand; so they called him with greater earnestness; but he stood reeling and wavering as if he knew not whither he should stand or fall, or which way to go. Then they called him with exceeding great vehemency, all of them, one and another: after a little while he turned in, staggering as he went, with his Armes stretched out, in either hand a Gun. As soon as he came in, they all sang and rejoyced [sic] exceedingly a while. And then he upon the Deer-skin, made another speech unto which they all assented in a rejoicing manner: and so they ended their business, and forthwith went to Sudbury-fight. To my thinking they went without any scruple, but that that they should prosper, and gain the victory.

Sudbury was a smashing success for the Indians. They destroyed the town, killed seventy-four English, including two Captains, and lost no more than six warriors. But ominously, the returning warriors were anything but their usual celebrating, boastful selves after a victory when they returned, on a Sunday. Instead, they appeared grim, shaken up, completely lost. Rowlandson wrote that the shaman who had kneeled on the deerskin during his invocation of Hobbamock before the battle "came home…as black as the Devil."

Mary described this event as follows:

> When they went [to the battle], they acted as if the Devil had told them they should gain the victory: and now they acted, as if the Devil had told them they should have a fall.

Cotton Mather later interpreted the Indians' strange behavior as the consequence of shamanistic divinations of a negative nature that took place following the battle. From the battle of Sudbury on, the Indian defeats piled up, one after another.

In early May, the colonists negotiated Mary Rowlandson's release. Just prior to her release, Philip apparently attempted to extort money from her in exchange for putting in a good word on her behalf with the Indians who were negotiating the deal. His tactic proved ineffective, however, and the release went ahead as planned. Mary returned to her husband, and the wreckage of their lives. Their remaining three children were still held by the Indians, and they had lost all their worldly possessions in the attack. But her God was good to Mary after her ordeal. Miraculously, her children were returned unharmed, and the Christian community took her and her family in, and provided her with financial support for the rest of her life.

The men of Bridgewater had been the first on the march in the war, with seventeen of them eagerly going to the aid of fellow settlers when nearby Swanzea was first attacked. Bridgewater residents had been strongly urged by their fellow Puritans, as residents of a wholly interior colony, to desert their town and flee to the coast for protection, but they had refused. Nearby residents in Middleboro, and all those along the Taunton River down to Assonet, fled.

On May 8th, after some earlier harassment, a powerful force of 300 warriors led by Tispaquin approached the town, defended at the time by only 26 men, with the intent of destroying it. The Indians set fire to several homes, and things looked grim. But the men of Bridgewater emerged with such furor from their garrison houses that they somehow managed to repel Tispaquin's forces. Then, suddenly, the heavens opened up, and a tremendous rain shower extinguished all the flames. Tispaquin halted his force, and he and his warriors communed with Hobbamock, who appeared to them in the form of a bear, walking on his hind legs.

As a result of this apparition, despite his overwhelming advantage in numbers, Tispaquin led his forces away. The Indians later said that if Hobbamock had appeared as a deer, the warriors would have destroyed the town and all its inhabitants. To the Puritans, it appeared that the Holy Settlement had been saved by the hand of God.

And later, throughout the region, the Puritans marveled at the good fortune of Bridgewater. Despite being the first to take up arms and fighting consistently throughout the war, often in the role of aggressors, none of the Bridgewater men ever died. And despite multiple attacks on the town, none of its residents were ever killed. These facts were viewed by the Puritans as a sort of miracle.

On May 18th, Captain William Turner attacked a large band of Nipmucks on the Connecticut River and killed many of them. The Nipmucs surrendered.

Upon hearing this news, Philip left Mount Wachusett together with Weetamoo, Quinnapen, and Tispaquin, who was leading his warriors. Together they attacked towns in Plymouth and Rhode Island.

On June 6th, Benjamin Church, after celebrating the birth of a son, rejoined the war. He found that Plymouth had suddenly warmed to his idea of deploying a combined Puritan and Indian force, but they were planning on having Bradford lead it. Church did not want to fight under Bradford, whose military tactics were far more conventional than his own, so he chose to go back to Rhode Island. When he got there, the independent thinker decided to make a radical move and try to form an alliance with Ashawonks, the female sachem of the Sakonnets. Ashawonks had just returned home after abandoning Philip on the warpath.

Alone, with only a bottle of rum to aid him, Church put himself at tremendous risk and met with the sachem and her warriors, who were, at first, hostile. Somehow, Church was single-handedly able to secure an alliance with the Sakonnets against Philip. This momentous action would later prove devastating to the combined Indian forces, because the Sakonnets knew their ways. It was particularly difficult for Philip to bear, for he considered the Sakonnets his own blood.

On June 16th, Philip's forces burned Swansea. He was headed towards Plymouth with about 1,000 men to try and recover stores of buried corn. During this attack on Swansea, Philip's warriors killed Thomas Willet's son.

The Willets were another family that Massasoit had asked his sons to spare in the event of hostilities, in addition to the Browns, because they were his friends.

On June 27th, Bradford's troops arrived at Pocasset. He told Church he would not sanction his alliance with the Sakonnets until it was approved by Plymouth. Church was eventually able to secure this approval, but with heavy conditions. Plymouth refused to pay his men; they must pay their own way with plunder and Indian slaves.

This put Church in a difficult position, for he did not believe in selling Indians into slavery, at least most of them. He did feel that Philip and his followers had dragged New England into the war, and as a consequence deserved the worst. But he also believed that other Indians who had been pulled into the war, including some Pokanokets, should be treated humanely when captured.

Church's men included a small core of *Mayflower* descendents, who were young and resourceful. To them he added his Sakonnet allies, who taught the English how to fight like an Indian in the woods and swamps. One of the things the Indians told Church was "never come out of a swamp the same way you went in, or you will be ambushed." Church's decision to use friendly Indians against the enemy encouraged a trend that proved to be a major turning point for the Puritans in the war.

In July 1676, Major John Talcott from Connecticut surprised the Narragansetts and slaughtered several hundred of them, showing no mercy. Talcott then allowed his Indian troops to torture to death a young Narragansett man they had captured. He did this partly to appease their wishes, and probably to witness their methods firsthand as well. The event proved to be a stunning exercise in brutality, and left little doubt in the minds of the Puritans as to what might happen to them should they fall into enemy hands.

One of the saving graces for the colonists in this area was that while some western tribes were later known to rape female captives in wartime, Eastern Indians were prohibited by taboo from doing so. They believed that any such acts would negatively effect them in battle.

In the summer of 1676, the combined English forces increasingly began to follow Talcott's brutal example by slaughtering Indians whenever possible. They did this because they sensed victory, and they were desperate to end the war using any means they could. If enemy captives weren't killed, they were sold into slavery to fund the war. Most of them probably ended up on sugar cane plantations in the West Indies. Mosely and his band of pirates were particularly brutal to the Indians, as were the Connecticut Indian allies of the Puritans in Connecticut.

On July 11th, Church led his men to Middleboro, where with the help of his Sakonnets he captured an enemy band of Indians. His successes continued, unabated, from that moment forward. In late July, Governor Winslow granted Church more autonomy to bring in Indians, and he did. Church appears to have been blessed with great personal charisma. Using a policy of rewarding traitors, he was able to convince the Indians to turn each other in with great success. To the Puritan leaders back in Plymouth, it must have seemed that Church had been granted by God the power to single-handedly deliver Indians out of the Wilderness.

Bradford's troops, fighting in a more conventional English manner, also continued to pursue Philip and the enemy, as they had since the start of the war. The son of Governor Bradford, like his father had before him, believed himself to be an instrument of God. The younger Bradford stated on several occasions that his overall success was granted to him by the Lord, as were each of his victories over the Indians in battle. Bradford tolerated, but did not condone, the unorthodox Indian fighting tactics of his rival, Church.

On July 18th, Plymouth formally renewed a holy covenant that their *Mayflower* ancestors had made with the Lord God before leaving Leiden. They confessed to the Lord that they had degenerated, and that they were too proud, and begged for his forgiveness.

After this great repentance, the Puritan forces began to experience unprecedented successes in battle, which continued until the close of the war.

By this time, both Bradford and Church were keenly aware that Philip's days were numbered, and they both wanted to capture him. Bradford had come close to Philip in the backwoods many times. On July 25th, he tried to capture him again, but failed. The Indians were desperate, and now nearing the end. Church and his Sakonnets were hunting them down in their most hidden lairs, deep in the woods and swamps.

On July 30th, Benjamin Church was attending church in Plymouth when a messenger arrived and informed him that Indians were crossing the Taunton River in an attempt to destroy the towns of Taunton and Bridgewater. As Church sped west, two Bridgewater patrolmen saw two Indians crossing the Taunton on a fallen tree. They shot the older one, who turned out to be Philip's uncle and advisor. The younger one escaped, and they later found out it was Philip himself.

The next day, July 31st, the men of Bridgewater began capturing Indians at will. They were just giving up. The next morning, after a battle, they were surprised to see an Indian sitting on a stump near the scene. A marksman nearly took him down, but stopped because a friendly Indian told him he was on their side. The man escaped, and it turned out, once again, that it had been Philip.

Church came across the Taunton on the same fallen tree that Philip and his uncle had attempted to use. He found a band of Indians, but Philip had run, this time deserting his wife and nine-year-old son. Philip's wife and son were captured, and later held for their own protection in the Reverend James Keith's house in Bridgewater, which had been turned into a garrison. Church chased Philip south down the bank of the Taunton, but eventually had to give up in order to get his prisoners back to Bridgewater. The next day, he went back, with his Sakonnets leading, and found the Wampanoag sachem camped with numerous Indian followers. On the way, Church's men had come upon many stragglers, including women and children, that had been left behind by Philip.

Church decided to let Philip camp for the night. He sent his Sakonnets to make contact in the morning, but they found that Philip and his warriors had fled into the swamp. Church told his men to surround the swamp, and they started catching Indians as they came out. Then the Sakonnets managed to trick Philip's warriors by convincing them they were a large army. Church went into the swamp to get Philip, and ran right into him. But while his warriors stood and fought, Philip ran, and managed to escape through the English perimeter.

Church then found Totoson, the sachem that had attacked Dartmouth, and personally fought him. But this sachem, like Philip, also managed to escape. However, in the end, this encounter proved a massive victory for Church. His small group of 40 men had somehow captured 173 Indians. True to his nature, that evening in Bridgewater, Church entertained both his troops and the Indians he had taken captive.

The hand of God seemed to continue to work against the Indians. On August 6th, Weetamoo and the remnants of her Pocassets were attacked by English troops. Mary Rowlandson's cruel former mistress managed to get away, but she drowned trying to cross the Taunton River. Weetamoo's naked body later washed up on the shoreline of her father Corbitant's ancestral village. There, a colonist found it, cut off her head, and sent it to Plymouth. Her head was prominently displayed, much to the distress of the Indians who recognized it as belonging to their queen.

Just a few days later, Quinnapen, who had returned home to Narragansett Bay, was captured. He was subsequently executed in Newport, Rhode Island. Shortly after, Totoson died of disease. Several other sachems turned themselves in to the English. They were all executed, including one who was tied to a tree on Boston Common and shot.

By August 11, 1676, the English were firmly in control. They had disbanded almost all their forces, except for Church's. But Philip was still out there. Church was trying to visit his wife when an Indian formerly crossed by Philip betrayed him, telling Church the sachem was hiding at the base of the Mount Hope cliffs. Church led his core group of *Mayflower* descendents and his Sakonnets, along with a defector from Weetamoo's band named Alderman, to get him.

That night, Hobbamock sent Philip, ensconced deep in the Assowamset Swamp near Mount Hope, a dream. He had been betrayed. At dawn, the sachem tried his best to get his warriors to run. But this time, Church had anticipated Philip's behavior and had set an ambush. When Church attacked, Philip left his warriors and ran away. Annawon, an old warrior that had fought for Massasoit, famously shouted "Ioutash! Ioutash!" ("Fight! Fight!") in attempt to inspire the Indians to hold firm, but Philip ran anyway—straight into Church's ambush. Caleb Cook then tried to shoot Philip, but his gun misfired. Alderman, the Pocasset Indian, was the only other man there. He fired two shots at Philip, one of which passed through his heart and killed him.

Church had Philip's body dragged in through the mud. He took a good look at him, and then pronounced him to be "a doleful, great, naked, dirty beast." The sachem's body was butchered in quarters by Sakonnet Indians, and his head was cut off. On August 17th, the Pastor John Cotton was leading the Plymouth congregation in a Day of Thanksgiving. At the end of the day, most unexpectedly, Church rode in to town with Philip's head. The church recorded that "…in the day of our praises our eyes saw the salvation of God."

Meanwhile, two legendary Indian warriors, Tispaquin and Annawon, were still on the loose. Church went after them. On August 29th, he captured Tispaquin's wife and children. Knowing Tispaquin's invincible reputation as a "powaw-sachem," Church left a message for him saying that if he turned himself in, Church would make him his Indian Captain and take him to Maine to fight the Abenakis, his next foe. Tispaquin came in.

Church next chose to go after Annawon, with just six men. Those who knew the old warrior warned him that this was madness, but Church went anyway. In a daring escapade that involving repelling down a high rock face, Church captured Annawon, and slept next to him by his fire that night. The two had a sort of conversation, during which Annawon told the Englishman that the course of the war had convinced him that "a great god rules over all." He also handed over to Church what remained of Philip's personal belongings.

Later, when Church left to go to Boston to discuss his Indian-fighting campaign in Maine, the Plymouth authorities acted. When Church returned, he found both Tispaquin and Annawon had been beheaded. Later, Church did go to Maine, with his Sakonnets, and he had a long, successful career as an Indian fighter there.

At the close of the war, most of the Indians in Southern New England were gone, either killed or sold into slavery. The lives of Philip's family were spared, including his young son and heir, after a spirited debate regarding their fate among the Puritan Ministers. The Reverend James Keith of Bridgewater, who had formerly sheltered them in his home, argued successfully to spare them. They were sold into slavery instead, and due to the reputation of the North American Indians as defiant and unsuited for slavery, they may have ended up as far away as North Africa.

The combination of the plague that had preceded the Pilgrims and the war had completely decimated the People. After 12,000 long years, they had finally lost their New World Paradise.

YELLOW DAY
1881 A.D.

It was the morning of September 6, 1881. Two Bridgewater farmers stood knee-deep in black mud on the edge of the Hockomock Swamp. In a desperate effort to improve the fertility of their rocky, New England fields, they were excavating cartloads of stinking swamp mud with which to top-dress them. They dragged the cart up the slopes of their fields using a team of big, brown-and-white Clydesdale draft horses. They typically did most of this work in the Fall, after the hay was in. The two reckoned that they had hauled close to 5,000 cartloads of the wet muck in the last few years alone.

It was 5 a.m., just before sunup, that special time of the morning characterized by "gray light," when all is peaceful and there is just enough light to see. Sam, the hired man, saw it first, as he peered out from under the drooping gray limbs and scarlet leaves of the swamp maples.

"Good Lord Mose," he rasped, pausing his shoveling to catch his breath. "Take a look at that."

Moses Nash, the farm's owner, glanced up just in time to see a giant red orb solemnly clear the eastern horizon. As the light of this strange red sun illuminated the land about them, they saw that the moist ground fog that had been wisping around their feet extended out over the fields as far as they could see. Then, as the two watched spellbound, the entire sky—every inch of it—turned bright red. Moses, not taking his eyes off this surreal vision, planted his shovel firmly in the muck next to Sam's.

"In all my years, Sam," he said hoarsely, " I've never seen anything like that."

Sam's eyebrows went up, and he nodded wordlessly. Both of the men were wondering what was going to happen next. A chill settled down Moses' spine, and after a quick look over his shoulder into the shadowy swamp behind him, he quietly muttered an impromptu prayer. "Lord, save us. Nay, protect us…from this place."

After a while, the two men resumed work, digging out the heavy shovelfuls of mud, pitching them into the cart, cajoling and urging the team up the slope, then doing it all over again under that searing, blood-red sky. Soon, the breeze went out of the world, and the morning became hot, humid, and oppressive. The long-sleeved cotton shirts of the men were stained dark with mud, and soaked through with sweat. They worked quietly, on edge, trying gamely to focus on the task at hand and not look up at that horrid sky.

"Funny Mose" said Sam, breaking the silence. "I ain't heard a bird sing all morning."

So it went on like this, the day, until just before noon, when the sunlight, such as it was, began to fade, and a great gloom began to gather. Moses and Sam, up spreading mud on the fields, were trying desperately to calm their skittish team. The horses were spooked good, stamping their big, white-feathered feet, tossing their huge heads, and snorting loudly through flared gray nostrils. Moses clenched Bill's bridle, and reached up to stroke his nose and murmur comforting words, at the same time nervously eyeing the sky above. Then, as the light faded to near-twilight, it happened.

The entire sky turned from red to yellow, and a strange and terrible golden light descended from the heavens, illuminating all things with an unholy glow. The fences ringing the fields, the trunks and leaves of the maples in the swamp, the roofs and walls of the farm buildings, the team, the men themselves—all were electrified in a shimmering, brassy glow, as if they were about to implode into fire.

"What…what the hell…Mose, WHAT'S GOING ON?!" roared Sam.

Moses didn't answer. His brain was churning, memories of childhood flashing unbidden across his consciousness. He heard again his Father's Sunday readings from the Book of Revelation, about the burning chariots, the serpents, the seven horsemen, the coming of Christ, and the end of the world. If this wasn't it, Moses didn't know what was.

"Hang in there, Sam," he managed to blurt out, in a voice broken by fear. "Just keep workin'—there's nothin' we can do about it."

And that's exactly what they did, as soon as Moses checked in on his wife, Mary—they just kept working.

Later, the men broke for their mid-day meal, listlessly chewing their chicken, potatoes, and apple pie while sitting on the back of the muddy cart. They stared in disbelief at the once-familiar objects around them. The yellow blossoms of the flowers of the fields, buttercups and golden-rod, were now gray. The emerald grass of the pasture beside them was blue. It might have seemed like Heaven, then, bathed in that enchanted light and all, if the day had not kept growing hotter, if the scene had… well, just changed a bit, for the better somehow. But it didn't. Everything held, and the awful day wore on.

Up in the farmhouse on top of the slope, they saw a light flicker on. It was Mary, lighting a gas lamp at mid-day. The men couldn't see any chickens milling about up there in the farmyard, so they knew the birds must have returned to their roosts in the henhouse, duped into believing it was nightfall by the low light. After lunch, the two returned to work until around mid-afternoon, when they paused after hearing shouts from across the field.

"Jesus," growled Sam. "What now—Christ, that looks like Danny Ames!"

Danny Ames was a troubled soul, the Bridgewater drunk, who had recently turned farmer. He had settled in to the deserted Reeves farm next door, mostly because the owners were gone and nobody else seemed to want it. Rumor was he slept on bags of grain in the barn, with just his bottle of Tennessee whiskey for company.

"Fly, fly away! It is the time of the coming of the Lord!"

Moses froze at this unnerving salvo from the rapidly-approaching Ames. Then, he and Sam watched as the distant figure suddenly pitched over and disappeared into a *furrow. A cloud of fine dust rose from the spot, sparkling and glittering in the weird yellow light. Then, for all the world like a puppet on strings, the stick-figure of Danny Ames jerked straight up, erect, and moved rapidly toward them, gangly knees and elbows flopping, poking out of torn sleeves and pants.*

As he drew closer, Moses and Sam could see that he was clutching a bottle in one hand, and what appeared to be a Bible in the other, held up in front of him like a church hymnal.

Finally Ames stopped, just a few feet away. His long, unkept brown hair was matted. He was missing most of his teeth, his body was shockingly thin, his clothing filthy. Ames reeked of booze, and was swaying slightly from front to back. His eyes, glassy and red, stared fixedly, even accusingly at them. What happened next did little to improve the already-suffering morale of Moses and Sam.

"Blessed is he that readeth, and they that hear the words of this prophesy, and keep those things which are written therein; for the time is at hand!" screeched Ames from behind his good book, which he now pressed directly against his face.

Moses swallowed hard, recognizing the verse from the Book of Revelations.

"Behold, he cometh with CLOUDS! And every eye shall see him…"

At this, the filthy marionette doubled over to hack and cough, a sick man's hack, before spitting out blood onto the earth of the field. He wiped his mouth with the back of the hand holding the bottle, which the men could now see was whiskey. Danny took a good belt from the bottle, fixed his accusatory stare on them once again, and resumed his inspired preaching.

"And I turned to see the voice that spake with me. And being turned, I saw seven YELLOW candlesticks; And in the midst of the seven candlesticks one like unto the Son of man, clothed with a garment down to the foot, and gird about the paps with a GOLDEN girdle…And his feet like unto fine BRASS, as IF THEY BURNED IN A FURNACE!" He paused. "Look about you, FOOLS!" shrieked the filthy marionette. "What do you see?!"

By this time, poor Sam had had enough. Looking nervously about him, taking in the golden clouds hanging overhead, and the brassy, unearthly glow clinging to all, he panicked.

"Jesus, Mose!" he screamed in terror. "Maybe he's right! Maybe…"

"You BE QUIET Sam!" shouted Moses, cutting him off. "You know as well as I do that there's been smoke in the air for days. Most likely, all this is caused by those forest fires they say are still burning out West."

But although Moses sounded brave, in his heart he wasn't really sure what was going on.

At any rate, the reaction that he had roused from his neighbors seemed only to encourage Danny Ames. His gangly arms and knees began to jerk wildly up and down as he worked himself into a frenzy and delivered his crescendo: "FOOLS!!" "And when I saw him, I FELL DOWN AT HIS FEET AS IF DEAD!"

Suddenly, as if he had orchestrated his own demise, the stick figure pitched rapidly forward, arms tight to his sides, face down into a pile of black Hockomock muck next to the cart, and lay perfectly still.

By now, Sam had backed up a goodly distance from the podium of this bizarre sermon. Moses pulled himself together, walked forward, gingerly inserted his boot tip under Danny Ames' chest, and kicked hard, flipping the drunk onto his back. He felt as light as a rack of bones. As he lay there, all jumbled up in the mud with his Bible and his whiskey, Moses could see that Ames was still breathing.

"Stone drunk is all," he announced, matter-of-factly. "It's a wonder he ain't dead after drinking all that whiskey. Let's get him in the cart, Sam. C'mon…"

There was nothing left for them to do but load up Danny Ames and head back to the house. Night was coming soon, and only God knew what else lay in store for them. Both Moses and Sam were tired, and badly shaken by the events of this strange, yellow day.

"Save the whiskey Sam," muttered Moses as they pitched the drooping marionette into the cart. "Might need it ourselves by the time this damned day is through." He shouted loudly at the team, "Haw!" urging them up the long, furrowed slope. "See you up at the house, Sam," he shouted over his shoulder at his companion, who had stayed behind to gather up their tools.

As Moses and the team approached the little white farmhouse on the rise, the sky, like a portent, slowly shifted back to its infernal, blood-red hue of the morning. The yellow gloom lifted, and the same bright red sphere of the sun appeared once again, now setting in the West.

As the spooked horses thundered up the hill, eyes rolling white, with the drunken Danny Ames banging about in the wooden cart behind him, Moses began to recite the 23rd Psalm loudly in a clear, unwavering voice. "Yea, though I walk through the shadow of the valley of death I will fear no evil, for though art with me…"

By 1881, families like the Nash's had farmed lonely plots on the edge of the Hockomock Swamp for more than 200 years. Their ancestors had moved there after the town was granted the Hockomock lands, which lay to the west of the original Bridgewater settlement, by Plymouth in 1662. They had quickly put what they could of this "large and valuable tract of swamp and meadow lands" to the plow. Many of their ancestors had successfully defended these farms, along with the fledgling community of Bridgewater, from King Philip and Tispaquin during the war.

After the war ended locally in 1676, the Indians were no longer a threat, so more farmers had come to the Hockomock area. They settled places that had up to that point been considered too dangerous because of the numerous Indians, places such as "Scotland," that was named for the numerous settlers there of Scottish ancestry, such as the Keiths. The farmers in that area, near the Hockomock River, were now residents of West Bridgewater, which had been set off from Bridgewater and incorporated in 1822.

Bridgewater, reacting to an expanding population, had divided itself politically after almost two centuries, following the division of its original parish, or church, starting in 1712. East Bridgewater had been incorporated in 1823, and North Bridgewater, which would later be incorporated as Brockton, was set off in 1821. The town that remained as "Bridgewater" was what had originally been the Old South Parish.

It is generally considered to be at this time, when the other parishes were incorporated as towns, that the new "Bridgewater" was said to have "inherited the name and traditions of the ancient town," thus, by default, assuming this mantle from its neighbor West Bridgewater, which was the original settlement.

The Hockomock land that the new farmers put to the plow was less productive agriculturally than the high, fertile land on the Town River, which had been the prized centerpiece of the original Bridgewater land grant from Plymouth in 1645. The Hockomock farms tended to grow steadily in size, as their owners converted land over from the Hockomock Swamp in attempts to increase productivity. These lowland Hockomock farms were usually planted in hay, a crop which had significant value at the time.

During the American Revolution and the Civil War, the men of Bridgewater once again distinguished themselves in the service to the United States military, but in these conflicts, as opposed to King Philip's war, some of them were indeed lost. After the Civil War, young men were scarce around the Hockomock. This was the case in small towns all across New England—many young men enlisted to fight, but not many of them came back—they were simply killed.

Of those who did come back East, many quickly pulled up stakes and went back to the West. Congress had just passed the Homestead Act that granted 160 acres in the West to any American who could occupy the land for five years and pay a modest purchase price. Most of these modest requirements were waived for veterans. The Homestead Act, and related settlement incentives offered by the railroads, were enough to lure most of the young blood of the Hockomock towns away forever.

All over New England, it was the same. Strong young men riding West, abandoning family farms by the hundreds, or leaving only elderly family members to hang on as best they could. Initially, after the war, they were lured away by the Homestead Act. But later, a devastating combination of market and technological forces descended on the New England farmer, that resulted in widespread ruin.

To the farmers, this situation appeared to be the classic "carrot and stick" situation of reward or punishment. Go West and prosper, or stay in New England

and face hardship and possible financial disaster. Unfortunately, for those who chose to leave, it was not that simple. Many of these pioneers found out the hard way that there were no guarantees of success on a farm in Illinois, either.

In the end, this new set of challenges, combined with those the New England farmers had always faced, the most difficult of which was the infertility of the rocky land, proved enough to finish almost all of them. The only farmers who survived were the few who had been fortunate enough to inherit fertile, well-located land, and were also capable of innovation. Unfortunately for the farmers of the Hockomock, the "fertile lands" part of this equation did not include their lowland properties. Most of the New England migration of farmers to the West came from infertile or isolated farms, just like those in the Hockomock.

By leaving, these young men spawned major social and environmental changes in New England. They hastened the decline of the rural villages that were poorly situated geographically. And when these farms and villages depopulated, the wilderness crept back in. In the Hock, the birches, pines, spruce, and bull briar re-colonized land on which hay had stood for generations, and hid the long, double-row walls the farmers had built of uprooted field stones to border their fields.

The Hockomock Swamp encroached again, flooding the deserted fields. Whitetail deer, muskrat, and other native wildlife roamed over them. Second-growth forests reclaimed nearly all of the land that the settlers had taken from the swamp with their sweat and blood. A few scattered, remnant bands of Wampanoags remained in the swamp even then, as they always had, long before the English settlers came to the Hockomock.

The farmers who remained in Bridgewater began raising cows instead of sheep, to supply butter and milk for the waves of people who were now leaving the villages and migrating to the cities.

Deer in the Hockomock were protected by law, and "bears and wolves were found only in the wildest places." Pollution had started to creep into the region as well, from Bridgewater's booming industries that included paper mills, small arms, cannon, tools, and shovels. Shoe-making was the largest business of all. Many of the streams in the area were fouled with effluent dumped from paper and lumber mills, wool-cleaning plants, and cotton-print works.

The Yankee farmers who would survive did so by applying their intelligence, ingenuity, and work ethic. One of the ways they did this was through automation. Because of the severe shortage of labor during the war, New England farmers had adopted new technological inventions to help them cope. These machines included hay spreaders, hay mowers, horse pitchforks, and wheel horserakes.

These innovations greatly reduced the labor required to run a farm. Two farmers could now unload a tow of hay in six minutes using the horse pitchfork, versus the hour it had formerly taken them by hand. And the new hay mower replaced a small army of men at harvest time. These modern machines marked the end of the era of traditional, handmade and blacksmith-made farm tools such as the bullrake, that were far less productive. The "hired man" of the late 19th century farm in New England was also vital to the survival of many farm families. He helped keep the operation together in both difficult and prosperous times.

Although the new technological wonders helped farmers cope in the late 1860s, ironically they also contributed significantly to the underlying social problem they faced, which was the depopulation of their communities. That's because these new working machines replaced working men. No longer able to find work due to the machines, these men simply left town along with everyone else.

Many farmers had also altered the traditional mix of crops they grew on their Hockomock plots to meet the demands of a market driven by war. They planted heavily in potatoes and onions, both of which were in high demand as food for the troops. At first, after the war, these crops held their value, as did hay, which had always been a mainstay on the lowland farms. Hay indirectly met the demand for dairy products generated by the hordes of people who had emigrated to cities like Boston after the Civil War. These city people had a seemingly insatiable need for milk, cheese, and butter, all of which are perishable products that were best sourced at the time from local farmers. As a result, farmers found a good source of income in their hay crops, some of which were sold to feed the dairy cows of other farmers, some of which was fed directly to their own herds. The milk from the herd also found a ready market, and provided a new, welcome source of income.

Then the railroads went through, opening up the great agricultural markets of the West. Eastern markets were flooded with cheap products. The grain crop from the Hockomock, though it had never amounted to much, was now rendered simply unprofitable. It was the same with the traditional corn crop. New England farmers' aspirations to expand their growing livestock operations of horses, cattle, and sheep were now dashed. To top it off, during the same period, the mainstay crops farm families had depended on during wartime—potatoes and onions—were made worthless by a new crop disease and intense competition. It turned out that everybody had the same idea.

By 1870, New England farmers were truly suffering. The thirty years that followed, up until about the turn of the 20th century, have been described, from their perspective, as "three decades of unrelenting gloom." Still, the farmers who remained kept fighting, mostly by changing their focus nearly completely to those aspects of their operation that met the growing demand for fresh, local products such as dairy. Some began experimenting with improving their poultry flocks, and expanding them to meet a growing demand for fresh eggs and meat. In this case, however, the farmers' labor did not produce a payoff. The real economic boom in this area would prove to be far in the future. An additional burden to farmers at this time was that taxes on their land were as high as any area farmer could recall.

A major change for women occurred at around this time as well. The role of the farm wife changed significantly. Basically, her daily workload drastically increased. This change was caused by the general market shift to fresh, local products, the burden of which was shared by farm wives across New England, particularly by those living on the less-productive farms that were facing financial hardship. This was because much of the new work, such as making butter, and growing vegetables, was left to the women out of sheer necessity. The men had to be out working in the fields and tending to the livestock. So, these new tasks were added to the already-full daily routine of the farm wife, which included cooking, cleaning, washing, tending to the children, the hired man, and any other farm help, as well as countless other domestic duties.

Many struggling farm wives responded to these new market conditions by starting butter-making ventures, driving their wagons to town each week to sell their hard-won product to the general stores. They also expanded the farm's kitchen garden to include cabbage, lettuce, cauliflower, celery, strawberries, cucumbers, beans, and many other vegetable varieties. But growing vegetables proved to be intensely difficult labor. To grow them productively, farm wives learned that they needed to regularly haul large quantities of water from the well. In addition, they had to fertilize their crops heavily, which forced them to shovel, transport, and spread large quantities of horse manure.

Some of these farm wives also grew perennials for the Boston cut-flower market, which the new train had made possible. In the end, the butter-making may have been the most difficult cross for the women to bear. The work was physically grueling and time consuming, an exercise in sheer drudgery.

One bright spot for farmer's wives at this time was the investments in new, labor-saving technology, which benefited them as it did the men. The hay mower and other machines guaranteed that their husbands, with perhaps a hired man, could harvest the hay crop, which eliminated the need to bring in immigrant labor. The burden of feeding and general care of these laborers had previously fallen to the women. In addition, there were now big iron cook stoves to replace the brick ovens, which eased their labor in the kitchen and also kept them warm while cooking on cold winter days.

Tin ware, the ice chest, and the washboard, all recent additions to the New England farm scene, likewise eased the predicament of the farm wives. New hand pumps at the wells outside helped them with their watering, cooking, and other domestic duties, and some even got a newfangled sewing machine to replace the old spinning wheel that reigned over the living room.

But the things that helped the farmers' wives most, the real luxuries, most farmers of the Hockomock were simply unable to afford. At the top of this list were indoor bathrooms and hired help, like the girls from Nova Scotia who were so helpful to their wealthier farm brethren.

As the decade of the 1870s wore on, it is quite likely that the place itself wore on the Hockomock farmers as well. For although the lonely Hockomock farms in Bridgewater were just a few miles from the more prosperous farms on the Town River, it may as well have been a continent. For the land there was not high, dry, and full of light, but low, wet, and dark. Some of them probably never quite came to terms with the isolation, the mysterious, wandering balls of foxfire, the quicksand, and the insatiable mosquitoes.

And always, in the backs of their minds, must have lurked their grandfathers' saying about the Hockomock Swamp from Colonial days: "The Devil lives in there—always has."

By 1880, the economic situation on most Hockomock farms was truly grim. While before there had been no extra money after meeting the mortgage and the taxes, now many farmers were struggling to meet, and occasionally missing, their monthly bank payments. Many of the farms had already been abandoned. Their elderly occupants, left to shift for themselves by younger family members, had finally given up, and gone to live with relatives in town.

Most of these townspeople were by now employed in Bridgewater's burgeoning new manufacturing industries. While the Hockomock farmers had been struggling stalwartly to eke out a living on the land, Massachusetts's economy had undergone a fundamental shift from farming to manufacturing. This shift, a result of the Industrial Revolution, had left them and their agricultural brethren far behind in the process. Bridgewater had quietly transformed itself from an agricultural town into an industrial powerhouse.

In one sense, this change had been a natural one, for the citizens of Bridgewater had always valued enterprise and industry second only to religion. There is no doubt that they viewed the replacement of their primeval forests by fine houses, roads, and industries as Progress. The mechanical arts flourished in Bridgewater, so much so that the nation now viewed the town as one of the cradles of much-vaunted Yankee ingenuity.

A handful of companies, such as Bates and Hyde and Continental, manufactured cotton gins, a labor-saving device that separated cotton flax from seeds. These Bridgewater-made machines were sold all over the world and revolutionized the Cotton Industry. The first cotton gins were made at a factory near the Satucket fish weir, the spot that had acted as the center of the original Bridgewater land purchase from Massasoit in 1649.

Shoe factories started in Bridgewater with W.F. McElwain prior to 1872. These factories employed large numbers of Irish, Italian, and other foreign immigrants for labor, immigrants that would stay and forever alter the character of the Yankee village. The shoe factories were vast in size, produced inconceivable numbers of shoes on a daily basis, and remained profitable ventures in town well into the first half of the 20th century.

Some of the most successful shoe manufacturers were the descendents of original Bridgewater settlers, including the Keiths, Southworths, and Aldens. Shoe ventures produced large fortunes and palatial residences for their owners, and many fine public buildings for the town. In 1870, North Bridgewater, incorporated as Brockton in 1881, produced more shoes than any town in America. The owners of these factories prided themselves on the "moral and physical well-being" of their employees. Paper mills were yet another significant industry in Bridgewater during the second half of the 19th century.

Perhaps the most important industry of all to the Bridgewaters in their industrial heyday, with the possible exception of shoes, was iron. After the Old Colony Railroad came through in 1845, Bridgewater became known as an "Iron Town." The first firearms and solid cannons in America were made there. Along the Town River, where the first iron works had blossomed after the American Revolution, there now rose stupendously large iron works. They were worked by big, strong men and even bigger, stronger teams of oxen.

One of these operations, the iron works on High Street, dammed and flooded the river to create a millpond in 1695, and subsequently became Bridgewater's most renowned and long-lasting industry. In 1863, the Lazell Perkins Iron Company was the second-biggest iron rolling and forging facility in the United States. The operation is best known today for producing the iron that was used to build the pilothouse of the USS *Monitor*. The Stanley Iron Works, which provided iron plate and other parts for Stanley factories in Connecticut, and the Bridgewater Iron Works were other major local iron operations.

Unfortunately, however, iron, like farming, was an industry that was ultimately doomed in Bridgewater. It would hold on another fifty years or so, but by then the same railroad that had allowed the industry to flourish in town would destroy it, just as it had done to most of the local farms. For the railroad resulted in the migration to and consolidation of the Iron Industry in the American West in the 1880s, which spelled eventual ruin for the great iron works of the East like those in Bridgewater.

In addition, all the raw iron worked by these immense operations was local bog iron, dug in stupendous amounts right out of the bottom of Bridgewater ponds and swamps, and much of this local iron was simply used up. The Stanley Works closed down its Bridgewater operation in 1928.

The typical New England farmer of the late 19th century was educated, respected, and a vital part of community life. These were men and women of substance, quite capable of reckoning the vast economic and social forces that were arrayed against them. But their keen knowledge of their dire predicament could only have served to drain their resolve. Around the wood stove at the general store, the traditional gathering place for men, the common refrain must have been "How do you fight the inevitable?"

Two particularly onerous events emerged to further plague the Hockomock farmers at the end of this already-devastating era. In 1878, the gypsy moth was accidentally introduced from Europe. The ravenous caterpillars of this winged pest, squirming in their white silken nests, literally ate their way across Eastern Massachusetts, defoliating every tree in their path. They ate the leaves off the shade trees on the farms, leaving the beleaguered farm wives at the mercy of the hot summer sun as they tended their vegetables.

And in 1880, an event occurred which shook all the farmers to the bone: a tuberculosis scare in the state's dairy herds. According to an article they read in the journal of the new Massachusetts agricultural college, in Worcester, a farmer had lost his whole herd to the disease. The Hockomock farmers knew that if they lost their dairy cows, one of the few paying operations left on their farms, they were finished. This event was doubly troubling because at that time, tuberculosis was a deadly disease in humans as well, with no cure. As they soberly considered all these challenges, the farmers of the lonely Hockomock plots, many of whom were the direct descendents of the devout original settlers of the plantation, must have felt that their Lord had turned his back on them.

The practical result of these challenging conditions for all New England farmers was still more work. Men worked the fields relentlessly, from before sunup to after sundown. The women tried to increase production from their butter making operations, hauled more manure, and carried more water for their vegetable gardens in attempts to increase their harvest. And so the long, gloomy decade of the 1870s passed by the farmers of the Hockomock in this manner, until finally, in the end, came to them the gloomiest, darkest day of them all—Yellow Day.

While her husband and Sam were hard at work spreading swamp muck, Mary Nash had set about her butter making. After a brief stint outside that morning in her vegetable gardens, under that God-awful red sky, she had retreated to the relative sanctity of the farmhouse. Now, on that gloomy, suffocating, humid day, she faced her most dreaded task. She set to work morbidly, woodenly, in the light of the gas lamp's unnatural glow, the same light that Moses and Sam, down on the fields, had seen flickering. She was sweating even before she started. Mary tried not to look out the window, at the yellow luminescence clinging to the outbuildings; she tried hard to focus on her work.

First, she poured the soured cream she had put out to sit the day before into the tall, stoneware churn until it was about half-full. Then she began to pump the dasher—like a broomstick with a cross on the bottom to agitate the cream—up and down, methodically, once a second. Over the last year, depression had rendered her physically incapable of singing, but the melody of the traditional butter-making song still ran unbidden through her head while she labored:

> Come butter, Come butter, Come!
> Peter—standing at the gate!
> Waiting for a Buttercake!
> Come butter Come!

After half an hour of pumping the dasher, her arms, shoulders, and back started to ache. After an hour of pumping thus in the close, fetid heat of the kitchen, she was drenched in sweat, nauseous from the smell of the soured cream, and praying for the butter to come from the milk. When one of her arms grew too tired to pump, she switched to the other. Mentally, Mary was hurting as well. The butter churning had become a horrid metaphor for her. It seemed to represent her entire life on the farm—endless labor for results that seldom materialized.

Finally, by peeking into the churn, Mary saw that the butter had gathered from the cream. She lifted the lid and gently herded the floating lumps together with the crossed ends of the dasher. Then came the next round of drudgery: working out the buttermilk from the lumps of butter. Lifting out the lumps with a butter paddle—a large, wooden spoon—she placed them in a big wooden bowl. Then she poured off the whey, and began working the butter hard against the sides of the bowl with the spoon.

As she beat the buttermilk out of the lumps, Mary poured it out of the bowl into jars for drinking. When no more buttermilk came, she poured a small quantity of cold water into the bowl to wash the butter, worked the lumps again, and then poured the water off. She repeated this cycle several times until the water ran off clear.

At this point, the dedicated farm wife was nearly exhausted, and her hands hurt badly from her arthritis. But she knew that if she didn't work the buttermilk out well enough, the butter would later spoil, ooze, and run. After the buttermilk was gone, to complete her product, Mary added five teaspoons of salt, packed it into a butter mold—hard, so she wouldn't be accused of cheating anyone—and finally, pushed it out of the mold and placed it in a five-pound box.

In the end, exhausted, sweating, reeking of sour cream, and bathed in all that unholy yellow light streaming in through the kitchen window, Mary sat at the table and stared impassively at her box of butter. "After all that," she thought, "it's no good." The cream had been too hot. As a result, the butter was too airy and soft.

Damn this day, Mary thought. She knew that Mr. Straffin, the kind owner of the general store in town, wouldn't have the heart to turn her away, wouldn't tell her, as she suspected, that her product could not compete with the hard, dense butter now being shipped in by rail from the Midwest. But she also knew full well that as a sharp Yankee businessman, he wouldn't pay her much, either, and wasn't that the whole point of her labor, to make money to help pay the bank what they owed?

Over the last several months, Mary had been plagued by involuntary thoughts of suicide, something she had told no one. The urge would come on her uncontrollably, a symptom of her never-to-be diagnosed depression. She would envision a half dozen scenes of her own death, that involved cutting her wrists, shooting herself with Moses' war revolver, drowning herself in the farm pond, losing herself in the swamp, diving headfirst into the well, or taking an overdose of the laudanum Doc Merrick had prescribed as a cure for her afflictions.

At these times, she had been desperate for someone, for Moses to notice—but somehow, he never had. Maybe, she thought, he had just been too busy fighting his own demons. Now, sitting alone, in that gloomy kitchen, gazing out of the window, where, between the apple trees, she could see the crimson leaves of the swamp maples, the swaying, tufted reed beds, and the mosquito-infested, dark pools of the Hockomock, the thoughts of suicide came again. The hot tears streamed down her face. Mary could feel the eyes of the dark spirits of the place watching her.

"I HATE this place!" she cried aloud, finally acknowledging a thought long-suppressed.

Then, a voice came into Mary's head, from out of the dark green cedars, from deep within the rustling, mysterious reeds of the swamp. It was the voice of Hobbamock, the Spirit of Death. "KILL YOURSELF. END IT ALL NOW."

Mary swallowed hard, and sat there looking woodenly out the window as the gas lamp sputtered and went out, leaving her alone with her box of butter in the darkness.

She watched as the surreal yellow gloom outside deepened, then lifted and disappeared, and the sun, that same hateful, blazing red ball of the morning, started to drop down in the West. Then, as her husband hurried up the slope outside, bravely chanting the 23rd Psalm, the entire sky turned blood red. Mary, without hope now, knew this to be a sign from God. It was over.

She would be no longer of this "Place Where the Spirits Dwell." She stood up, and with all the resolve and dignity she could muster, walked over to the black soapstone sink and picked up her largest kitchen knife.

When Sam made it back up to the farmhouse, Moses was sitting in the darkness on the granite stoop, sucking whiskey straight out of Danny Ames' bottle. With the blood on his shirt and arms and all, even Sam gave his friend a long, searching look.

"She's up in the bed, Sam," slurred Moses in reply. "I put her up there. To bed. Mary. She just couldn't go on anymore, I guess."

This outburst was followed by an imploring, grief-stricken glance at Sam, and a torrent of tears down Moses' mud-stained cheeks.

"It was my fault, Sam, me. I neva shoulda brought a beautiful creature like Mary to a God-forsaken place like this. Knew better, I did." He paused for a ragged breath. "Oh God, why... why this..."

After a glance inside the kitchen door, Sam quickly slammed it, and sat down, visibly shaken, right next to Moses. He pried the bottle from his friend's fist, and lifted it to his lips for a long swig. Together, the two old friends sat there, in the heat of the night, and drank down the remaining whiskey in silence, their minds reliving the bizarre events of the day. At length, Moses stood.

"I'll be going now, Sam," he said hoarsely.

"I'll ask you to do one last thing for me," he said, and gestured towards the kitchen, eyes downcast.

Sam nodded, then rose, went into the house, and began cleaning up after Mary. Afterwards, he went back out to the cart, dragged out the unconscious Danny Ames, and dumped him unceremoniously into the pile of hay in the barn.

The next morning, Sam, a loyal hired man to the last, got up early and rode into town to fetch Doc Merrick. Moses, after rising and dashing his head several times into a bucket of icy-cold water from the well, went to see his last remaining neighbor, Mr. Buck, and made arrangements to sell his land.

"Can't pay you much, Mose. I'm sorry," said Mr. Buck gently, with great sympathy.

Moses didn't argue. "Just drop off the money with Sam," he said quietly. "And thank-you, John. My farm will at least make you a good woodlot. Maybe it was never worth much more than that anyway," he added reflectively, as he shook his neighbor's hand.

Then Moses rode home and paid his last respects to Sam. "I'll trust you'll take care of the place," he said. "Mr. Buck sure won't want Danny Ames looking after it."

"You know I will Mose," replied his faithful friend.

Moses asked Sam to send the payment to a forwarding address that he would provide later, then, after hesitating, added, "And take from it the money you feel you're due. You're a good man, Sam."

Moses climbed the steep, narrow steps to the attic of the farmhouse, dusted off his Civil War musket and sword, and pulled out his honorable discharge papers from an old wooden chest.

And then, Moses Nash rode away, away from his family's ancestral farm, away from the Hockomock, the "Place where the Spirits Dwell," rode fast and hard until he no longer felt either its presence or Mary's pain, rode out towards the Big Sky, the open plains, and all that bright light of the American West, until finally, at last, he was free.

FRIGHT NIGHT
1908 A.D.

"Sweet Jesus, Phil, look!"

The driver of the carriage glanced upwards, in the direction of his companion's frightened gaze, as he hauled in the team of horses. "Whoaaaa…Easy girls.…"

A very bright light, like a lantern, hovered low in the sky up ahead over the Stanley Ironworks, where bars of pig iron lay stacked on pallets like cordwood along the railroad tracks. It was 3:10 in the morning, Halloween, 1908. "What the Hell is that, John!?"

"Ain't no aeroplane, I can tell you that for sure," replied his fellow undertaker nervously. "Not even Orville Wright could make a plane hang still like that, and even if he could, he's all smashed up from his fall. Must be a balloon."

"Then he must be some sort of lunatic balloony, flying at night, and way out here over that cursed swamp," commented the driver. "He goes down in there, even his rich city friends won't be able to save his skin."

The two men watched, in silence, as the craft dropped suddenly lower, and began to move methodically, as if it were controlled by an outside force, up and down, and then in a circle.

Phil Prophett cleared his throat. "Can those hot-air balloons do that?!" he blurted out in a strained voice.

"Don't think so," replied his companion, very slowly. "That's somethin' else. We need witnesses for this, John…"

"Well, he's not gonna be any help," replied Prophett dryly, jerking his thumb over his shoulder towards the pine box resting behind them, while steadily eying the light above. "Cause he's dead."

"Hey! You there! You with the light! Who are ya?!" shouted Flynn loudly.

There was no answer. Then the light began to bauble around inside of the craft. It was at that point that the mystery looming overhead began to get the best of John Flynn. "What…what if…that's one of those Martians, Phil?" he gasped.

"Martians? Like in Wells's book?" queried his companion incredulously.

"Yeah…yeah…I been readin' it these past few days…it's been sittin' heavy on my mind. Wells said they might come back, those Martians—make more attempts to take us over—fire more canisters from Mars and all…don't you remember?"

"But that book was fiction, John…it weren't true!"

"Well, it seems like it could be true, and what the hell else is that thing, Phil? Balloons can't move like that!" replied John earnestly. "Remember, in the book, the Martians knew how to fly? Figured out our gravity and all, and launched that huge circle-thing they used to spread the BLACK SMOKE, before our diseases wiped them out? What if they drop the BLACK SMOKE, Phil? We won't even be able to see it,

in this darkness!" The petrified man was babbling now, barely coherent. "And what if they got one of those RAY-GUNS a-board?! WHAT WILL WE DO THEN? GET IN THE RIVER...I TELL YA THAT'S THE BEST THING TO DO WHEN, YOU KNOW THOSE THINGS EAT—"

"Enough!" roared Phil. "You start talkin' crazy nonsense like that, to anybody but me, who's known ya since you been a whelp, and they'll have us both committed to the new Asylum over at the State Farm. It's a balloon, God-dammit, and that's that." Raising the reigns, he roused the team with a loud "Giddyup!" and got them moving.

The creaking dark carriage lurched down Main Street in West Bridgewater, heading towards the town center. After all, they had a body to deliver for a burial in the morning. As the carriage creaked away, the two men huddled together on the seat watched, transfixed, as the mysterious lighted craft overhead moved slowly away, towards the Southeast, right out over the dark, brooding vastness of the Hockomock Swamp.

The UFO case involving John E. Flynn and Philip S. Prophett, which occurred on Halloween morning in West Bridgewater, Massachusetts, in 1908, is well known in UFO circles. The incident occurred during an exciting time period in the history of aviation. It was the era of the balloonists, known today as the "Airship Era." Planes were still very much experimental aircraft.

Orville Wright, an American, had just made the world's first successful powered airplane flight five years earlier, on December 17, 1903. On Halloween day of 1908, Orville had finally left the hospital after a crash a month earlier had left him with a broken leg and four broken ribs, and his passenger, Thomas Selfridge, dead as the first airplane crash fatality in history. Meanwhile, Orville's brother, Wilbur, was busy setting new flight records in France for an audience that had formerly been highly critical of the brothers' "first-in-flight" claims.

H.G. Well's best-selling book *War of the Worlds,* which electrified the world with its plot of a nearly successful Martian attack on the Earth, and which so successfully seeded the fear of Aliens in the public consciousness, was celebrating its 10th anniversary.

The national fervor around aviation at the time of the Bridgewater UFO sighting is amply borne out by a sampling of articles from the *New York Times* of November 1st, 1908. One of these, "Balloon for Milwaukee," describing the shipment of a New York-made balloon to the Milwaukee Aero Club, states that:

> The shipment of this balloon to the West indicates the increasing popularity of old-fashioned ballooning despite the facts that the leaders in aeronautics are disposed to frown upon mere ballooning as productive of little practical results. But it is a leader to other things, and the unusual interest in aeronautics this season in New England has been

due primarily to the number of new clubs that have been organized since the first of the year and the many ascensions. Springfield, North Adams, Pittsfield, Hartford, Worcester, and Boston all have aero clubs, and there are prospects that a few more will be formed within the next few months.

Another *Times* marketing rag, thinly disguised as an article, states that;

A serviceable airship is actually cheaper than a fast automobile or a fancy horse. If one is content to take out his air craft for but one or two flights a week the cost of maintenance is less than for motoring, and but little more expensive than driving.

And in *Duchess Aboard Airship*, the paper notes that on November 2nd, in Friedrichshafen, Germany:

Count Zeppelin made a most successful trip in his new airship to-day around the Lake of Constance. He was accompanied by several women, including Duchess Vera of Wurtemberg and his own daughter. The airship was aloft for one hour.

The same *New York Times* edition also lauds fledgling advances in airplane flight, including those of the French. After having been forced to eat crow by Wilbur Wright's undeniable flight demonstrations, they had apparently not yet officially conceded defeat to the American innovators. On October 31st, the same day that Flynn and Prophett saw the alleged balloon in Bridgewater, the following article appeared:

Farman Wins Height Prize: His Aeroplane First to Leave the Ground of its Own Power

Mourmelon, France—Henry Farman today won the height prize…offered by the French Aero Club for the first aeroplane leaving the ground by its own power and making a flight over the tips of a series of captive balloons which were attached to the ground by a cord about 80 feet long. Wilbur Wright was not eligible for the prize.

Directly above this article is another, likewise dated Halloween Day, 1908, that describes Orville Wright's medical progress subsequent to his prior crash:

Washington – Orville Wright, the aviator who was injured by the fall of his aeroplane at Fort Myer, Va., on Sept. 17th, left to-day for his home in Dayton, Ohio…While his condition is considered to be exceptionally good by the surgeons who have attended him, they do not expect that he will regain the full use of his left leg for several months. There is practically no shortening of his leg as the result of the thigh fracture.

The night that Prophett and Flynn saw their mystery craft, the daily Brockton, Massachusetts *Enterprise* of October 31st noted that:

> High above this town (in Bridgewater), a big passenger balloon, equipped with a powerful light, was seen floating between 3 and 4 o'clock this morning…It may have been the same mysterious airship that has been reported as seen at night in various parts of New England the past two months.

The rival Brockton newspaper, the *Times*, on the same day reported the incident and stated that: "Why a balloon should be seen over Bridgewater this morning is a peculiarly hard question to answer." This article describes, in detail, the paper's unsuccessful attempts, in conjunction with the *Associated Press*, to identify the craft.

After accounting for the whereabouts of all balloons in the area, they concluded that:

> There are no other known balloons in this part of the country: at least none which could have reached Bridgewater without traveling a part of the time by day, and being plainly seen and reported for many miles. Every one of these has been queried this morning, and all of them are accounted for in a way that bars the slightest possibility of their being over or near Brockton or any of the towns in this part of Massachusetts.

After alluding to the rash of recent, night balloon sightings in other parts of New England, the *Times* noted:

> The balloon appears capable of speed and directness of travel which are out of the ordinary, and suggest that it might be fitted with a power-driven fan or propeller, but none who have seen it ever heard any sound indicating the presence of machinery.

The following are excerpts from Flynn's account of his sighting in the *Times* article:

> We saw the light, not exactly a searchlight but an unusually strong lantern of some sort, over the Stanley works. We stopped the team and for ten minutes watched it, and saw it was moving, and coming nearer and nearer to earth. At last, with the stars bright, and occasional bits of light from the lantern, we caught a glimpse of the shape of the balloon. We shouted toward it, but heard no response or sound of any sort.
>
> The balloon dropped down and the light moved about, perhaps as though they were trying to get their bearings. Then it slowly rose, and moved directly off to the east, or slightly south of east."

Flynn was later able to watch the light receding for more than one-half hour after he got home, and noted his surprise that although it had to be nearing the sea at that point, it did not appear to drop down in an attempt to land.

The weekly *Bridgewater Independent* on November 6 added that Flynn and Prophett were "out on legitimate business," though the paper never mentions the actual nature of their morbid errand, and that they "hadn't been electioneering, hadn't been to a smoke talk, and were in their right senses. They say the balloon was in thorough control, and they are backed up by other reliable citizens."

Oddly, the *Independent* article attributes the "creepy feeling" experienced by townspeople in response to this incident to the following:

> Some lunatic is sailing a balloon around and about and over in the dark hours of the night, with a possible anchor dragging along, apt at any moment liable to catch in the neckband of our "nightie" and yank us away to the mysterious one's mysterious hiding place.

Local residents initially seemed to have settled on the idea that the two undertakers had witnessed a balloon that had originated from the nearby Brockton Fairgrounds. And at first glance, their assumption seems warranted. At any rate, it certainly seems safe to say, based on the fledgling status of airplanes as well as their inability to hover, that whatever they saw in the sky early that Halloween morning could not possibly have been a plane. Hot air balloons, on the other hand, were becoming popular at the time, and it seems quite possible that some intrepid balloonist, perhaps from the new aero club in Boston, was experimenting with night flying, willingly or unwillingly, in his newfound aircraft.

In his *The Book of the Damned: The Collected Works of Charles Fort*, Fort, widely recognized as the first serious investigator of unexplained events, mentions the Bridgewater incident, in the context of a discussion examining a UFO theory based on the proximity of the planet Venus. Fort was quick to raise one of the obvious problems with the "balloon theory," the fact that when the press checked around, all the balloons that had made ascents in Massachusetts that day were accounted for. And what's more, Fort points out, a search throughout Southeastern Massachusetts revealed no further trace of the craft. If it had been over Bridgewater at all, the strange balloon had seemingly disappeared into thin air.

The second, and perhaps more serious problem with the hot air balloon theory, however, is that many of the actual witnesses did not support it. Flynn, in particular, apparently took issue with this assessment. In a subsequent letter to the *Brockton Times*, published on November 10th, Flynn wrote the following:

> The report has become current about town that the balloon seen by Philip Prophett and myself on the morning of Oct. 31, while we were driving home from a house where we had been called on business was a hot-air balloon. This statement is untrue and I have absolute proof of it...I could see the outline of the large bag, and it could not have been a hot-air balloon, for it remained stationary and then moved up or down, seemingly at the will of some individual.
>
> I claim that a hot-air balloon could not move in a circle or perpendicular, as this one did...When first seen, it hovered above the Stanley Iron Works, seemingly about 100 feet from the ground, but when we returned (to Bridgewater at 3:10 a.m.) it was going in the direction of Plymouth. Prophett called his father and he got up to watch this lighted bird as it soared slowly away. All were in their right minds and several reputable citizens of the town have since told me that they also saw it and they also are sure that it was not a hot-air balloon, William Prophett included...Its identity remains a mystery to me, but I have seen many hot-air balloons and I am positive that this was not one of that type.

Flynn appears to be saying that he *saw something that looked like a balloon, but it wasn't a hot-air balloon*. For he saw, or at least thought he saw, a bag. But the movements of the craft that night, among other things, clearly convinced him that despite appearances *it could not possibly have been a hot-air balloon.*

So what was it, exactly, that those two undertakers saw in the Hockomock that Halloween morning in 1908? It was certainly a credible sighting, for at the time the Prophetts were one of Bridgewater's prominent families. Was it an experimental balloon of an advanced type unknown by the public at the time? If so, then how did it get there at night, without anyone seeing it pass over during the day somewhere en route?

The fact that no propulsion noises were heard by Flynn or Prophett, or any other New England observers, if in fact it was the same craft seen by all, also seems to make this theory problematic. Was it perhaps *something that wanted to look like a hot-air balloon*, but didn't have it quite right? And was it simply by chance that the craft was hovering directly over the ironworks?

We may never know the answers to these questions, but we do know one thing for sure. The Bridgewater UFO sighting of 1908 was the precursor to a multitude of documented UFO sightings in the Hockomock region—so many documented sightings, in fact, that many modern UFO researchers consider the Bridgewater Triangle, as they and other paranormal researchers know the area, to be the prime hotspot for UFO activity in all of New England.

GRASSY ISLAND
MAY 21, 1927 A.D.

Wet sand and muck was flying everywhere. Professor Edmund Burke Delabarre, sweating in the heat of the early July morning, paused to wipe his brow and lean on his shovel. This was Delabarre's seventy-third trip to Grassy Island, which lay in the Taunton River very close to Dighton Rock. The professor had started coming here several years earlier, in 1918, one year before his final paper on Dighton Rock was published, the one that launched his controversial "Portuguese Theory." The low-lying, tiny island, covered by only spartina grasses, was submerged by the waters of the Titicut at high tide, so Delabarre typically came at low water in order to get as much digging time in as possible.

With all the torn-up shoreline around him, Delabarre might easily have been mistaken for a hard-working clam digger. But the few passersby on the river obviously knew better, because they gazed curiously at him and pointed as they passed in their rowing dories or catboats. To them, he was the Mad Professor of Grassy Island.

The locals knew that the objects in his clamming basket were Indian artifacts, not shellfish. Grassy Island was covered in these types of things, and its tiny beach had always been a popular location for picking up arrowheads. But few people actually stopped there nowadays, at least while the Mad Professor was there, for a few years back, Delabarre had actually bought the island. He had made one of the earliest sites of human habitation in all of New England his very own. And the professor had, quite literally, torn the place, or at least a portions of it, to pieces.

As an archeologist, Delabarre had tried to keep it professional, at first, by staking out measured dig sites and all, but the rising water had kept washing his marker stakes away. Then he started finding artifacts everywhere, and realizing that the whole place was covered with them, he concluded that test pits were unnecessary. Delabarre eventually succumbed to the fever of the dig and just started excavating wildly. He was always racing against his enemy, the rising tide.

As he resumed his digging that sweltering July morning, Delabarre eyed his enemy, the shimmering tidewaters of the Titicut, as they advanced steadily up the beach of the tiny island towards his dig site. He checked his gold pocket watch dangling from the vest of his 1920s-style brown suit. There was only about an hour left before the river would force him away. He had better get moving. Heaving his wire quahog basket up the beach, the professor starting excavating an area of beach that lay under the leading edge of about four feet of peat, which had been created by centuries of decayed marsh grasses. Within just a few seconds, out from the sand layer beneath the peat slid yet another Indian artifact.

This time it was not the typical, easily-recognized point, but a much larger stone, shaped roughly like a square. Delabarre's eyes gleamed, and he quickly seized the stone, dashed down to the water, and washed it off. Squatting there, gazing intently at it through his round spectacles, the professor could see that one of the edges of the dark stone had been roughly chipped into a sharp edge. It looked like an axe head, or maybe an adze head. (An adze is a woodworking tool that is like an axe, but uses a blade that is fixed horizontal as opposed to vertically.) Delabarre proudly walked his prize over to his shellfish basket and placed it carefully inside, where it joined five points, both arrowheads and spearheads.

Delabarre was ecstatic. But his joyous mood was not in the least on account of that beautiful summer morning on the Taunton River in July of 1925. The coursing, shimmering currents of the Titicut, the startling pink sunrise that had earlier blessed the eastern sky over Assonet Neck, the majestic flight of the surprised Blue Heron, the fields of green, aromatic spartina grasses stirring in the morning breezes, all went completely unnoticed by him. For Delabarre was focused on just one thing—connecting with the past. He did not notice these things because before his eyes lay something entirely different; a scene that had played out perhaps 1,000 years before, in one of the earliest settlements of the People. With the aid of his muddy prizes, in his mind's eye Delabarre was peering deep into the past.

Delabarre didn't leave Grassy Island until the waters of the Titicut rose up behind him to the edge of the peat, which covered the entire surface of the island except for its edges, and filled up his sturdy, Brockton-made leather shoes with a warm brine. Then the professor hastily gathered up his tools and his basket, and sloshed over what remained of the beach to his wooden skiff, which he had purposely anchored to the higher edge of the peat. The boat was now swinging in the current. This wasn't the first time that Delabarre had been pushed off Grassy Island by the tide.

After awkwardly clambering into the skiff and shoving off, Delabarre, completely coated in mud, leisurely stowed his gear and washed up the best he could in the waters of the Taunton, letting the current sweep him down from the northwest side of the island, where he did most of his digging. When the skiff cleared the southern tip of the island, which looked like the point on a high, wide wedge of pie, he manned the oars and started pulling across the current. He was heading for the east bank and Assonet Neck. But in his mind, Delabarre was not in an early 20th century rowing dory at all. Instead, he was paddling a mishoon, one that had been crafted out of a great white pine felled at the edge of the Hockomock Swamp just to the north. He was moving with the ancient rhythms of the Titicut, just as the People had 12,000 years before him. And it was their tools, now in his possession, that had taken him back.

Grassy Island lays about fifty-six rods, as Delabarre described the distance in 1925, or 924 feet north of Dighton Rock's original resting place on the east bank of the Taunton River. The island lays just off Assonet Neck, the peninsula that was sacred to the Indians and that now divides the Taunton and Assonet Rivers and forms the southerly part of the Town of Berkley. Grassy Island resides in that broad, shallow part of the Taunton River historically known as Smith's Cove, just before the river narrows drastically upstream and enters the Hockomock Swamp.

Since 1640, when its ownership was first assigned to an English settler based on its value in hay, the island was always described as composed of roughly three acres. But by the time Delabarre did his archeological excavations there in the 1920s, he estimated that it was just over an acre. He described the island as roughly triangular in shape.

In one of his papers on the subject, published by the *American Anthropologist* in July of 1925, Delabarre describes the island as "entirely submerged at the highest tides, and its level surface is covered wholly with salt-marsh growths, underneath which there is peat overlying what was once doubtless an exposed surface before the peat-growths began, but which is now exposed only at low tides along the edges of the island where the peat has washed away." Professor Delabarre called this sandy, stony ground beneath the peat the "ancient surface."

Delabarre had become interested in Grassy Island upon hearing a report, dating back to 1910 or 1905, that described a "pocket" of Indian relics that had been discovered and subsequently removed from there. Like those locals who had explored the place long before him, Delabarre found many of his stone artifacts, perhaps half of them, simply scattered on the beaches that extended out from the edge of the peat at low tide.

The others he found by digging into the "ancient surface" in places where it was exposed under the edges of the existing peat due to erosion by storms, currents, and other natural forces. He found the excavated artifacts either on the surface of this previous, "ancient" surface, or down to a depth of about nine to ten inches below it.

The Professor's finds, based on his approximately seventy-five trips to the island between 1918 and 1925, were extensive. In addition to a "large number of chips, flakes, broken fragments, cores, and unworked pebbles of materials used in manufacture," Delabarre uncovered approximately 400 complete artifacts. About three-quarters of these artifacts he classified as "chipped objects:" spearheads, arrowheads, perforators, and knives.

Other kinds included stone axes, adzes, round "hammer stones," pestles or celts, mortars and grinding stones, gouges, sinkers, and hoes. Due to the sheer number of artifacts, and also the evidence of tool manufacture, which typically took place only when the Indians were in large groups, Delabarre quickly became convinced that he was excavating a village site.

The professor also knew that it could not be a place that had existed within the *known history* of the region because its surface lay under several feet of peat. It had to be *prehistorical*, perhaps even pre-Algonquin. And as he slowly accumulated his treasure-trove of artifacts, the professor's finds began to prove out his theory. They were different in several significant ways from the obviously more modern local artifacts that he was used to finding, such as the arrowheads that turned up regularly in the plowed fields on nearby Assonet Neck.

Most of the arrowheads and spear points that Delabarre found were small, or rather ordinary in size, with only one, an unusually perfect one made of rhyolite, that was large—almost four inches long. And like all the later Indian artifacts, these varied greatly in quality, from splendid works of art to crude hack jobs. But the Professor noticed two major differences between the Grassy Island points and the others found locally.

Most of the arrowheads turning up in the fields were white, made of quartz. The majority of the island points were made of darker stones, such as rhyolite, a green shale that weathers into gray, with far fewer of them made of quartz. And most of the later, pale quartz points were triangular in shape, while most of the darker, island points were stemmed. There were several clear differences between the two groups, all of which Delabarre took as corroboration for the prehistory theory.

The other, or "non-chipped" artifact types, such as the hammer stones, also displayed features that set them apart from modern, local artifacts. In general, they were very crudely made.

Most were just natural stones, totally unshaped. The only reason Delabarre knew these stones had been used by the Indians as tools was that a great many of them showed signs of use, either from striking or grinding. Only a few of the stone tools were grooved, such as a sinker and a blunt axe, only a few were notched for hafting on a handle, and there were very few among these that showed serious attempts to alter the shape of the stone. The people who lived on Grassy Island seemed to be content, for the most part, with using found stones for doing their work.

Delabarre also concluded that many of the types of stones used by the tool smiths on the island must have come from far away, strongly suggesting trade.

Other objects of interest Delabarre had uncovered on Grassy Island by the time he published his first, 1925 article on it in the *American Anthropologist* was a lump of pure graphite, a few very small red ochre particles, both of which were used by the Indians to make paint, a two-foot-by-four-foot pavement, or hearth of stones, and stains from sulphate of iron on a gouge. This last may have meant that the gouge had come in contact with a firestone of iron pyrites, possibly due to its placement in a grave.

Delabarre must have felt he had gained at least a partial understanding of who these ancient people were. They made fine projectile points and primitive tools, they most likely farmed and traded, they probably painted their bodies, and they used fire. And then he found the bones.

On May 21, 1927, Professor Delabarre unearthed a small, disk-shaped mass of bones, located about ten inches beneath the ancient surface of Grassy Island, near where he had found the hearth, the graphite and red ochre, the gouge, and the shallow mortar. All of these finds were within twenty-five feet of each other. The disk of bones measured one to two inches in thickness, and about one foot in diameter.

The bones were in tiny pieces, two inches long or less. Some of the bones were so small—"the merest speck"—that they could not even be collected by Delabarre.

There were hundreds of these bone fragments, all jumbled together, with the spaces between them filled with dirt. There was no evidence of ash or charcoal with the bones, and no evidence that they had ever been placed in a container. Delabarre dug up a seventy-five-square-foot area around the bones and found nothing else of significance, with the possible exception of his earlier finds such as the hearth, to shed light on their nature. The bones were isolated.

When Delabarre dug them up, he carefully recorded the dimensions of the disk, the bones' appearance, and their surroundings. But at the time, he didn't place that much significance on them, so he didn't collect every last one. That's because he didn't realize that they were human. When the Professor later had the bones analyzed and realized they were human, he went back and collected all that he could, which was a challenge because they had been reached by the tides and strewn about the beach.

Delabarre later said he was confident that he got all the bones that had been in the disk, but he also said it was possible some of the bones he collected may have been from an outside source. The professor apparently thought some new bones had shown up on the beach between the time he found the original deposit and the time he returned to collect the remainder.

Most of the bones showed "checking," or markings, which the experts who Delabarre had analyze them said were probably the result of long exposure to the weather or the "action of fire." They were so fragmented that it was hard for anyone to identify them. But there was no doubt that some, if not most, of the bones were human, and that some were animal. There were pieces from a human arm, leg, and foot, and definitely many from a human skull. The American Museum of Natural History tried to reconstruct the skull, but failed.

And it was certain that the human bones represented far less than a complete human skeleton. The most glaring absence of all was the complete lack of human teeth. Teeth are the hardest part of a skeleton, and they would not have been lost when other parts of the bones were kept. Even after burning.

The bone experts included Professor H. H. Wilder, Barnum Brown, and C. C. Willoughby. Willoughby had recently published his article "An Ancient Fish-

Weir," which documented his discovery of ancient fish traps in Boston's Back Bay while the Boylston Street Subway was being excavated. He and the other experts were divided on any further interpretations of the find.

It seems that the person to whom the bones belonged was not too old, but perhaps not that young, either. There were animal bones mixed in with the human bones, but no one seemed sure what kind of bones they were. Maybe a scapula and a vertebrae, possibly from a woodchuck or a rabbit. Just how the bones had ended up there at all was the biggest mystery of all.

Delabarre, in conjunction with his experts, entertained a few possibilities about "how he may have perished" and how the finely-fragmented deposit of bones came about. His first theory was that the bones were part of a kitchen midden—as in the unfortunate "he" was eaten. But Delabarre quickly dismissed this possibility, because a midden would have presumably held a greater number and a more varied collection of bones. It also would have been spread over a larger area, and included broken pottery and other artifacts.

His second option was that the person was a prisoner burnt at the stake. But Delabarre thought that this theory was hard to reconcile due to the number of missing bones, the inclusion of the animal bones, and the neat, disk-shaped pile, unless it was merged with the next option—cremation. Delabarre may have believed, at least as the most plausible explanation, that the bones were the result of a cremation, after which the bones were buried in some sort of perishable container. But he points out, as weaknesses of this theory, the mysterious presence of the animal bones and the fact that most of the skeleton is missing.

The last two theories that the Professor entertained were that the disk may have been the stomach contents of a carnivore, such as a wolf, or the contents of a shaman's medicine bag, both of which were known for being extremely eclectic. But in the end, the Mad Professor took a pass.

In his second, 1927 article in the *American Anthropologist*, titled "A Prehistoric Skeleton from Grassy Island," Delabarre draws only one, firm conclusion about the bones, which is this: "these bones are certainly those of an Indian who lived in Massachusetts not less than ten to fifteen hundred years ago." The professor was content to contribute his discovery as evidence for the ongoing scientific effort to provide confirmation for the theory of a pre-Algonquin culture in New England.

Between 1939 and 1942, a number of scientists in New England were struggling to determine the relationship between ancient human habitation in the area and the position of sea level. The problems they were working on had been first raised by the rediscovery of the Boylston Street Fish Weir in 1915.

Two of the scientists working on these problems, Frederick Johnson of the R. S. Peabody Foundation in Andover, Massachusetts, and Hugh M. Raup of

Harvard University, were aware of Delabarre's work, and they decided to include a study of Grassy Island as part of this general scientific effort. The last part of their overall study, which started with the Boylston Street Fish weir, was Stuart's Island in Marion, Massachusetts, the site of another ancient Indian encampment that had been located below the peat of the current marsh, and below the high tide mark.

By the time Johnson and Raup began their study, the owner of Grassy Island was a Mr. Stuart Robertson of Taunton. It seems that the owners after Delabarre used the island as a duck blind.

The archeologists obtained permission to dig on the island from Robertson, and then began collaborating with the aging Professor Delabarre, who enthusiastically supported their efforts, mostly by writing letters. Delabarre would pass away a few years later, in 1945. In their "Grassy Island" study, published in 1947, Johnson and Raup made a point of it to mention Delabarre's incredible, almost unbelievable, attention to the minutest detail. They describe his catalog of his collection and record of specimens as "extraordinarily complete."

By the early 1940s, a few things had changed on Grassy Island. Erosion had taken a toll on the island's size. And the new group of archeologists couldn't even dig on the north end of it, where Delabarre had located the majority of his artifacts, presumably because all his digging there had caused most of it to wash away. Instead, they dug four trenches on the southwest part of the island. And they had some better scientific instruments. But all in all, these new diggers did pretty much the same thing that Delabarre had done. They rowed out across the Taunton River to the tiny island each day and dug under the peat, and then watched with frustration as the relentless tide rose to flood their work.

Archeologically speaking, the Johnson and Raup dig added few major finds to Delabarre's. They found some projectile points, lots of stone chips, and a hearth, and not much more. They found no bones, no skeletons, and no graves. But they did corroborate most of Delabarre's conclusions, which was important because apparently, as they mention in their study, his overall work had been denied the scientific attention it rightly deserved. In fact, current scientific thinking at the time seems to have practically ignored Delabarre's publications on Grassy Island.

Based on his research there, Delabarre had made his conclusions regarding sea level rise at a time when scientists were still not sure whether the land around Boston had sunk or the sea had risen. This latter eventually turned out to be the case.

Using a then-current idea that sea level had risen at about one foot per century, he dated the occupation at Grassy Island at a time that "cannot be later, and may have been an indefinite time earlier, than about 1,000 years ago." This estimate would have placed the abandonment of the encampment due to sea level rise at the year 928 A.D., at the latest.

Johnson and Raup concluded that "beyond question, an ancient Indian camp of considerable proportions for this section of New England was once located on the surface beneath the peat." Their calculations indicated that the Indian village on Grassy Island may have been inhabited as early as 425 A.D., and was likely abandoned around 1200 A.D. The original settlement probably lay about 3.5-4 feet below the level of the existing peat surface.

It should be remembered that Johnson and Raup were really studying sea level rise and its relationship to human history. Finding artifacts was just one part of their study. The other parts included an account of the plant communities on the island, a study of the peat that overlay the ancient surface, and a geographical and mineral analysis of the island. In terms of Grassy Island history, these aspects of their study, together with a fine description of the Taunton River watershed and the local geology, is significantly more interesting and valuable than the archeological part.

Johnson and Raups' study did, however, serve to inspire later efforts conducted by the Massachusetts Archeological Society, including the excavation of the Titicut and Wapanucket sites. Frederick Johnson would later, in the summer of 1947, be invited to direct the dig at Titicut at the bend in the river in the far south of Bridgewater, the major human settlement dating from the Early Archaic. Titicut eventually yielded thousands of artifacts.

Grassy Island lays at the precise point in the Taunton River where the fresh water that has drained from the land meets the salt water that has been pushed up from the Atlantic by the tide. This brackish environment gave the island a unique variety of plant species. "Grassy" proved to be an apt name, for Johnson and Raup's team found no woody plants on the island, nor any historical evidence of there ever having been woody plants.

In the early 1940s, Grassy Island was covered entirely with marsh plants and algae that grew on top of the peat. At high tide, according to the scientists working there, it was "nearly or completely covered with water that is at least brackish."

Plant species included largely the Spartina grasses that are typical of saltwater environments. But there were also notable, missing saltwater plant species, and also a significant number of freshwater species that disappeared forever just downstream. The peat under which the ancient settlement had been found was apparently made from a mix of saltwater and freshwater grasses and herbs.

Johnson and Raup's team studied the peat of the island, as well as its pollen, in an attempt to decipher the natural history of the island after the ancient settlement was abandoned due to rising tides. In the end, however, they seem to have been frustrated by its complexity.

But the scientists did figure out some interesting things about the natural history of Grassy Island. For example, it may have originally been the leading edge of a marsh that extended out from the east bank of the Taunton River, where the Shove's Creek marsh now lays. This marsh was probably eroded away by currents, leaving as a remnant the part that forms the island. The scientists also discovered that Grassy Island appears to be slowly migrating towards the east bank of the Taunton. They estimated that the original island may have sat 850 feet to the west.

The Johnson and Raup study was ended prematurely in late 1942 due to the second World War. One of the scientists joined the Navy, and travel by the others was inhibited by gasoline restrictions. They did continue the study for a brief period, about three days, when they finally could return to the island in 1945. They published their results in 1947.

Professor Delabarre did not live to see the Johnson and Raup study published. This was unfortunate, for their study validated most of his work in regards to Grassy Island. Like his work on Dighton Rock, Delabarre's academic work for Grassy Island was destined to remain ignored or undervalued during his lifetime. Independent corroboration of both these bodies of work would come only after he had passed away. Edmund Burke Delabarre would never experience satisfaction from either public acceptance of his theories or professional validation of his work by his peers.

And what did Johnson and Raup have to say about the mystery of the fragmented human bones that Delabarre had discovered? Not much. They state merely that:

> The conditions under which the discovery was made and the character of the material recovered prevent any satisfactory explanation of the occurrence…Recent inspection of the bones…led to the inexpert opinion that a large majority of the bones were not human and that many had been burned.

Many had been burned.

600 A.D. The warm summer breezes licked the green spartina grasses on Grassy Island and rippled the brackish waters of the Titicut, waters that divided on the island's north side and rejoined on its southern tip on their long journey downriver to Narragansett Bay. The light hung golden and sublime over the small cluster of round bark wetus clustered on the northern end of the island. Blue plumes of smoke rose from the wetus. Dusky squaws in doeskin, carrying infants, could be seen moving in and out of the huts. They stopped occasionally to tend to the men who lay reclined on rush mats outside the dwellings.

Several warriors in leather breechcloths, carrying throwing sticks, moved along the beach on the west side of the island. They were carefully watching the west bank of the river, which lay just a short distance across the rushing current. The People in the village were watching the sun as it started to descend over that western bank, illuminating the river with ethereal colors of red, orange, purple, and green, just as they had watched it descend for nearly 12,000 years.

Grassy Island, known to the People then as the "Place where the Sweetwater Meets the Salt," was peaceful and incredibly beautiful that afternoon, a little piece of Paradise highly prized for its abundant fish and other natural resources. But the scene on the island the day before this one had been far different.

The Strangers had come from the south and the west, the directions they always came from. Never had they come from the east, a narrow area inhabited only by other members of the tribe and bound by the vast Atlantic Ocean. Some of the Strangers had come on the incoming tide, awkwardly manning primitive rafts that they must have hastily assembled downriver. Their other half had come from the western bank on similar craft, across the northward-flowing currents.

The People had little warning, for it had been many years since invaders had come to the area, and they had been caught by surprise. The women had been down on the eastern beach of the island, gossiping and cleaning the many striped bass, fluke, and bluefish they had collected from the large fish weir that extended out into the Titicut from the marshes on the eastern bank. The men had been lounging around the wetus in the warm summer sunlight, smiling and joking, smoking tobacco in their stone pipes, discussing a successful waterfowl hunt that morning, as they admired the sparkling, pure blue waters of the Titicut pour up from the bay.

They had felt secure on their isolated little island, composed of about five grass-covered acres near the western bank of the Titicut, protected to the east as they were by their own people, to the west by the fast, deep currents flowing through the main channel of the river, and to the north by the vast Hockomock Swamp, a place through which only they could venture without becoming lost.

This false sense of security had cost them dearly. For to the south and west, the world as they knew it no longer existed. Times had changed. The populations of those tribes had burgeoned with their adoption of farming, and some of them were now migrating, looking for new places to call home. And as the People were soon to learn, they carried new, advanced weaponry as well.

A young Indian boy playing on the western beach had sounded the alarm with a short, stifled yell just before he pitched backwards, dead on the sand. A strange, short dart had passed through both sides of his throat. The men ceased their talk and leaped to their feet in disarray, shouting and casting about hurriedly for their throwing sticks.

Their war chief, who had been dozing on a deerskin couch, finally roared, "There!" and pointed towards the channel to the west, where three of the crude rafts were being paddled toward the island by grim-faced men. The Strangers were painted, and heavily armed with stone axes, spears, and strange, curved sticks that they held in their left hands.

The People knew instantly that these strangely determined men meant business—and business of the bloodiest kind. They were coming, clearly, to take away the People's little piece of Paradise. After shouting a hurried warning to the women on the eastern beach, the warriors ran down to the western beach, following their war leader, and yelled fierce threats at the invaders. But the Strangers did not reply, did not return their taunts. They just kept up their grim-faced, determined paddling, and drew ever closer to the island.

Then the invaders stopped, and somehow managed to hold their rafts fairly stationary in the rising floodwaters of the Titicut. They held there, just out of the range of the Grassy Islanders' atlatls, or throwing sticks. The islanders shouted more taunts at them, trying to lure them closer, but the silent, painted strangers just reached back into strange skin bags they wore over their shoulders and withdrew short darts. Then they raised the strange, curved sticks, and Death began to fall on the islanders out of the blue sky. For a few moments, the People just froze in disbelief, watching their friends and neighbors dropping to the ground, writhing, dead or badly injured, with fletched arrow shafts marking chests, throats, and abdomens where they had been struck.

"Back! Back!" shouted the war chief at last, when he realized the superior range of the Strangers' weapons.

The islanders backed up to the high tide mark, and watched with satisfaction as the next round of small projectiles bounced harmlessly off the stony beach. But six of the island men already lay dead or dying at the water's edge.

The Strangers didn't shoot any more arrows. Instead, they conversed with each other between the three rafts, in a tongue that was unintelligible to the islanders.

"Stay back," warned the war chief. "Wait." He was eying the rafts with keen interest.

The speed of the current was picking up with the rising tide, and the war chief knew that soon the inexperienced watermen in front of him, as deadly as they might be with their strange and powerful weapons, would no longer be able to maintain their position in the river. He signaled his remaining warriors, about twenty of them, to follow him, and began trotting along the upper beach towards the northern tip of the island. The braves strung out in single file behind him.

When they reached the small, sandy point on the north side of the island, the men crouched in a semi-circle around their leader.

"When they are pulled into the point by the current," he said grimly, "kill them all."

The war chief had been right. The once-confident strangers were now gesturing frantically towards each other, fully aware of what was happening to them. The Titicut had spun them about, and was moving them northwards, straight towards the point where their enemies waited.

"Come," said the war chief, and gestured towards a large piece of driftwood, the bleached bones of a large cedar tree that had washed up on the beach.

Six of the men dragged it into a horizontal position across the beach, facing northwest, the direction from which they knew the strangers must come as they were swept in to the beach with the current. Then they knelt down behind the sturdy trunk, notched their long-shafted darts in their throwing sticks, and waited for the Great River to bring them their victims.

And bring them it did, just as the islanders knew it would. The current, now running at nearly five knots, swept the strangers, despite their frantic paddling, right up against the point.

"Stay down," said the war chief, and the men grinned with satisfaction as they heard the thunk, thunk, thunk of arrows peppering the soft driftwood.

"Hold," he then ordered, and again, the islanders heard the barrage hitting the other side of the log.

The chief, who had been quietly counting to himself, timing the approach of the rafts, turned to his warriors when the volley ended.

"Now!" he screamed, as he vaulted over the log and ran pell-mell towards the waterline. Then the islanders, who were capable of dropping a mallard duck from high in the sky with their darts, launched their primitive, but deadly, weapons straight into the faces of the painted invaders. And the Strangers died there, every last one of them, in just seconds.

The current streamed red around the floundering rafts, now drifting aimlessly in the shallows and covered by dead men splayed in all manner of unnatural positions. Some of the Strangers were floating, face down and bloated, in the river. But the islanders had no time to relish their sudden and devastating victory, for shrill, faint screams were now rising from the east side of the island.

"The women!" cried one of them, and they all hastily gathered up their spent darts and sprinted down the eastern side of the point. As the braves cleared the north point and gained an unobstructed view to the south, they were met with a shocking sight. Three more rafts were in the shallows, and painted men were advancing towards the beach. The islanders realized then that the Strangers had launched a two-pronged attack.

The islanders could see that three of the Strangers had already reached the stony beach, fringed by marsh. They appeared to be holding about twenty-five women, along with several children, hostage in a tight pack. When they spotted the islanders, the Strangers waved stone axes above their hostages' heads, clearly threatening to kill them if the braves advanced. But the islanders knew what was at stake. Faced with the destruction of all that they loved, they advanced like a furious pack of wolves towards the invaders.

A couple of the islanders fell to the beach as they came, badly hurt by arrows, but they could see that only a few of the Strangers were shooting their strange curved sticks. The rest of them were wallowing helplessly in the deep mud flats off the eastern shore, sunk in over their knees.

For like their counterparts, they had made a grievous tactical error. This second wave of Strangers had tried to land on the eastern shore of Grassy Island, facing the vast eastern marshes, at low water. And now they were stuck.

The screaming horde of islanders descended on the Strangers holding their women with a terrible vengeance. They didn't even bother to use their atlatls, just brained them with their crude stone axes, and then kept going towards the main body of invaders, who were now terrified, trapped as they were like wallowing pigs in the mud of the tidal flat.

Badly off balance and panicked, the Strangers struggled with their bow and arrows, and were only able to get off a few desperate shots before the islanders were upon them. The Strangers' dark eyes widened with fear as the islanders crashed their rough-hewn war axes and crude stone knives down on them, smashing out their brains, hacking them to pieces, one by one, out there on the mud flats. For these were rough, primitive men to the eyes of the more cultured invaders, who hailed from warmer places far to the southwest. They practiced the gentler arts of civilization that had come to them with the prosperity and leisure bestowed on them by agriculture. To them, the islanders, with their crude weapons, throwing sticks, cheeks tattooed with animals, and chest amulets carved in the forms of beasts appeared little more than cave dwellers.

The Strangers who had been holding the squaws, now dead, had made the grave mistake of killing two of the women. If there had been any chance of mercy for the attackers, it was now gone. The islanders showed none. By this time, several canoes from a neighboring village on the high, fertile fields of Assonet Neck had arrived, and two dozen more warriors had joined the islanders in the slaughter.

"Halt!" roared the war chief, covered in crimson blood, when just one of the invaders remained alive, a large, skilled warrior who had been valiantly holding off a half-dozen islanders in the shallows. "Take him alive," ordered the war chief. "We will make this one sing."

The Stranger, covered in mud and blood, and wielding a beautifully-wrought stone tomahawk, seemed to sense what was happening. Wanting no part of capture he leaped forward, splashing the muddy waters and swinging his axe fiercely at his adversaries, urging them to strike. He wanted to die like the warrior he was. But instead, the islanders surrounded him and took him down ignobly in the mud, like a beast. Then they dragged him up the beach by his ankles, watching with satisfaction as the sharp stones and shells tore off his breechcloth, ripped his body, and streaked his arms and back with blood.

The Stranger wouldn't speak. Nor had the islanders expected him to.

"He will sing at sunset," said the sachem of the village.

Hearing of the capture, the village shaman, who had been cowering in the spartina grass on the southwest end of the island during the battle, made an appearance before the chief and demanded to have a part in the ceremony.

"When I was praying for our warriors during the battle," he lied craftily to the chief, "Hobbamock informed me that he is angry with our disrespect. That is why he sent the strangers to attack us. If we give him this man's soul, he may just be appeased."

The chief, a proud and noble man, stared at the shaman with contempt.

But the sachem's contempt was tempered by fear. For his nephew lay badly injured in the wetu next door, an arrow plunged deep in his belly, and he was sure to need the shaman's healing services in order to survive.

"All right," said the chief evenly. "You can have him. But the warriors get him first."

The shaman smiled darkly, for he knew full well that what he wanted from the captive the warriors could not take. The shaman spoke not a word, but rose and set off towards his wetu, set far away from the others, towards the southern end of the island, to begin his rituals.

Two of the warriors took a mishoon to the western bank of the Titicut that afternoon to secure the trunk of a cedar tree, for the largest woody plants on the island were the high-tide bushes and the bayberries that lined the beaches. They buried the nine-foot post they made from the cedar deep into the sand of the point at the north end of the island, where the first wave of the Stranger's comrades had died. According to the shaman's request, the captive was not to die facing the southwest, where his ancestors dwelt, but towards the north, towards the Hockomock, the abode of the spirits of Death and disease, the stronghold of Hobbamock.

As the sun began to slip down towards the tree line on the west bank of the Titicut, the People gathered on the north point. They lit a campfire on the beach on a small, rectangular stone hearth that lay about twenty feet away from the cedar post. It would have been a beautiful evening on the river, if it had been any other evening but this one, with the murmur of the Titicut, the splashing of the feeding bass, and the low flights of the night herons overhead.

But the People were in mourning. They had lost eight warriors, two squaws, and the boy who had cried out on the beach. And several of their men lay injured, some of whom would surely be dead by morning. And all they had to vent their pain and despair on was this one captive.

And he, so far, had refused to grant them any satisfaction, for he had not spoken a word. But he would, that they all knew for sure. He was a strong man, but he would sing. They all did.

The wails of women mourning slowly came to an end as the sachem rose by the fire and requested silence.

"Since the beginning of time," he began, "our people have dwelt here, at the Place where the Sweetwater Meets the Salt. It is a unique and special place, a place of great beauty, a place of great plenty, a place of peace. But today, our peace has been broken, and we mourn the death of our own.

"It is not the first time we have been attacked by strangers from the West, and it will not be the last. My father's father's father told him of such attacks, in days long past. We have grown unwary, and we must regain our wariness.

"But for now, we will mourn our fallen, and take our retribution on this dog who has been given to us by Cautantowwit."

Then he motioned to a young warrior, who ran to a nearby wetu and ducked inside. He emerged with another brave, and together they dragged the bound prisoner across the beach. They lashed him to the cedar post, and the chief nodded to one of the squaws whose husband had been killed by the strangers that morning.

Her face strained with grief and pain, the squaw and a throng of women advanced on the Stranger with mussel shells in their hands. They cursed and spat on him, and sliced his body with the sharp shells. They told him that he would never see his family again, that his wife would sleep with his best friend, that he would die a painful death, and that his soul would never reach Cautantowwit. They eventually had to be pulled away from the captive by the warriors. The Stranger had not yet uttered a sound, despite the wretched injuries inflicted on him by the women. Now the real torture was to begin.

But first the chief stood up and addressed the captive.

"If you tell us who you are, from whence you have come, and why you attacked us," said the chief, "we will have mercy on your body and your soul. Otherwise, we will hack you to pieces and prevent your soul from ever reaching Cautantowwit. And in the end, you will tell us what I have requested. It is your choice."

But the captive just stared at the sachem defiantly, and refused to speak.

The chief nodded, acknowledging the man's bravery. "Begin," he said simply, and sat down.

Two of the warriors, both of whom had lost brothers in the battle of the morning, had volunteered to be the torturers. One of them advanced on the prisoner, whose torso and upper legs were bound to the cedar post, with a large stone knife as the crowd watched with anticipation. Seizing his right wrist, with a deft move he took off the Stranger's thumb. The other brave, in the meantime, had pulled a firebrand from the now-roaring fire on the stone hearth.

While the other man held the prisoner's wrist, he pressed the flaming branch to the captive's thumb, thereby cauterizing the wound and preventing the loss of blood.

The onlookers smiled grimly as the prisoner blanched, and they smelled his singed flesh. One by one, in succession, the unfortunate captive's fingers were taken off, and then they cut off what remained of his hands. At each step, the amputated body part was cauterized, so as to prevent the prisoner from bleeding to death and escaping his fate too easily.

The man was very brave. Everyone could see that. He did not cry out. He just stared in quiet resignation towards the coursing waters of the Titicut, perhaps *imagining how his soul would cross them soon, and head west towards the land of his ancestors.*

The prisoner thought of his fair young wife, in the large village to the southwest, who by now probably knew that he was dead or captured. And he thought of his three young boys, the oldest of whom he had just taught to shoot a bow, of how much he loved them, and of how he would never see them again, at least not in this world, and he promised himself, yet again, that for their sake and the sake of his own soul, he would die with dignity, like the warrior he was. These beastly savages, with their primitive ways, would glean no satisfaction from him.

Encouraged by the crowd, particularly the women, his torturers then took off his arms at the elbows, burning as they went, then cut down through his shoulders and jammed firebrands into the holes to stop the crimson flow of blood. Then they started up from his toes. The prisoner tried not to look at the shaman, who was hovering on the edge of the crowd, leering at him, dressed in his full barbaric regalia, crows' wings fluttering from his skin skull cap, red ochre covering one half of his face, black paint the other. He was the one, the prisoner knew, who he must face in the next round, when his spirit was finally released from what was left of his mangled body.

Instead, he fixed his proud gaze on the eyes of the chief. And the chief returned his gaze with sad respect. For deep down, he knew that he was killing a strong, proud man of character, a man in a position that he, someday, could easily be in himself.

The two brave men kept their eyes locked until the very end, until the knife-wielding brave severed the second of the captive's legs at the joint of his hip, until he looked down at his pitiful remains, just a torso, really, tied to a post on that dark beach. And then, and only then, did the Stranger finally break, just a bit, and then only out of shame at what he had become. Looking out once again over the smooth rolling waters of the Titicut, he let out a long, wavering cry: "Aaaaaaaooooooooooooooww....."

His haunting, plaintive death knell echoed out through the calm, quiet night, over the beautiful, dark waters of the Titicut, drifted away towards the south, and was gone. The Stranger's noble spirit departed from his body, his head fell to his chest, and he was dead.

The People stacked brush high around the Stranger's remains and lit it on fire, burning him and the post in an enormous blaze that cast its light out into the darkness of the Hockomock Swamp to the north. The village shaman finally emerged from the shadows, chanting and dancing, and tossed several mysterious objects onto the pyre, including a live woodchuck and a rabbit that he had pulled from a small cage of sticks. They twisted and squealed horribly before succumbing to the flames. The shaman fell on the sand in a trance and went on his magical flight. He tried to capture the man's soul, and in the company of Hobbamock he very nearly succeeded. But in the end, the Stranger found the path to Cautantowwit, and evaded all attempts to force him into the Underworld.

The next morning, the shaman returned to the still-smoking ashes alone, scattered them, and retrieved most of the prisoner's bones, which had been reduced to ashes, including the remains of his skull. The shaman wrenched the teeth from the jawbone, and placed them in his medicine bag.

Then he put the small pile of bones he had salvaged into a skin pouch, and took them to a ceremonial spot on the northwest side of the island.

In a secret ceremony, he offered them as a consolation to Hobbamock, who was furious that the prisoner's soul had escaped him. Then he dug a shallow hole in the ground, and buried the skin pouch where he was sure no one would find it. And for 1,327 years, no one did.

The tiny hunter, clothed in a red hunting jacket and toting a two-foot shotgun, came around the bend in the deer trail too fast to see the cat. He was so small he didn't even have to bend down as he chased the whitetail down its tunnel-like passage. He would have seen the cat, had his head not been down, his eyes not focused so intently on the cloven tracks of his prey. But as it were, he nearly slammed straight into the pitch-black feline, crouched menacingly as it was over the carcass of a freshly killed buck.

The massive feline condensed down into a rippling sheen of muscle and then, in a heartbeat, launched itself at the little hunter, a streak of darkness through the gray Autumn dawn. But the hunter was faster still. The claws of the surprised cat batted only air, and then its broad, smooth head met the hard trunk of a white cedar. Stunned, its long, thick tail twitching, the cat shakily regained its feet and peered groggily about through the red slits of its eyes. Instead of the little hunter, it saw only a blinding sphere of light, hanging a few feet over the path on the far side of the buck.

"Hail, Little Chief," the cat finally said in a guttural, deep voice, eyes squinting into the glare. "It has been quite some time since we have seen you in the Hockomock."

A high-pitched chuckle emanated from the sphere. "It has not been long enough, Man-spirit," a nasally voice said. "Your memory must be short indeed to forget my powers so quickly."

The sinewy cat lowered its fat belly down onto the trail and began to groom its chest and paws, which were covered with the blood of the deer. "It seems," it replied with a sly grin, "that we seek the same prey."

"Hunting is but a diversion for us," replied the sphere curtly. "We take no joy in Death. There was no need to bring it upon this majestic creature."

The mature buck that lay splayed between them had been eviscerated, and drained of its blood, but no part of its body had been consumed.

The licking feline eyed the body of the dead animal with perverse pleasure. "All things have their time to die," it purred, "even you, Old One, though you pretend to be immortal.

"Anyway," the cat sniffed, "I was not referring to this simple beast when I referred to our common prey."

"Then what was it you were referring to, Filth?"

The cat frowned and its red eyes became slits. "Man," it purred, "our common prey is Man."

"You are mistaken, Death Spirit. I hunt not the Race of Adam," replied the sphere at once. "Men are our brethren in this place, though they know it not. We seek only to guide them."

"Guide them! Then why is it you have guided so many of them to their deaths?!" rumbled the cat. *"Your Glamour and your tiny arrows ended the life of more than one Wampanoag in the days of old."*

The light of the sphere grew more intense. *"Like Men,"* said the nasally voice loudly, *"there are those among us who have given in to their dark side. We too were created imperfectly. But these are few among us, and we do not sanction their evil ways."*

At this the feline snorted in disgust, and sat up on its hindquarters. *"Evil. What is it that you know of evil?! Tell me this, Little One, if you wish only to help Man, why do you terrify him with your beastly apparitions, and your shimmering spheres in the night sky?"* He regarded the orb for a few moments in disdainful silence. Then, receiving no response, the cat continued. *"I will tell you why. You may not kill, but you will dispel Terror. You seek to frighten Man away from these wild places that you hold so dear. So you see, you and I are not as different as you think. Don't you see what is happening?*

"Cautantowwit has imprisoned you both here on Earth, but Man is destroying it, destroying the garden that your god created, pulling it right out from under you. If you were smart, you would kill him too, before you are left without a home. You have it in your power. I tell you, our common enemy is Man, whether you will admit it to me or not, Little Chief."

"No," said the voice from within the sphere slowly, with great resolve. *"No—we will never join you, never exterminate the Others. For we too seek redemption from Cautantowwit, and our Commandments clearly state that we must not harm our brothers."*

"Someday, the Creator will come again to judge the Living and the Dead. And that means you, Man-spirit. You will be held accountable for your evil deeds on Earth, and you will be sent back to the Underworld, to be torn by the teeth of Demons for Eternity. For in the end, it is the Demons—not you, or I—that are the true enemy of Man. And you, Hobbamock, though you pretend otherwise, are but their wretched, despised slave."

After this condemnation, the panther commenced a long, low growling that seemed as if it would continue forever. Finally, he spat and hissed, then spoke. *"Listen, Oh Fallen Child of the Light. You should know that we are planning a Great Campaign. We are moving against Mankind."*

"We?" demanded the nasally voice from the orb.

"All of us, across the Earth," replied the cat softly, with intense malice. *"We shall shower fear and death on Man and his Dumb Creatures."*

"Dumb Creatures?"

"His cattle, his horses, and his other hangers-on. There are many now among us, Indian Spirits, that hate these beasts more than Man, and they have waited long to rend their flesh," the cat explained.

"These Men are much different from the People, as you must know," replied the sphere. "Your apparitions of Mohawks and Englishmen will no longer work."

The cat grinned slyly. "Never fear, we have our ways," he chuckled. "Am I dressed as a Mohawk now?" His long, pink tongue shot out and caressed his glossy black fur. "We have terrorized and brought Death to them in the Old World since their creation."

"And Death?" queried the sphere sharply. "Will you bring sickness among the children of the Light?"

"We will," promised the cat. "We have already bred Death here," he said, slapping a dark, stagnant pool beside the path, from which a thick cloud of mosquitoes rose. "And we will turn them against themselves to harvest the lives of their own."

"That implies followers, Wretch. If you haven't noticed, it's been pretty quiet around here, ever since Cautantowwit deprived you of your followers. You have no more shamans to twist with your lies."

The cat smiled triumphantly. "You have been hiding in your underground kingdom for far too long, Little One. The New Children of Nunkatest are not all followers of the Light. The witches have followed them here from the Old World. And some of them have even sought and found the ancient ways of the shaman. Once again, we have followers, as we always knew we would if we but waited.

"In exchange for power, these Men will gladly do our bidding. And even better—they are ignorant. The Demons will find it easy to gain entry through them into this world. The Hell Spawn will find and possess those that are willing to accept them, claim their souls, and also use them to slaughter their own. But why do I waste my words on you? You and your race are weak, caring only for joy, festivity, and beauty. You will doubtlessly submit to your fate at the hands of Man, with but a whimper."

The shimmering sphere was now changing color rapidly, from blue, to green, to pink, and back again. After some time, the Little Chief spoke. "We can never join you, Hobbamock. For we, though fallen, are creatures of the Kingdom of Light, and you dwell in the Darkness, groveling at the feet of the Evil One. But you do make a point. The humans are on a path to their own destruction, and if they are allowed to continue, they will destroy us as well. For alas, we cannot survive without wild places like this one. We have understood all of this for quite some time now."

The black, sinewy cat cocked his ears, and his eyes narrowed as he sensed an opening. "Then what will you do?" he purred in a soft, soothing voice.

The flickering, shining orb did not answer him at once. "It is a difficult situation. For Mankind labors under illusions which cloud his judgment. It has been too long since the coming of the Son. Man has forgotten that his task here on Earth is to have Faith, to prove to the Father that he is worthy of Redemption, of returning to the Spirit World from whence he has fallen."

The black cat, long tail twitching, stared fixedly at the sphere. "You didn't answer my question, Glamorous One," he snarled softly. "What is it that you will DO?"

"*Perhaps,*" *responded the nasally voice thoughtfully,* "*we will conduct our own campaign, to frighten Man away from the last wild places, the places that we treasure. But we will also seek to guide him, to teach him the error of his foolish ways.*"

At this, the cat chuckled. "*Then you will have your work cut out for you. The solitary ones, those of your kind who take the shape of the Man-beast, dislike even the company of their own. You will be hard pressed to form the few who are left into an army. And an ugly, bumbling army it will be even if you did.*"

"*They will comply,*" *said the voice from the sphere.* "*It is they, the solitary ones, who fear the loss of the wild the most. And perhaps you will witness more than just they.*"

"*What will we see, Oh Master of Illusion?*" *sneered the cat.*

"*Sky ships,*" *replied the sphere.* "*They believe us to be visitors from the stars. We will play on their belief to teach them, to give them wisdom, to send them a message that they must stop destroying this Earth. And perhaps, just perhaps, on Judgment Day Cautantowwit will take this compassion into account, and forgive us for our actions.*"

The black feline rose softly to his feet and smiled an evil smile, for he knew an unlikely and fortuitous deal had been struck. "*And that effort,*" *he said,* "*is something that I am sure you will not fail to enjoy. For your kind has always found pleasure in the flesh of man. Just be sure, after you steal your pleasures, to return them to this place.*

"*For we want our share of their souls, and they are no good to us lost in your Underground Kingdom. So it is goodbye for now, Little Chief. I will bring this news to my Masters.*"

And then, just as the morning sun broke the horizon, the great black cat leaped powerfully off the trail, and bounding from hummock to hummock, quickly disappeared into the seemingly impenetrable rows of swamp maple. The shining sphere that was the Little Chief rose up, and up, through the feathery green needles of the white pines, and higher still, until it disappeared into the fading stars that hung like a painted dome over the vastness of the Hockomock.

PART II: NEW TESTAMENT

THE BRIDGEWATER BEAR
APRIL 8, 1970 A.D.

Barry Horton gunned his GTO, or "goat" as this make of car is affectionately known, as he turned onto Bedford Street from Bridgewater Center. Bedford Street turns into Route 28 south of the center, and passes straight through the ancient Indian village of Titicut, over the Taunton River, and onward to Cape Cod. Route 28 was the "Old Road" to the Cape, that up until 1956, when Route 24 was opened, filled up with thousands of beach-bound tourists every weekend. They cursed and sweated through the traffic snarled around the Bridgewater Common, which was laid out to the exact dimensions of Noah's Ark by the devout citizens of Bridgewater in 1822, first in horse-and-wagon, then in Model Ts, before finally escaping south down Bedford Street.

Barry's repainted orange hotrod, two wide black stripes on the hood on either side of the jutting super charger, leaped forward with a roar when he hit the gas. He passed the latest Prophett Funeral Home, looming white out of the darkness, that had been moved south of the center and into a modern facility. As he did so, he snapped off the King Crimson tape that was droning monotonously on the radio. He shook his long, blond hair violently, as if to clear his head. You can only listen to so much of that crap, *he thought.*

This dark stretch of Bedford Street that passed the mental institution always freaked Barry out, so he turned the knob through the stations looking for a comforting voice, any voice, to keep him company in the darkness until he made it home. He overshot a talk station, hit some serious static, then rolled the big silver dial back until the newscaster's voice came in clearly.

Only half listening, he heard the following words:

In West Bridgewater, the need for a dog control regulation was emphasized when an Angus cow, which had just had her first heifer calf the day before, was apparently killed by a pack of dogs.

Horton shifted uneasily in his seat, which was still slick from the leather spray he had applied to it that afternoon. The newscaster's voice continued:

The Angus belonged to Everett Estabrook of Windy Ridge Farm, West Center Street, and was one of several being pastured at the Allen Foye property on East Center Street.

Mr. Foye had looked out his window to the far pasture, near the river and a wooded section, to see a dog circling around the small calf. He donned boots and made the long hike over rough terrain; also noting a number of dogs in the woods. After driving off the animals from the day-old calf, he began a search for the "mother" and found her dead in a badly trampled area where she had apparently not given up her fight for life easily.

"Damn...." Horton muttered in dismay, and switched off the radio in disgust. Now he was really freaked out. He just wanted to be home. And it was precisely then, as he zoomed past the access road that led to Bridgewater State Hospital, that he saw it, looming up in the headlights of the Goat, huge and hairy, lumbering across the road in front of him.

"SHIIIIIIIIITTT!!!!" screamed Horton as he locked up the brakes, skidded, and screeched to a halt. He sat their trembling, wigged out, and afraid, breathing burnt rubber, staring at whatever that thing was that was moving through the glare of the GTO's headlights. Then it turned and looked right at him. "What the—?!" cursed Horton, whispering now.

It was very big. The creature appeared to be more than seven feet tall, far bigger and more powerfully built than any man, and it was entirely covered in brown hair. Horton watched in horror as the creature strode, on two legs, across the highway, and then dropped quickly out of sight into the woods that stretched between Bedford and South Streets. Still shaking badly, Horton managed to get the car into gear, and drove off slowly through the darkness. He made it home in a daze a short time later. Then he called the Bridgewater Police and told them everything.

Bridgewater, April, 1970.

The holy settlement had transformed itself yet again. Once primarily agricultural, then industrial, the town had become Suburbia, like so much of America had after World War II. Town residents, other than those who worked at the State College, the state hospital, or downtown, got into their cars each weekday and took to newly built highways such as Route 24 that led to office jobs somewhere else. Bridgewater had become a bedroom community. But this label is somewhat deceptive, for Bridgewater, at the time, was anything but sleepy and peaceful. In reality, the town was reeling from a combined assault by war, drugs, and wild dogs.

Earlier in the year, the federal government had announced that more than 40,000 American soldiers had been killed to date in Viet Nam. The North Vietnamese and the Viet Cong were using guerilla tactics, in the darkness, in the fog, and seemingly everywhere else, with great success.

The U.S. Air Cavalry Division, stationed sixty-seven miles northwest of Saigon and just three miles from the Cambodian border, had been hit a few weeks earlier. The guerillas had killed four American GIs and wounded seventeen before they were driven off with tanks and armored personnel carriers. The Viet Cong left twenty-nine bodies behind. The Cambodian government was demanding that the nearly 40,000 Viet Cong guerillas who were in their country leave there at once.

Two-hundred and fifty miles to the northeast of Saigon, enemy saboteurs had just blown a massive, five-by-eighteen-foot hole in the American merchant ship *Amercloud.*

American protesters demanding an end to the war were holding regular demonstrations in Washington and elsewhere, creating an internal conflict that would come to a head one month later, in May, when Ohio National Guardsman would tragically shoot and kill four student protesters at Kent State University.

In the Fall of 1969, the United States Government had officially given up on UFOs by ending the Air Force's twenty-one-year-old Project Blue Book. Millions of dollars had been spent, including $539,000 for the study that ultimately recommended ending it. The study was led by Dr. Edward Condon, a University of Colorado physicist. The project had accumulated substantial files that documented reports of unidentified flying objects. When they announced the end of the study, the Air Force explained that "neither national security nor science was being served" by it. Condon said that although "there were plenty of kooks" who claimed otherwise, "nobody has produced a shred of solid, credible evidence to support the idea that these UFOs represent visitors from outer space."

One of the consequences of the program being shut down was that people no longer had an official, centralized place to report UFO sightings. The Air Force recommended that people "pass the information on to a scientist, check signals with the local air base, or call the Police Department." But essentially, they were saying that the public was now on its own when it came to dealing with those curious bright lights in the sky. This fact would soon become all too clear to those who would witness UFOs in the Hockomock region.

In April 1970, people everywhere were fighting for their rights. In Washington, the movement to lower the national voting age to 18 from 21 was in trouble, despite the fact that the Senate supported it. That was partly because the Chairman of the House Judiciary Committee, 81-year-old Representative Emanuel Celler, was fighting it tooth and nail. Celler, who had been in Congress forty-seven years, thought that young people saw things in black-and-white, and that they were too immature to vote.

In December of the previous year, 1969, 175 black students at Harvard finally left a hall into which they had barricaded themselves. The University had finally conceded to some of their demands.

The American Indian was a regular feature in the news. As a group, the Indians had never been in a worse socioeconomic condition. They were ranked the poorest group in the country, having fallen into abject poverty after years of seeing their reservations successively whittled down by conflicting interests.

The average lifespan of an Indian was age 44, at a time when other Americans could expect to reach 66. And they had decided to fight back by launching a movement to reclaim their ancient tribal lands.

To the average American citizen in 1970, it must have appeared that the Indians had gone crazy. For example, in March, there was an assault on historic Ellis Island in New York by fourteen tribes. It ended in failure when the boat the Indians were in developed engine trouble as they tried to launch it under the cover of darkness from the New Jersey shoreline. One of their spokespeople at the time announced that these Indians, members of a group called "Indians of all Tribes," were trying to claim the island, an abandoned Federal facility that had served as the gateway to America for millions of immigrants, in order to turn it into an Indian commune.

Other groups affiliated with the Indians of all Tribes had seized Alcatraz Island in San Francisco the previous year and were living on it. The Indians were also trying to take over Fort Lawton, which lays near Seattle on Puget Sound. "It's all part of the same movement" explained Mrs. Robinson, the Indians' spokesperson. She stated that the Indians wanted Ellis Island "turned over to the Indians of all Tribes." Jane Fonda was also working publicly with the Indians to promote their cause.

In 1970, Bridgewater citizens, like many other people across the country, were deeply concerned about the menace of drugs and cults. The two seemed to go hand-in-hand. Gallup polls showed that most American adults believed that organized religion had lost its meaning, and that the proportion of Americans attending church had dropped steadily since 1958. It was the Age of Aquarius.

Prior to 1970, most people probably thought that beliefs in Witchcraft had culminated with the Salem witch trials, and had passed away forever with Increase and Cotton Mather. But now they weren't so sure.

Benjamin Franklin's Age of Reason, which had taken hold of the country after the Mather era, now seemed to be at risk. Interest in cults was intense. The movement would make great strides in the coming decade, in fact becoming so powerful that at times, cults appeared to be a threat to national security. Evil would have its day.

Nationally, the cult situation was exemplified by the Manson trials, which were in full swing by April of 1970. In December 1969, in a desperate attempt to escape the death penalty, 21-year-old Susan Atkins had testified against her weird, nomadic cult brethren in front of a Grand Jury in Los Angeles. Charles Manson's "family" was accused of eight random and brutal killings, including that of the beautiful, blonde actress Sharon Tate.

After her testimony in LA, Atkins was asked how she felt about ratting out Manson. "Dead," she replied without hesitation.

Atkins's attorney later told the press that he feared her testimony would make her the target of Manson's "black magic and mystical spells" that the cult leader typically employed to control the members of his "family."

Other members of Manson's family also testified that the cult was held together by a kind of "black magic" that Manson used to control them. Atkins told her attorney that the cult members committed the murders while under this type of control. The slim, pretty brunette said that, under this influence, she and three other girls, along with a man that was not Manson, snuck into Tate's home and brutally murdered the actress, along with three of her guests and an 18-year-old boy. Atkins said Manson had ordered the killings. At the time, Sharon Tate was living in the rented Benedict Canyon estate with her husband, Director Roman Polanski. Thirty-five-year-old Manson and his followers were living on an abandoned movie lot. And they were doing a lot of drugs.

At Bridgewater State Hospital, two months earlier, in February of 1970, a Drug Symposium had been held to allay the fears of the citizens of the town and the vicinity about the growing levels of drug abuse, including heroin. The head of Massachusett's drug addiction program, Lawrence Gaughan, told a packed auditorium of locals that:

> The drug problem is everywhere and it is going to get worse in the next two to four years. There is little motivation for people to come off drugs. They don't want to return to the world of pain, tension, and trouble. They would rather "cop out."

A Brockton cop also spoke to the crowd about the social costs associated with addiction. He told them that the crime rate was rising, particularly violent crimes, break-ins, larcenies, and armed robberies. He added that the drug addicts were committing these crimes in order to fund their habits, and that often an addict would commit many such crimes before they were finally caught.

And as if war, protestors, flying saucers, cults, and drugs weren't enough for the citizens of Bridgewater to deal with in the spring of 1970, they had another pressing problem as well. Dogs. Crazed packs of wild and marauding domestic dogs were holding the town hostage. The main problem was that there were no leash laws in Bridgewater or the surrounding towns.

The neighboring City of Brockton, once North Bridgewater, was regularly the scene of chaotic dog chases that often ended in snarled traffic and property damage. Pictures in the Brockton newspapers from the period show frightening action shots of leaping dogs chasing children off playgrounds, with dog officers in hot pursuit. These dogs were generally domestic males chasing a bitch in heat. The understaffed and under-equipped dog officers would typically try to snare the fleeing bitch with a sort of lasso tied to a stick. The Brockton dog packs roamed the city at will, knocking down children waiting for the bus to steal their lunches.

In rural Bridgewater and neighboring Middleboro, across the Taunton River, the dogs went semi-wild, or even wild. They formed vicious hunting packs that preyed successfully on Massasoit's ancient deer herd in the Hockomock and the vicinity. Unafraid of man, and having experienced their first taste of blood, these vicious predators posed a real threat to residents.

One of the most frightening things I have ever experienced was an attack by a wild dog that had gone rabid. It was the late 1970s, and the wretched creature had burst out from some brush, surprising me and a friend, just kids, as we walked along a quiet country road in the summer heat. We heard it coming, and we knew that nothing moved that carelessly in the woods, at least nothing that was right, so we had a few seconds to mentally prepare.

But we weren't prepared *enough* for that thing. The monster that eventually emerged from the bushes and came straight for us was snarling and yelping horribly, and drooling heavy white foam. The hair around its neck was standing straight out, causing it to look more like a lion than a dog, and every bit as big. The dog's body was badly disfigured, with mangy clumps of hair and giant, swelling ticks hanging off it.

I will never forget how that creature walked. It heaved itself desperately towards us, in all its uncontrollable, pitiful madness, on the front side of its collapsed forelegs. My friend and I took one good look, and ran as we had never run before, with fear driven deep inside us. Later, we heard from our parents that some cops had come down and shot it.

The Bridgewater Police took Barry Horton's call describing the hairy monster in their newly-renovated digs in the Old Bridgewater Academy building. One of the many fine buildings that surround the Bridgewater Common, Bridgewater Academy was opened in 1799, during that golden age now known as the town's "Age of Enlightenment."

The police brought out the dogs: bloodhounds from the nearby Middleboro State Police Barracks. They were the same dogs that they had used to chase Albert DeSalvo, the professed Boston Strangler, when he escaped from the Bridgewater Hospital three years earlier and fled into the neighboring swamp.

The inmates who escaped from the facility never got far. The dogs would run them down, and they would be found, shivering and crying, torn by Bull briars, maybe in the torchlight of a low-hovering police helicopter. And that was just the start of their misery. They knew damn well that when they got back to the Hospital, they would be thrashed soundly, made an example of by the guards, who at that time of major prison reforms had a saying: "Bridgewater is the only prison left that isn't run by the inmates."

The cops who plunged into the swamp on the night of April 8, 1970, to chase Horton's hairy monster were no strangers to mystery animals, either. Just two weeks earlier, a seven-foot Boa constrictor had been found dead in the road off Pleasant Street. And just a few months earlier, in late 1969, the police had responded to a report made by Bridgewater State College students of a "monster" similar to Horton's. That giant, hairy creature had been sighted near the Great Hill Dormitory of the College, which lay less than three miles to the north of where Horton had reported his giant hairy creature.

Bridgewater State College, founded in 1840 as the "Bridgewater Normal School," a teacher's preparation school for the State of Massachusetts, was so close to Bridgewater Hospital, in fact, that the students there were careful never to say to someone that they went to "Bridgewater," because they knew if they did, they might be razzed about being an "inmate." The Bridgewater cops had launched a chase for the monster spotted by the students, too, and had been able to pick up some sort of tracks. But ultimately, they had been unable to catch what would later become known locally as the "Great Hill Monster."

Sergeant William Nicolas of the Bridgewater Police commanded the chase for whatever it was that Horton had seen. Police Chief James Elliott and representatives from the Massachusetts Society for the Prevention of Cruelty to Animals were also on hand. The cops first called all the residents in the South Street area, and warned them that "a bear" was on the loose.

Sergeant Nicolas then told his son, Patrolman William Nicolas, to get down there into the woods and track the thing. So Bill went in, and managed to pick up tracks of some kind. But he and his fellow officers had no luck running the bear, or whatever it was, down.

Meanwhile, calls from frightened residents of the South Street area were pouring in to the Bridgewater Police Station. Plenty of other people seemed to be seeing the bear, too. Most of the callers reported something quite large, dark colored or black, running through their yards.

One of the Bridgewater Patrolmen that responded to these calls, nicknamed "Frenchie," was sitting quietly in the darkness in his patrol car, not really sure what to expect, when suddenly the rear end of his cruiser was lifted entirely off the ground and dropped. Badly shaken, he twisted around and trained his searchlight between the nearby homes, and thought he saw something dark running away.

In the end, "the bear" had much better luck than escapees from Bridgewater Hospital typically did, for it got clean away. The cops finally knocked off the chase around midnight. The next morning, they told everybody that they had not received any more reports of the bear, and that yes, there would be school that day in Bridgewater. Everybody was asking.

There are no brown bears, or grizzly bears, in Bridgewater, Massachusetts. The grizzly is a species that inhabits Alaska, Canada, and the American Northwest. As for Black bears, in 1970, the year the chase took place, according to Massachusetts Wildlife's Black bear study, there were only 100 of the animals in Massachusetts, and those were presumably all in the western parts of the state. The species has now rebounded. There are approximately 3,000 black bears in Massachusetts today, and they have been seen recently wandering as far south as Cape Cod.

Bears, both the brown and the black varieties, can walk on two legs as the creature that Barry Horton described crossing the road that dark night was doing. But it is doubtful if either species would choose this gait to cross a major roadway such as Route 28 in Bridgewater.

Black bears typically only stand on two legs to get a better look at, or smell of, something. And people who have seen black bears crossing roads typically see them running, on all fours, not walking on two legs. And even if it was a black bear on two legs that Horton saw, the chances are pretty slim it would have stood seven feet tall. So, from a conventional perspective, Horton's description of what he saw does not make much sense. So then, what *did* he see?

Bill Nicolas, the son, firmly believes that what he tracked that night back in 1970, in the swamp near Bridgewater State Hospital, was a bear. Nothing more. And he's well aware what some people think it was. Bigfoot. Why does he think it was a bear? Mostly because of the tracks. The tracks, says Bill, were just not that big. "They were bigger than anything domesticated," he admits. But nowhere near, say, the 13"-18" prints typically associated with Bigfoot. "They were more like five, six inches long," he remembers, with some difficulty. It was a long time ago.

And what about that disturbing incident involving his fellow patrolman's car lifted off the ground? "Well," says Bill, between hearty laughs, "between you, me, and a lamp post, that was us."

"Who—the cops?"

"Yep—we did it. That was a prank. And it almost gave Frenchie a heart attack, too."

And as for the "Great Hill Monster" they had tracked a few months earlier, well, it had never been proven that the kids at the College had seen anything. And let's face it, it was 1969, and everyone knew what college kids were doing then. Drugs.

Bill Nicolas isn't the kind of person that doesn't believe in anything beyond what is accepted by science at the time. He told me, for example, that his uncle, who is a reputable person, saw a UFO in Bridgewater at the junction of Route 28 and Route 18, which, interestingly enough, lays just a few miles to the north of Horton's "bear" sighting. So he thinks there may be a real mystery associated with that phenomena.

But a Bigfoot in Bridgewater? Nah…despite all the crazy stories he heard over the years when he served on the Bridgewater Police force, Bill doesn't think so.

So, assuming there were no bears in Bridgewater in 1970, exactly how did it come to pass that he was tracking one, that dark night in the woods near Bridgewater State Hospital, back in those dark days of war, drugs, wild dogs, and insane escapees?

"We think what happened was that somebody raised it (the bear) as a pet, then released it."

"Kind of like what happened with the Boa constrictor?" I asked.

"Yeah, kind of what like happened with the snake," replied Bill.

WONDER WETLAND
MAY 1, 1971 A.D.

Hockomock: Wonder Wetland. This is the title of a booklet that Massachusetts State Senator John Ames III made sure hit every legislator's desk in 1971, in support of a bill to preserve the Hockomock Swamp as conservation land. The original booklet, somewhat rare today, was an attractive little thing, with nice photos and interesting sketches of wetlands, turtles, and bog flowers.

It was also a thoughtful and factual piece of work, written by highly capable people, such as Kathleen Anderson, then Director of the Manomet Bird Observatory, formerly an ornithologist for the Encephalitis Field Station in the Hockomock, and later, as an octogenarian, a leader in Massachusetts environmental affairs. Ted Williams, then Managing Editor of the Massachusetts Division of Fisheries and Game's *Massachusetts Wildlife* magazine, whose later accomplishments include several books, wrote the fine history piece.

Wonder Wetland fulfilled its purpose admirably by helping to ensure the passage of the preservation act championed by Ames, and it is still routinely referenced today when people discuss the Hockomock. The booklet talked a lot about water.

H_2O. Two atoms of hydrogen joined to one atom of oxygen. A simple molecule that, in one sense, is what it's all about. Our planet, our civilizations, our cities and towns, and our bodies are all dependent on water for their very existence. And water is certainly what the Hockomock is all about. *Wonder Wetland* did a very good job of communicating to skeptical state legislators and the public the practical importance of the water in the Hockomock to the region. This was an especially difficult task in the early 1970s, a time when water was not generally a concern on people's minds.

That mindset has changed quite a bit since *Wonder Wetland* was published. With a greatly increased world population and the added recognition of global warming, most of us have become far more aware of the importance of water to our lives. And with that new-found awareness has come widespread concern. The facts are readily available, and quite sobering.

The Earth is covered in water, but most of it, more than ninety-seven percent, is salty. Almost two percent of the rest is unavailable to us, locked up in snow and ice. That leaves less than one percent that is available for our use. Much of this available water is in aquifers, or underground sources of water. We are currently depleting the world's aquifers more quickly than they are recharging from rain and other natural sources. And with the earth's population growing at the rate of some 83 million people each year, demand for water will continue to outstrip supply, barring major behavioral changes on our part.

This gloomy forecast doesn't even take into account the effect of global warming. The Tibetan Plateau is a place of glaciers on the top of the world that supplies much of the water for the great rivers of Asia. These glaciers are steadily melting. It's only a matter of time, and perhaps not that much time, before countries such as China and India face extreme water shortages. Scientists at China's Institute of Tibetan Plateau Research are *currently predicting ecological catastrophe* based on current rates of glacier shrinkage. Scientists currently estimate that by 2025, *1.8 billion* people will live in places where water is extremely scarce.

These dire circumstances we have encountered in recent times only increase the importance of water storage areas like the Hockomock Swamp. *Wonder Wetland* describes the Hockomock in the following manner:

> A self-perpetuating 7½ billion-gallon water storage and flood control project that didn't cost a dime to build or operate—and never will if it is preserved.

Most of the water held in the Hockomock is from rain: 7½ billion gallons is the estimated amount of rain that falls annually on the swamp. Paul T. Anderson, another contributor to the booklet, derived this number from a simple equation that involves the land area of the swamp, which is roughly ten square miles, and the average amount of rain that falls on Southeastern Massachusetts each year, which is forty-four inches. Neither the average rainfall in the area nor the land area of the swamp has changed significantly since 1971.

The 7½ billion-gallon estimate is also based on the fact that in Massachusetts, in general, about one-half of the rainfall percolates into the ground, and the rest runs off. However, in the Hockomock, which is a flat wetland, the amount of rain that runs off is far less. Thus, a vast quantity of rainwater is trapped in the swamp, which acts like a huge sponge. The water builds up until the swamp is saturated, at which point, it is slowly and naturally released down the Hockomock River that flows into the Town River, that flows into the Matfield, then into the Taunton, or Great River, which eventually empties the water into the sea at Narragansett Bay in Rhode Island.

The swamp's absorption of heavy rainfall also ensures that sudden flooding is avoided or minimized in all the towns located in the flood plains of the region's rivers, such as the Bridgewaters, Taunton, and Middleboro. And without the Hockomock Swamp holding all that water, even places as far away as Dighton, Freetown, and Fall River would face significant damage to residences and commercial properties from flood waters racing down overburdened river channels.

In March, 2010, all of these largely hypothetical claims were vindicated when southeastern Massachusetts was deluged with record amounts of rain. Over eighteen inches of rain fell on the area in three subsequent storms, more than had ever been recorded since record keeping began in 1885. It may have been more rain than has fallen annually in several hundred years. Route 44, a major highway on the Raynham/Taunton line, was closed due to flooding. Homes were flooded, businesses were destroyed, and schools were evacuated throughout the region.

On March 30, 2010, after the final, devastating storm that dropped 5.64 inches of rain on rivers that were already on the verge of flooding, some of the 850 National Guardsmen fighting the flood were called in to Freetown, where a major road and a bridge were swept away by racing floodwaters.

They also responded to a crisis in Middleboro, evacuating residents as water crested and breached the dam at Pratt's Farm. State emergency officials piled up sandbags in East Bridgewater at Harvard Street and Pleasant Street, and throughout the region in areas of road closures.

Rivers in the state were racing four-to-five feet over flood levels. The mayor of Brockton declared a state of emergency as homes and streets flooded and homes were evacuated. In the Bridgewaters, receding flood waters left feces from flooded sewer systems, gasoline, pesticides, and assorted other dangerous contaminants that threatened human health. Many of these contaminants had washed off new roadways.

President Barack Obama toured the area personally and subsequently declared it a disaster, making residents and businesses, many of whom were already financial disasters from the Great Recession of 2007-10, eligible for Federal assistance. The towns in the area began thinking about regional ways that they could comply with newly-proposed Federal EPA requirements designed to make towns and cities improve storm water control measures.

And unseen, behind all of the suffering and mayhem of this "Monsoon March," abided the Hockomock, like a massive sponge, safely and efficiently holding in check billions and billions of additional gallons of floodwaters, just as it has done for thousands of years.

In Easton, the Department of Public Works Director Wayne Southworth, Sr. was busy leading the fight against the flood. Ironically, Wayne is a direct descendent of Constant Southworth, the man who along with Samuel Nash testified to the Plymouth court in 1662 that their committee had indeed bought the Hockomock from Ossamequin as part of the original Bridgewater plantation purchase. "It would have been a complete disaster without the Hockomock," says Wayne, when I asked him about the flooding in Easton.

Still, that March Wayne saw floodwaters moving in ways that he had never seen before.

And that's significant, because before he became head of the DPW, Wayne was head of the Easton Water Department for many years. Wayne says there was more, and different kinds of flooding in town that Monsoon March because of all the recent development in town, especially the blacktop.

Wayne knows the Hockomock intimately. He lived on Howard Street in Easton for many years, on the edge of the swamp. He remembers his friend, an amateur archeologist, showing him ancient hearths, or campfires, that he had unearthed on a high sand esker left by the glacier back in the swamp. It was picturesque up there, remembers Wayne fondly, so much so that it wasn't very hard for him to picture Indian families looking out over the swamp from their campfires thousands of years ago.

He also recalls vividly three twenty-foot black racer snakes coming through the field towards him out back of the house. They were so long that their heads were raised three feet above the ground as they coursed through the grass. Wayne also fondly remembers the joy of picking wild cranberries in the nearby bogs with his children.

It was the same all throughout the Hockomock region that Monsoon March. Without the vast Hockomock wetland, the destruction would have been unimaginable, perhaps even closer to the scale of Hurricane Katrina, when flood waters destroyed most of New Orleans. Some towns, such as Freetown, which had been waiting with bated breath for the 300-year-old Old Forge Pond Dam to give way, an event that would have caused the evacuation of the town center, would have been literally washed off the map without the swamp. The Hockomock was that valuable to the beleaguered region as a flood control system.

During more typical years, the consistent water storage provided by the Hockomock Swamp maintains the region's water table at a high level, which ensures the consistent availability of clean water to communities for drinking, bathing, and cooking.

This storage also ensures the year-round flow of the region's rivers, by recharging them even in the summer and times of drought. It is also worthwhile to note that the historical economy of Southeastern Massachusetts, as witnessed by the traditional mill industries of Bridgewater and the surrounding Hockomock towns, was largely based on water power—energy created by damning its rivers and streams.

By keeping these rivers flowing, the Hockomock Swamp lays at the very heart of the traditional economy of the region. These streams were also historically vital to local agriculture as well as fisheries, mostly alewives, that were a major source of food for the region's people.

In today's global economy, the small rivers and streams of southeastern Massachusetts are not as important to the region as they once were. But perhaps soon, in a post-oil world, they may prove vital to the area again.

Today, much of the farmland along Route 106 in West Bridgewater near the Hockomock River has been converted to business uses. But descendents of many of the old farming families still live there. The families living on the West Bridgewater/Easton line, an area that was part of the Hockomock land grant by Plymouth in 1662, have seemingly been there forever. In true New England fashion, the residents in the neighborhood don't know each other particularly well. But they do know a fair amount about local history, including the history of their own, and their neighbors' families.

Wayne Legge lives in a fine white farmhouse on the north side of Route 106. Wayne and his wife, Marilyn, bought the house in 1959. At that time, there were five working farms in the area. Today, there are none. Stuffed full of old clocks and other homey New England antiques, the house dates back to 1918. Their land is bordered on the east by the Hockomock River. The land behind the house was originally owned by a truck farmer, who sold his vegetables at a stand across the road on the very edge of the swamp.

Wayne's front door opens onto to a wide farmer's porch and a view to the south over Route 106 straight into the Hockomock Swamp, land now owned by the Massachusetts Department of Fish and Game.

When Wayne bought the property, there was a permanent farm stand out by the road that the previous owner had used to sell home-grown squash, pumpkins, strawberries, carrots, and other produce. Wayne, who is not a farmer, moved the farm stand out back and converted it into a shed. When he bought the home, the property was still farmland, treeless except for the six Norway maples that still border the house on the east and west sides. So Wayne planted it with fifty trees, mostly white pines, which now loom tall.

Wayne's property is classic Hockomock farmland. One hundred and fifty years ago, the place might easily have served as the model for the fictional Moses Nash's farm. Wayne remembers his daughter pushing a baby carriage with pet rabbits in it across a great green field out back, all the way up to the high White pine island on the north side. Now all that's visible between Wayne's property and those pines in the distance is an immense tangle of low brush, briars, reeds, and water—in short, swamp. When the truck farm ended, the Hockomock had quickly reclaimed lost ground.

Wayne knows that the Wampanoags once inhabited his land. Many years ago, he and his son, Geoffrey, decided to do some digging on the property because he suspected as much. Wayne asked himself, *Where would I have lived on this property if I was an Indian?* He chose a high spot in the fields, near the river, and began to dig and sift. He found what he was looking for, all right—but not for the reason he expected. Wayne started hitting rocks, big rocks, including one with a flat side. Pretty soon, he discovered that he was excavating an old foundation. Wayne was later able to tentatively date the foundation at 1710-50 by measuring the inside diameter of the many broken pipe stem fragments left by the early colonial inhabitants.

Wayne first found the old bottles, dishes, toys, and coins inevitably found at colonial-era residences. Then the Indian artifacts began to come up. It didn't make a whole lot of sense for them to be there, but there sure were plenty of them. Wayne figures that at some point, one of the property's owners must have scraped soil off the top of the surrounding fields to fill in the old foundation. This resulted in a "dump" of sorts, which naturally contained Indian artifacts.

The stone artifacts he found included numerous projectile points. One, made from white quartz, was tiny with serrated edges. Wayne figures that one was used as an arrowhead for birds. There was also a hand gouge, a "leaf knife," which really looks like a leaf, assorted scrapers, a large, broken, gray pestle for grinding, and a "dibble," which is a three-to-four-inch tool with finger grips and a short plug coming off it at an angle. The dibble is just the right length for poking a hole in the soil to plant a kernel of corn.

But Wayne's prize find, the one he keeps in its own shoebox, is a true work of art. Large and exquisitely formed, his Susquehanna Astabula projectile point of black chert shocked the archaeologists down at the Massachusetts Archeological Society, who helped him identify his finds.

"You couldn't have found *that* in your yard," they told him. "Where did you buy it?"

"Yes I did," replied Wayne. "I *did* find it in my yard."

The archeologists just shook their heads.

It wasn't so much the fact that the large black blade was so very thin, or that it was obviously the work of a highly skilled artisan, or that it may be as much as 6,000 years old. It was the material from which the blade was formed that surprised the archaeologists. Black chert, they told Wayne, is only found near Lake Champlain, in Vermont, or across the lake in New York. Not in the Hockomock.

Wayne figures this only proves that those Archaic people living on his land back then had an advanced trading network, that stretched far to the north.

At the same time he was digging for evidence of previous inhabitants on his land, Wayne was looking for well water. He and his son dug up an old thirteen-foot well near the old foundation and rebuilt it.

What surprised Wayne about that well was that the water in it didn't come from the direction of the Hockomock River on the nearby eastern border of his property, but from the west.

"That's not surprising," an old farmer who lived to the west of his property told him. "You've got an old spring running under the bottom of your driveway."

Wayne decided he would try to find that spring, so he asked a renowned dowser and friend at his Methodist Church in Brockton for assistance. The dowser, then in his advanced years, declined a trip to Wayne's property, but asked him "Can you draw me a map?"

So Wayne drew the dowser a map of his property, complete with topographical estimates. The dowser laid it on the hood of his car and went off to get his special equipment. When he came back, the man waved his rod over the map and immediately said "Yep, there it is." He pointed to a spot directly at the bottom of Wayne's driveway. Wayne could hardly believe it. He hadn't told the dowser anything about what the farmer had told him regarding the placement of the spring.

Wayne remembers when his part of West Bridgewater was so rural that nobody looked twice when animals broke out of their pens, and parades of pigs, or cows, or chickens, would come strutting down the middle of Route 106. Marilyn would call the police department, and it was pretty funny watching the cops trying to herd the cows around. There wasn't much traffic for them to stop back then.

One time, the cows at the Michelson's big farm to the east broke out and invaded their yard. It looked like a hurricane went through. Everything living had been smashed and broken. Wayne had recently planted a bunch of small trees, all of which had been trampled flat by the cattle. It was the type of event that helped fuel the Wampanoag's anger against the English colonists in the mid-17th century.

Farmer Michelson came down, looked it over, and said, "Yep, looks like they did a number on your trees." Then he handed Wayne $300, which made good on the damage.

Wayne also recalls that back then, in the 1960s, the Hockomock River ran low for quite a while. It was nearly dry some years.

"Now it's always at what I call 'high tide,'" he says. "Ever since they built up all the farmland and put in all that blacktop, like on Manley Street in Brockton. I used to be able to cross over," Wayne remembers, nodding towards the river, "but I can't ever do that today."

This change seems to have occurred at about the same time as the increased traffic.

Neither Wayne nor his wife have seen anything "funny," or out-of-the-ordinary in the area. But Wayne admits he was never much for hunting or fishing, and hence never ventured far into the Hockomock Swamp on his own. One time, he did take the tractor up onto the high pine island in the swamp across the street, though—the one to the south that you can see from his front door. There were folks living up there, on that island, back then in the 1970s. Young folks, living in lean-tos. As Wayne recalls, it was mostly a seasonal thing.

Marilyn doesn't remember any UFOs, in 1979 or any time else, but she does remember vividly standing on the farmer's porch out front, looking south towards the swamp, and seeing a line of lights coming in low over the treetops. But that turned out to be just low-flying planes. The flight pattern into Logan International Airport in Boston was much lower then, Marilyn recalls, before they made the jets fly higher, and farther off to the east.

What the Legge's do remember coming down from the sky in grand style, though, on May 1, 1971, was a helicopter. It landed in a field of Michelson's farm, near the banks of the Hockomock River. Wayne recalls proudly how he and his son and daughter joined a flotilla of thirty canoes headed south down the river that day, led by Massachusetts Governor Francis Sargent and State Senator John S. Ames III.

The group was on a grand tour of the Hockomock Swamp that afternoon in a bid to raise public awareness in support of the pending bill to preserve the swamp as conservation land. Wayne, who has taken photographs all over the world, including Korea and Japan, even created a color slideshow of this historic event that he treasures to this day.

I met Wayne when I mistakenly knocked on his door. At the time, I was attempting to locate the wife of John Baker, a man who had run into Bigfoot, or something like it, in the early 1980s in the swamp nearby. Wayne heard me out patiently, his front door cracked and firmly held. Then, surprisingly, he invited me in, and showed me some old newspaper clippings about, among other things, a giant mystery cat spotted in the area four decades earlier. Ultimately, Wayne offered to show me his slideshow about the governor's canoe trip. About a month later, after having read about the impact of this canoe trip on the passage of the 1971 bill that saved the Hockomock Swamp, I took him up on it.

The canoe trip was a publicity event organized by John Ames III. Ames arranged the excursion and obtained the personal support of the governor, in an attempt to build public support for bill S-780, which was still awaiting a green light from the state legislature. Ames was leading a bi-partisan contingent of area state representatives in a behind-the-scenes efforts to get the bill passed. A similar bill in 1970 had failed to obtain the blessing of the Ways and Means Committee, the same committee that was now considering this one. If the bill passed, it would provide the money to preserve the Hockomock Swamp forever. But there was real concern, even during the canoe trip, that the bill would not get through.

Ames, a freshman legislator at the time, had been looking around for something to do to help his district. He had taken up the cause of saving the Hockomock Swamp because "it was a hell of a regional resource" and also because it was the public water supply for Taunton. In addition, Ames knew there was a lot of environmental degradation going on there at the time.

There were many people, and diverse types of people too, behind the initiative, including hunters, environmentalists, and historians. There were many people in the region who loved the place, who were familiar with the rich history there, including Ames.

"At that time," John recalls, "there were still a bunch of old characters around that would go in there with a gun and a bottle of whiskey and come out with their deer."

The cause to save the Hockomock was "all motherhood and apple pie," according to Ames. In other words, it was hard to be against it. But the reality was that there was no money to fund it. Then Jimmy Kelly stepped up to the plate. If Ames was the naïve, freshman Legislator at the time, then Kelly was the proverbial old, sly fox. A senator from western Massachusetts, Kelly was the Chairman of Ways and Means, and he had an appreciation for conservation. He "took an interest in the thing," as John puts it, although John didn't even know him at the time.

Kelly slipped in a percentage increase on hotel rooms and funded the bond issue, which raised the necessary funds. Meanwhile, Ames had formed "The Friends of the Hockomock," a nonprofit group that he and other benefactors, including many conservation commission members from the local Hockomock towns, used to raise the money to print *Wonder Wetland*. Somebody else printed up "Don't Knock the Hock" bumper stickers, and distributed them to the grassroots supporters in the area.

When the senior members of the senate figured out that John intended on distributing his booklet in the chamber, they told him, "You can't do that." Apparently, it just wasn't something that was done. But John did it anyway. And then Ames got up there in his earnest manner, and talked about the swamp, its value as a natural resource to the people.

On September 27, 1971, the Massachusetts State Senate approved a $5 million bond issue that had been approved a week earlier in the House, and Governor Sargent subsequently signed it.

The act mandated that the purchase be administered entirely by Massachusetts Fish and Game, the organization that had previously designated the 6,000-acre Hockomock Swamp as its first priority in the event the bill passed.

Ames said that, at the time, the purchase of the ten-square-mile swamp was worth it "as simply a water resource and flood control project," but that the additional value lay in preserving the ecosystem for generations to come "in essentially the same condition as it was when Indians were the only inhabitants of southern Massachusetts."

Ames also recommended that the Hockomock be used on a limited basis, perhaps for hunting and fishing, but that care should be taken by the public not to overwhelm the area and its many residents. Senator Ames also noted that "thousands of individuals and organizations" had contributed to the passage of the wetlands act. Somehow, by all working together, they had pulled it off. The "Place Where the Spirits Dwell" had been saved forever.

There was some major irony in the fact that it was John Ames doing the saving. That's because John's great, great grandfather was Oliver Ames, Jr., who lived from 1807 to 1877. Oliver, Jr. was raised in Easton, and rose to prominence in the family business, Oliver Ames & Sons Shovels. This was a hugely profitable operation that provided many of the shovels and other tools for the construction of the transcontinental railroad in the 1860s. Oliver, Jr. later became a major financier and developer of railroads on the national level, most notably, the Union Pacific Railroad, with which his brother Oaks was also associated.

Oliver Jr. did some railroad work locally as well, in his capacity as a director of the Old Colony & Newport line serving southeastern Massachusetts. By the mid-1860s, Ames and the other directors were looking to expand this line, which had reached Easton a decade earlier, from Randolph in the north to Taunton in the south.

In Oliver Jr.'s personal diary, there are numerous references to his role in the construction of this new line, which ran "through the swamp on the boundary of Easton and Raynham"—that is, through the Hockomock Swamp, including the following:

• Thursday, August 11, 1864: "Pleasant and Warm. Day Hammar Shop not running on a/c of heat. Surveying out the RR between here and Taunton—suffered very much from the heat in running through the Swamp."

• Monday, September 26: "Went with Mr. Winslow to try the mud in the Cedar Swamp prepared irons and had 2 men go to try the mud and carry the irons. Met Mr. Gilmore there, found the mud 25 feet deep in one place."

• Thursday, October 6th: "Spent the day in looking over the line of RR between Swamp and C Gilmore's. Both lines walked over. The westerly line has 20 feet less Elevation and is the best line, but does not accommodate the people as well."

• Saturday, October 8th: "Cloudy morning a light Shower in the night...went to Boston today. Meeting of RR Directors to take into consideration the Route through Raynham...decided to adopt the middle route."

Little did Oliver Ames, Jr. know that just over a century later, his great, great grandson would be the man to forever preserve the wild beauty of the swamp through which he so painstakingly ran a railroad.

John Ames III got a bluebird day for the canoe trip. The little round helicopter, white with red seats, came down with great fanfare in the green grass of Michelson's field, just across the river from Wayne's. Sixties-era cars lined the side of quiet Route 106, also known as West Center Street, including some big black towncars.

Governor Sargent, tanned, rugged-looking, and dressed as an outdoorsman, smiled and shook hands with Ames, tall, young, and patrician-looking, in front of the news cameras. The two went over a map of the terrain they were about to cover. More than thirty canoes, many of them wooden, launched with great fanfare from the south side of the bridge on 106.

Senator Ames and the Governor paddled away in the lead, setting a rapid pace. The craft behind them was paddled by Arthur Brownell, Commissioner of the Department of Natural Resources, and Jim Shepherd, Director of the Division of Fisheries and Game, who were both strong supporters of the pending bill. Several other State Legislators were in the trailing canoes, along with several local families that supported the bill, including Wayne Legge and his son, Geoffrey.

Nobody actually tipped over at the launch, but the canoe holding U.S. Representative Hastings Keith, from West Bridgewater, got sucked into the current stern first. It seemed sure to capsize before it was finally turned about.

The flotilla drifted south with the current, down the twisting course of the river into the wild expanse of the Hockomock. It's not an easy stretch of the river to paddle. Wayne recalls vividly a time he did it with friends, and they all got lost because they couldn't identify the channel. They had eventually wandered out of the channel into some sort of floodplain that stretched deep into the tangled undergrowth. The group barely made it out. Marilyn and the other wives, who knew what time they expected to be back, nearly had a fit.

The little white helicopter, owned by the Department of Natural Resources, was full of newsmen that didn't wanted anything to do with canoes. It hovered persistently, like a tern, and swooped low and noisily overhead. The copter buzzed the canoes, and flushed panicked mallards and black ducks out of the marsh. The canoes wove through the swamp, strung out over a couple of stretches of open water, and navigated cautiously under the overhanging limbs of Red maples that were just budding out crimson.

They portaged over the now-defunct Maple Street that runs into the swamp from Pleasant Street. But they stopped there first for coffee, to swat pesky mayflies, and to chat about the swamp.

The long line of canoes then proceeded down the Hockomock River to where it met the Town River, and then followed the Town northeast, away from Lake Nippenicket, that last remnant of ancient Glacial Lake Taunton. Ames and his party were celebrating a traditional river passage, one that had been routinely made by the dugout canoes of the Wampanoags for thousands of years. They followed the Town River under Route 24 towards West Bridgewater Center. The two-hour paddle ended, after a tight squeeze under a stone bridge, at the Canoe Club, an historic Bridgewater paddling establishment, where Representative Ames hosted lunch.

The canoe trip was a smashing success. The resulting press coverage, including a television broadcast and newspaper articles heavily splashed with photographs depicting committed politicians and the wild beauty of the Hockomock, was well received by the public, and ultimately helped ensure the passage of the wetlands bill through the Legislature.

The acquisition of the swamp by the state proceeded very slowly. The pace made the local environmentalists crazy, in part because the Inlands Wetlands Act that had been in place in the state since 1968 had proved largely ineffective as a means of protecting similar areas against land developers.

The first major Hockomock land purchase occurred in March of 1974, roughly coinciding with Governor Sargent's announcement that a four-lane extension to Route 495 would be built. This extension, which was built to speed traffic from I-495 to Cape Cod, runs east across the southwest corner of the swamp just south of Lake Nippenicket.

The 495 extension further hemmed in the Hockomock, which was already sliced by Route 24 running north-south on the eastern side, by Route 28 also on the east, by Route 123 in the northwest, by Route 138 running north-south down the center, by Route 106 east-west on the north side, and by Route 104 on the south.

The swamp was also bisected north-south by the now defunct railroad line built by Oliver Ames, Jr., which had been abandoned in the 1950s, and southeast-northwest by Montaup Electric's power lines. And all of the roadways had promoted suburban housing development, which had been chipping away steadily at the edges of the Hockomock since World War II.

Part of the reason the state moved so slowly acquiring the land in the Hockomock was that titles to the individual pieces of property were infamously hard to find. But in the end, the state got the job done. Fish and Game purchased the swamp and established 4,833 acres of it as the Hockomock Swamp Wildlife Management Area, which is now a place for hunting, fishing, and the preservation of habitat for a vast number of plant, animal, bird, insect, amphibian, reptile, and fish species.

The Wildlife Management Area is shaped very roughly like an inverted crescent, with the thick part to the north and the two horns facing south. It includes wetlands of cattails and marsh grasses, shrub swamp, maple swamp, cedar swamp, and some uplands that include farmland and mixed tree stands of hardwoods, hemlock, and pines. The area includes three canoeable rivers, including the Hockomock, the Town, and the Snake.

A preliminary survey of species in the area made in 1970, before the passage of the bill, included 170 species of birds, twenty-four species of fish, sixteen species of reptiles and amphibians, and thirty-seven species of mammals. At least thirteen of these species are now listed by the state as Threatened, Endangered, or of Special Concern, including Blue-spotted salamanders, spotted turtles, Blanding's turtles, Eastern box turtles, New England Bluet damselflies, Kennedy's Emerald dragonflies, gypsywort, and two-flowered bladderwort.

These are just *some* of the *plant* species in the Hockomock Swamp, a place of such great natural abundance and diversity that at first glance it seems incredible.

Field Horsetail. Staghorn Club Moss. Running Pine. Ground Cedar. Royal Fern. Interrupted Fern. Cinnamon Fern. Sensitive Fern. Marsh Fern. Massachusetts Fern. New York Fern. Spinulose Woodfern. Boott's Fern. Crested Fern. Marginal Woodfern. Hayscented Fern. Lady Fern. Virginia Chain Fern. Netted Chain Fern. Bracken. Eastern Hemlock. White Pine. Pitch Pine. Atlantic White Cedar. Dwarf Juniper. Red Cedar. Common Cattail. Narrow-leaved Cattail. Common Bur-reed. Broad-leaved Arrowhead. Jack-in-the-pulpit. Arrow Arum. Wild Calla. Skunk Cabbage. Asiatic Dayflower. Pickerelweed. Wild Oats. Canada Lily. Corn-lily. Canada Mayflower. Indian Cucumber-root. Carrion-flower. Greenbriar. Larger Blue Flag. Pink Lady's-slipper. White-fringed Orchid. Purple-fringed Orchid. Snake-mouth Orchid. Grass-pink Orchid. Crack Willow. Pussy Willow. Bigtooth Aspen. Northern Bayberry. Sweetfern. Black Walnut. Shagbark Hickory. Ironwood. Black Birch. Yellow Birch. Gray Birch. Beech. White Oak. Swamp Oak. Red Oak. Scarlet Oak. Black Oak. Scrub Oak. Swamp Smartweed. Mild Water-pepper. Arrow-leaved Tearthumb. Halbert-leaved Tearthumb. Red Campion. Evening Lychnis. Bladder Campion. Deptford Pink. Bullhead-lily. Fragrant Water-lily. Common Buttercup. Bulbous Buttercup. Tall Meadow-rue. Marsh-marigold. Goldthread. Sassafras. Field Mustard. Pitcher Plant. Spatulate

Sundew. Round-leaved Sundew. Common Witch-hazel. Meadowsweet. Steeplebush. Red Chokeberry. Wood Strawberry. Silvery Cinquefoil. Dwarf Cinquefoil. Common Cinquefoil. Japanese Rose. Swamp Rose. Carolina Rose. Choke Cherry. Wild Indigo. Red Clover. White Clover. Alsike Clover. Hop Clover. Cow Vetch. Creeping Wood-sorrel. Staghorn Sumac. Smooth Sumac. Winged Sumac. Poison Sumac. Poison-ivy. American Holly. Common Winterberry Holly. Red Maple. Ashleaf Maple. Box Elder. Spotted Touch-me-not. Common Buckthorn. Virginia Creeper. Common St. Johnswort. Canadian St. Johnswort. Marsh St. Johnswort. Marsh Blue Violet. Common Blue Violet. Northern Downy Violet. Northern White Violet. Lance-leaved Violet. Purple Loosestrife. Sour Gum. Virginia Meadow Beauty. Fireweed. Narrow-leaved Willow-herb. Common Evening Primrose. Bristly Sarsaparilla. Wild Sarsaparilla. Dwarf Ginseng. Water-hemlock. Spotted Cowbane. Wild Carrot. Queen Anne's Lace. Flowering Dogwood. Red-osier Dogwood. Red-panicle Dogwood. Sweet Pepperbush. Coast Pepperbush. Spotted Wintergreen. Shinleaf. Indian-pipe. Pinesap.

Swamp-honeysuckle. Mountain Laurel. Sheep Laurel. Swamp Sweetbells. Leatherleaf. Wintergreen. Tall Deerberry. Common Highbush Blueberry. Large Cranberry. Whorled Loosestrife. Yellow Loosestrife. Tufted Loosestrife. Starflower. White Ash. Green Ash. Bartonia. Swamp Milkweed. Common Milkweed. Hedge Bindweed. Dodder. True Forget-me-not. White Vervain. Blue Vervain. Narrow-leaved Vervain. Woundwort. Rough Hedge-nettle. Bee-balm. Bugleweed. Butter and Eggs. Blue Toadflax. Turtlehead. Square-stemmed Monkey-flower. Golden Hedge-hyssop. Cow-wheat. Beechdrops. Greater Bladderwort. Partridgeberry. Buttonbush. Northern Wild-raisin. Nannyberry. Northern Arrowwood. Mapleleaf Viburnum. Highbush-cranberry. Bedstraw. Cardinal-flower. Joe-Pye-weed. Boneset. Downy Goldenrod. Early Goldenrod. Gray Goldenrod. Elm-leaved Goldenrod. Rough-stemmed Goldenrod. Canada Goldenrod. Lance-leaved Goldenrod. Slender Fragrant Goldenrod. White Wood Aster. Purple-stemmed Aster. Heath Aster. Bushy Aster. Small White Aster. New York Aster. Daisy Fleabane. Horseweed. Pearly Everlasting. Black-eyed Susan. Yarrow. Ox-eye Daisy. Firewort. Golden Ragwort. Black Knapweed. Gall-of-the-earth.

This physical uniqueness of the Hockomock Swamp as an ecological treasure trove, first officially recognized by Senator Ames and his supporters in the early

1970s, is, in today's environmentally aware world, obvious and undeniable to most. But the supreme irony of the Hockomock is that while on the surface it is a natural paradise representative, perhaps, of divine goodness, beneath the surface lays an equally-potent underbelly of evil.

The great natural diversity of the Hockomock, its unique *physical* aspect, can be adequately explained by the geologic circumstances that formed its origins and subsequently allowed it to survive development, circumstances which typically involved massive quantities of water.

Much harder to define is what makes the Hockomock unique in a *metaphysical* sense. Specifically, what is it, exactly, that draws so much *evil* to the Hockomock?

For the first part of the answer to this question, I believe we need look no further than the obvious. It is, of course, the same thing that empowers the *physical* uniqueness of the Hockomock, the natural diversity. *It's the water.* The "Wonder Wetland" part. Specifically, I believe it's mostly about the springs.

Water is a sacred element in many religions. The Bible tells us that Jesus was infused with the Holy Spirit through his baptism in water by John the Baptist, and water remains a major aspect of the faith today, as evidenced by the continued use of holy water in baptisms and other sacred ceremonies. The majority of all Native American religious rites involve some use of water.

For the second part of the answer to our question, I believe we must turn to world mythology. Based on the prevalence of parallel accounts in numerous cultures, it seems likely to me that there exists some sort of world between heaven and hell, that lays beneath my feet. *Under the ground.* According to many religious traditions, this world is where the spirits of the human dead, both good and evil, abide, at least for a time. I believe that other, non-human spirits, such as nature spirits, may abide there as well.

It seems that, for one reason or another, and from time to time, there briefly appear *openings* between our physical world and this spirit world, through which, or at which time, certain things can pass freely between the two worlds. There are also well-established methods, that have been available to humans since the time of the ancient shamans, for making this passage into the spirit world at will, and also for calling, or summoning spirits from this world into our own.

I do not profess to understand the relationship between spirits, water, the physical world, and the spirit world. But I do know that people, such as shamans, who profess to have made passages to this underground spirit world in spirit form consistently describe starting their journey by *going down through openings in the ground.* And these openings are generally said to exist in our physical world as holes, cracks, caves, *caverns of water, or springs.*

Springs. A spring is an above-ground relief point for an underground body of water. It's like a leak. The source of underground water usually sits higher than the spring, and may be quite far from it. The underground water can reach the spring by a circuitous route, such as by sliding down a long rock ledge. It's sort of like the rainwater from a leak in your roof finding its way through a ceiling on the opposite side of your house. The Hockomock Swamp is perforated with springs, like a giant piece of Swiss cheese. Countless springs, that sometimes lead far down, through groundwater, to bedrock, into the very bowels of the earth. And into the spirit world, perhaps.

For the final part of our answer to the question of what makes the Hockomock special on a metaphysical level, we might speculate about the spirits that populate the spirit world that lays beneath it. For a clue, perhaps we need look no further than the literal translation of the Wampanoag place name itself. "Hockomock: Body enclosure." The Hockomock Swamp, a traditional burial ground in the first region of New England settled by prehistoric man, just might be the mother of all Indian graveyards.

We know from the Wampanoag's beliefs of Hobbamock that the Indians historically believed that most of the spirits that gathered in the Hockomock were evil, the harbingers of death and disease. We also know from the area's troubled history, especially the history of King Philip's War, that some of the Indians buried in the Hockomock in relatively recent times were brutally killed, or otherwise terribly oppressed by the European colonists.

And so to summarize, what the Hockomock might be on a metaphysical level is a vast network of spirit pathways leading to and from a densely-populated spirit world composed mainly, but not completely of evil spirits originating from the human dead, the goals of which are to inflict fear, disease, death, and related agonies on humans. And at least some of these spirits possess a special hatred of our kind.

The ancient Maya had rich cultural traditions involving water. They were a highly advanced civilization that existed from Mexico to Honduras, on what is now known as the Yucatan Peninsula, which separates the Caribbean Sea from the Gulf of Mexico. Mayan cities reached their height between 250 and 900 A.D. Among numerous other cultural achievements, including advanced systems of astronomy, math, art, and architecture, the Maya had the only known fully-developed written language in the Pre-Columbian Americas. In other words, they were the only Indians that could truly write.

Water was tremendously important to the Maya on both the practical and religious levels. The Yucatan Peninsula is mostly a high, flat area, underlain by limestone that is densely riddled with subterranean cave systems. Because most of the surface water runs off into this underground system, the land there is highly prone to drought. For this reason, to ensure a reliable water source, the Maya built their great cities beside the few available surface waters, which are a kind of sinkhole now known locally as "cenotes."

Cenotes resemble small, circular ponds with sharp drops at the edges. They are created by the collapse of a rock ceiling over an underground water source. Under the entire Yucatan Peninsula lays a vast, coastal aquifer system, composed of a fresh water lense floating on salt water. Cenotes link to this underground water table, and sometimes to major underground river systems as well. These beautiful, remote, and vast caverns of pure water are explored today by adventurous cave divers.

No one's going to dive into the groundwater of the Hockomock Swamp unless, perhaps, they are in magical flight. That's because the subterranean waters of the Hock, though vast in quantity, are not nearly so accessible, or picturesque, for that matter, as the haunting underground cenotes of the Yucatan Peninsula. There are no underground rivers there, unless maybe you counted river water flowing through areas of extremely loose gravel. And there are no watery caves. The water's all in the soil.

All of the groundwater in the Hockomock moves north to south, in the same general pattern as its rivers, or surface waters. The groundwater feeds into, and sustains the flow of these rivers, such as the Snake, the Town, and the Matfield, and it all ends up, like the rivers, eventually draining out to the Taunton River and onwards to Narragansett Bay.

Some of the groundwater, like that trapped in the sand and gravel, moves surprisingly fast. Some, like that trapped in clay, moves so slowly it may take years to flow off. But it's all moving, and most of it is connected. It was groundwater that did much of the damage in the Hockomock during March 2010, rising as it did to flood peoples' basements days after the rain stopped.

Under the groundwater of the Hockomock lays bedrock. The bedrock in the area of the swamp is perhaps fifty to sixty feet underground. This is significantly farther down than the bedrock in the northern portions of the Taunton River basin, up near Stoughton and Sharon, for example. Wayne Southworth, who once helped locate wells for the Town of Easton, remembers that the best wells they found were usually near rivers, in groundwater located in deep beds of sand and gravel, which were probably the geological remains of ancient rivers. Wayne particularly remembers one potential site in the Hock like this that he considered a perfect candidate for a well, but they never built it because it was just a half mile from the Town Landfill.

For the ancient Maya, there was more to cenotes, or surface waters linking to subterranean waters, than just water for drinking, bathing, and irrigation. Much more. For, to the Maya, the most culturally advanced Indians of the New World, cenotes were sacred places. They were the portals, the routes, to Xibalba, the

"Place of Fright." The Underworld. Xibalba was the home of the *sinister gods of Death and Disease. In other words, the Maya believed that these natural wells of water led to the same Evil deity whom the Wampanoags knew as Hobbamock.*

The preservation of the "Wonder Wetland" known to us as the Hockomock Swamp in the 1970s was not a comprehensive solution for preserving wild lands in the greater Hockomock region, but it did turn out to be a good start. In 1989, a group of Bridgewater residents, led by Gail Price, submitted an application to the state to formally designate the Hockomock Swamp/Lake Nippenicket area an Area of Critical Environmental Concern, or ACEC.

The group submitted the application in the hopes of blocking the Bridgewater Crossroads project, a proposed shopping mall and office park on 142 acres of land across the street from Lake Nippenicket, off Routes 495 and 104. Price and the other residents cited concerns about the impact of this large project on local water supplies and natural resources. The mall proposal, however, enjoyed strong support from Bridgewater town officials.

The proposed ACEC covering 17,000 acres, significantly more geographic area than the area saved in the 1970s, included the towns of Bridgewater, Easton, Norton, Raynham, Taunton, and West Bridgewater. In addition to the Hockomock Swamp, this area consisted of several other wetlands and water bodies, including Lake Nippenicket, the Hockomock, Town, and Snake Rivers, several ponds and brooks, and the Dead, Little Cedar, and Titicut Swamps.

An ACEC designation is made by the Massachusetts Secretary of Environmental Affairs, as a means of protecting and preserving unique natural, or cultural, areas of state or regional significance.

To meet the criteria, the proposed area must incorporate features such as fisheries habitat, inland wetlands or surface waters, a water supply area, wildlife area, an underdeveloped natural area, or have special scenic or recreational qualities. The purpose of the designation is to recognize the critical environmental value of an area and to put the public and regulatory agencies on notice that any development there must meet higher standards in the form of a closer environmental review.

In early 1990, Massachusetts Secretary of the Environment John DeVillars officially designated the area an ACEC. He cited the protection of local public wells, including Raynham's and West Bridgewater's, and the overall area's value for flood control as his main reasons. In fact, there were probably few, if any of the ACEC acceptance criteria that the Hockomock area did not meet.

The Massachusetts Division of Fish and Wildlife, which had managed the 1970s purchases of Hockomock lands, together with the citizen's group had also spoken favorably on behalf of the ACEC designation. It was the largest inland section in Massachusetts ever to have received this designation.

In mid-July 1990, DeVillars rejected the Crossroads developer's Final Environmental Impact Report, based on the more stringent environmental regulations imposed by the ACEC designation. He requested that the developer complete a supplemental report based on the exceptional quality of the natural resources in the Hockomock area.

DeVillars had apparently asked the developers to reduce the footprint, or size, of the mall in order to protect the nearby wetlands, and they had failed to do so. The ACEC designation, together with competition from a permitted competitor in the form of Taunton's Silver City Mall developer, ultimately sunk the Crossroads development project.

The ACEC designation was a powerful tool in preserving the Hockomock, but like the 1970s acquisition, it is only another piece of the conservation puzzle. This is because the designation mainly affects only larger development projects in the area, or activities that require a state license. A comprehensive, ongoing approach to conservation is necessary for long-term success.

A good example of this new kind of preservation effort occurred in 2008, involving 102 acres of land on Lake Nippenicket abutting the Hockomock Swamp Wildlife Management Area.

It was accomplished by the Campanelli Companies, which donated the land, the Wildlands Trust, which now owns it, and the Nature Conservancy, which now holds a Conservation Restriction on it. This group effort was also noteworthy in that it included the Nature Conservancy, the mission of which is to protect the biodiversity of the planet. This international group officially recognized the land on and around Lake Nippenicket as a habitat and ecosystem with world-class biodiversity value.

The ACEC designation, as valuable as it is to the Hock, does nothing, however, to prevent suburban sprawl. Developers are in hot pursuit of the remaining open spaces in Southeastern Massachusetts, including the Hockomock region. Developed land in the region increased from twenty percent in 1971 to twenty-nine percent in 1999. The region also lost almost nine percent of its forested land during that period.

Since 1999, smaller-scale commercial, industrial, and residential developments have continued to nibble away at the edges of the Hock. Much of the development in the interior of Southeastern Massachusetts has been along highway corridors such as Route 24. These highway corridors experienced sixty percent growth in development from 1971-1999.

New housing developments continue to spring up everywhere, on old farmland once proudly cultivated by the likes of Edsons, Aldens, and Leonards. Some of the new houses, like some in the old Scotland section of West Bridgewater, look as if they were dropped from the sky. They could have been built anywhere in America. In the shadows of the original, once-proud farmhouses, they crouch together like confused immigrants, staring out forlornly at the edge of the remaining meadowlands that made up the original Hockomock grant.

The conservation forecast for Southeastern Massachusetts is bleak. According to the Woods Hole Research Center, even if the region enforces "smart growth," which would include significant changes in the way it grows and higher density in the areas developed, by 2030 it can expect to see an increase of twenty percent of developed land. This would leave the region with a total of about fifty percent of its land developed. With a model of "Unmanaged Growth," meaning it proceeds with "business as usual," the area can expect to see an increase in developed land of thirty-four percent, leaving some sixty-three percent of its total land developed.

The towns in the Route 495 corridor, including those that border on the Hockomock, such as the Bridgewaters, Taunton, and Raynham, are expected to continue on their current pattern of major population growth, due largely to the construction of Route 495, the renovation and expansion of commuter rail lines, and the fact that they are relatively close to Boston.

Interestingly, the Woods Hole study recommends that the five major watersheds of the region should provide the basis for development planning. The Taunton River watershed, which includes 562 square miles and 43 cities and towns, is the biggest in the area. As it turns out, the region to which the earliest inhabitants of the region first came, some 12,000 years ago, is the same area that holds not only the key to the future of the Hockomock, but to the entire Southeastern Massachusetts region.

The Taunton River is, in this sense, as vital to the region's inhabitants today as it was to the first Paleo hunters that settled the region. The way in which the land in the Taunton River watershed is developed in our lifetimes will have a major impact on the quality of life of all future inhabitants of the region.

In 2009, President Obama signed the Omnibus Public Lands Act, which officially added the Taunton River to the National Wild and Scenic Rivers System. This action was the result of twenty years of sustained effort by local environmentalists and politicians, including Senator Ted Kennedy, and it was extremely good news for the environmental health of the river and the region. The law means that any major development projects in the Taunton's watershed that require Federal permitting will face stricter regulations.

It also means that the forty miles of the river must be preserved in free-flowing condition, and that it must be managed to protect and enhance its outstanding values.

On a more somber note, one of the major environmental threats to the Hockomock Swamp today is the currently-proposed rail service between Boston and the cities of Fall River and New Bedford. Governor Deval Patrick has thrown his support behind this project as a means of providing residents of the state's South Coast region a viable means of commuting to good jobs in Boston and points north.

Ironically, the Massachusetts Bay Transportation Authority's preferred route for this rail extension, known as the Stoughton Alternative, would leverage the now defunct rail line built by Oliver Ames, Jr. in the 19th century that runs from Easton in the north through Raynham in the south. The new rail extension would essentially cut the Hockomock Swamp in two.

Despite stiff opposition from area residents looking to safeguard their wells and powerful environmental groups, this route is still very much on the table, partly because the MBTA bought the old rail bed in the 1970s. For John Ames III, the adoption by the MBTA of this route after he worked so hard to preserve the swamp as conservation land would be a strange bit of irony indeed. It is almost as if his great, great grandfather Oliver, Jr.'s indomitable capitalist spirit is reaching out from the grave for revenge.

But was Oliver Jr. and his 19th century capitalist brethren right? Is life really all about "progress?" Residential and commercial development, although often viewed as progress and evidence of a community's worth, has today been shown by many studies to be more trouble than it is worth.

This is because the numerous problems associated with suburban sprawl are sure to come with it. In reality, residential developments often cost towns more in required services such as police, roads, and schools, than they collect in new tax revenues. And the benefits that open space provides in terms of recreation, well being, and our overall health are lost, oftentimes forever.

The conversion of natural lands to developed lands also carries with it significant threats to watersheds, wildlife, and other natural resources. Wildlife is forced to retreat into more broken-up habitats. Air and water pollution increase. More land is paved, creating imbalances in rivers and other water bodies, such as the one Wayne Legge pointed out by noting that the Hockomock River is now "always running at high tide" after nearby residential paving had been completed.

And finally, one of the greatest threats to the preservation of the Hockomock Swamp today is the same one that it faced in 1970. Ignorance. For some strange reason, almost nobody seems to know that the Wonder Wetland is there. And even the few that do are hard-pressed to define it. What is the Hockomock, exactly? And where is it, exactly? Few people can answer these questions.

A good part of this may have to do with the fact that today, many of the travel routes around the Hockomock are highways. The vast majority of the thousands of commuters that pass by the Hock at high speed each day on Routes 24 and 495, for example, probably have no idea that they are just feet from one of the largest wetlands in New England. If people do not know the land, they cannot love it. And without love, there is no public support to preserve it. Ultimately, it is only through the support of the people that conservation is made possible.

When Ted Williams wrote his "History" portion of *Wonder Wetland*, he related a story about a man named Harvey C. Ellis of Bridgewater. Ellis, an amateur archeologist, trapper, hunter, and fisherman, grew up on a large farm bordering the Hockomock Swamp, and knew it intimately.

Harvey and some friends once hacked three Indian dugout canoes out of ten feet of peat in the Hock. These blunt-ended "mishoons" were so well preserved that the young boy with them was actually able to paddle one of them out of the swamp.

Around 1970, Ellis told Williams that when the "expressway" went through, it "went right through our gunning stand and they drained our pickerel pond and tore down our camp."

He went on to say:

> Most of the swamp's still the way its always been. Last time I trapped was in '68 and I took 100 muskrats. I still hunt and fish the Nip pretty heavy and nothing's really changed. Funny thing is, though, most people don't know the Hock's there. They ask me how come I don't go North and I don't say too much. Shucks, why go North when I've got it all right here?

Got it all right here. With those words, Harvey Ellis just may have unknowingly defined the Hockomock. For the great secret of the Hock is that everything is right there, from the goodness of Heaven to the evils of Hell. And the reason why everything is right there is the water.

THUNDERBIRD
SUMMER, 1971

The lightning is the flash of his eye.
The thunder is the boom of his voice.
You cannot see him for he is wrapped in cloud.
He is Wakinyan Tanka.
He is the Great Thunderbird.

— Sioux, Plains

It was a few minutes past midnight. Police Officer Downey was driving home after his shift, which had just ended. Tom wasn't thinking about much other than going to bed. He was driving east on Maple Street in Mansfield, Massachusetts, headed towards his home in the town of Easton. Maple Street was a dark, country road back then, with few streetlights and mostly just woods on both sides. As best as Tom can recall, he was traveling at about forty-five miles per hour.

Nearing Bird Hill in Mansfield, Downey reached the point where Maple Street intersects with Winter Street on the right, and Bird Road on the left. It was then that he saw it—the dark figure of a man, about six feet tall, standing motionless on the right side of the road.

Tom figured the man was hitchhiking, so he swung his car wide to avoid hitting him. Then, as he approached, Downey saw enormous wings erupt from the dark figure, and it flew straight up, over the treetops, and was gone. And that was it.

There have been several documented sightings regarding spectacularly-large flying birds in the Hockomock. But perhaps the most credible sighting, and the one that best conforms to classic Thunderbird accounts, is this sighting by Norton Police Officer Thomas Downey, which occurred in the summer of 1971. Tom has thought a lot about this incident in the forty-plus years or so that have passed since it happened.

After he got home, he tried to convince himself that it had been just a stork, a heron, or something of that nature. Or that maybe the light, or the darkness, had somehow tricked him into believing the creature was much larger than it actually was. Or maybe that it had been some sort of hoax. After all, the police had just nabbed some crackpot in Mansfield that had been running around dressed in a sheet, generating ghost sightings, something he had apparently been doing for years. One night the "ghost" had leaped out in front of a cruiser, and almost gotten himself shot.

But in the end, Tom's rationalizations didn't work. He just couldn't convince himself that any of these explanations accounted for what he had witnessed. He had gotten a good look at the figure, and it stood as high as a man. But it could not have been a man, for he had seen it leap up into the air and fly away over the treetops. This pretty much eliminated the possibility of a hoax as well. So Tom did what he felt what the right thing, and called the incident in to the station. And then, later on, he told people about what had happened.

Going public with his sighting opened him up to ridicule by the other officers on the force and from the general public. The strange coincidences involved in the sighting didn't help his case. After all, his name was "Downey," and he had seen the creature very near "Bird Hill." It was as if some sort of cosmic joke had been played on him.

Tom, if he didn't pick up on these coincidences right away, was quickly made aware of them by others after speaking out. By now, he's been called just about every "big bird" name in the book, most notably "Thunderbird." After the sighting, he particularly remembers some annoying prank phone calls, all of which he now attributes to a single individual. But perhaps worst of all was when the "Monster Hunters" showed up uninvited on his doorstep. To him, they all seemed crazy.

But although at times he may secretly regret going public, Tom doesn't hesitate to say that he would do it all again. He didn't receive much more ribbing from his fellow cops than he would have expected from any bunch of guys, given the circumstances. He certainly wasn't run off the police force or anything drastic like that. He just dealt with it. But the incident will never leave Tom, really, and he is well aware of that. "Every five years or so, this thing seems to come back to haunt me" he told me when I first called him.

After the sighting, Downey did some investigating in the neighborhood of Bird Hill, and was surprised at what he discovered.

"No Sir," the locals told him matter-of-factly, "you're not the first one to see that thing."

As it turned out, people around Bird Hill had been seeing the giant, winged creature for years. Tom also did some research on Thunderbirds and related phenomena, and learned that down South, they are often seen in the vicinity of power lines and water tanks. The neighbors pointed out that both power lines and a water tank lay close to Bird Hill.

If you follow the dirt access road that runs under Montaup Electric's power lines northwest out of the Hockomock Swamp, from where the power lines cross over the Hockomock River near the Easton/West Bridgewater town line, after about 4.5 miles you will reach the Bird Hill area in Mansfield.

Tom Downey's not the only one who thinks that in some fashion, the power lines that traverse the Hockomock play some role in the bizarre sightings that occur there. The nature of any role electromagnetism may play in these sorts of events, however, is an enigma in itself.

Thunderbirds are giant, bird-like creatures that people have witnessed for thousands of years, often in conjunction with violent storms. The Native Americans of the United States and Canada have a rich mythological tradition regarding these creatures. Most of these tribes believed that Thunderbirds were nature spirits—sort of a cross between a biological creature and the divine.

The Indians often referred to these beings as "Thunderbirds" because they usually appeared and disappeared with violent storms that brought strong winds, rain, thunder, and lightning. The Indians believed that the Thunderbird actually created the thunder by flapping its wings, and the lightning by opening and closing its eyes. In the majority of tribal traditions, Thunderbird was considered a benevolent and wise spirit, even a protector of Man. The Indians sometimes referred to it as "Grandfather," and they generally revered it.

The Plains Sioux version of Thunderbird lived in their sacred Black Hills. They were led by the Great Thunderbird, Wakinyan Tanka. The Sioux believed that Thunderbird had saved them from a race of water monsters, the Unktehi, that had tried to drown them in ages past. The Great Thunderbird had led his brothers and children, clothed in black rolling clouds, and wielding thunderbolts and lighting darts, into battle against the Unktehi. The Thunderbirds set the forests alight with fire, burnt the land, and boiled the rivers where the Unktehi dwelt until the water monsters were no more. The Sioux people, hiding up in the hills, were saved.

Interestingly enough, in an 1890 article in *American Anthropologist*, A.F. Chamberlain stated that the Algonquian Tribe, of which the Wampanoags of the Hockomock region are a part, shared remarkably similar ideas with the Sioux about Thunderbird, despite the fact there is no known link between the two tribes. The Algonquians believed Thunderbird was divine, and that it used the lightning it made by flashing its eyes to kill serpents, or monsters, that it took "from under the Earth." The Algonquians typically described it as a "great eagle," and attributed storms and tornadoes to its anger, and good weather to its happiness.

There is, however, another creature found in Native American "big bird" mythology, that is of a very different nature than the benevolent Thunderbird. The best-known example of this creature is the "Piasa" of the Ilini, a tribe from Illinois. The name Piasa means "the bird that devours men." Although overall this creature physically resembled the Thunderbird, it had the hooked talons that are typically found only on eagles and other members of the raptor family. The Piasa had a nasty reputation for carrying off and devouring deer and humans, especially children.

The Wampanoags in the Cape Cod area of Massachusetts had similar legends of a giant devouring bird, first documented by Alden in 1798, that persisted in the region until the 20th century. In 1915, an anonymous local author wrote the following:

> And twice each year since time began, once in the Moon of Bright Nights and again in the Moon of Falling Leaves, the Great Devil Bird from over the South Sea had come to levy his awful toll on the tribe, by grappling in his terrible talons the half-grown papooses; sometimes even seizing young braves who were old enough to handle a tomahawk, and bearing them away to his lair in the Region of the South Wind.

In legend, this creature was later killed by the Wampanoag's culture hero Maushop, in its lair on the island we know as Martha's Vineyard.

In modern-day America, there have been thousands of sightings of massive, dark birds, sometimes from the ground, other times from planes. Many of them are probably just great blue herons, vultures, or other known creatures seen in the darkness, storms, or other poor conditions, and mistaken for something else. But enough of these sightings have been experienced by credible witnesses, in sufficiently clear conditions, to leave little doubt that *something* very large appears to be flying over North America. These sightings have many traits in common, and interestingly, they often conform remarkably well to descriptions of the Thunderbird and the Piasa-like creatures found in Native American mythology.

The majority of the modern "big bird" sightings involve a creature typically described as black or dark-colored overall, with a torso four-to-six-feet tall, a large, ugly beak, and an immense wingspan of approximately twelve to sixteen feet. A significant percentage of the people who see this creature in flight describe it as the "size of a Piper Cub." A Cub is a small, common, two-seater plane.

Observers typically believe that they are watching a plane in flight until they see it bank, like a vulture, and only then realize they are looking at a bird. Or at least something that looks like a bird. Their next thought is often, "But do birds *get* that big?"

Usually, the big bird sighting is brief, and relatively uneventful, like Tom Downey's. Typically, a monstrous creature simply erupts into the air off a dead animal on the road in front of the witness, or is seen swooping and tilting its way over storm-tossed trees, or soaring effortlessly away through the stratosphere towards the horizon. However, some modern sightings, that seemingly involve the Thunderbird's evil counterpart, are far from uneventful.

The most famous of these events in recent history is the case of Marlon Lowe, that occurred on July 25, 1977. At the time, Marlin, a 10-year-old boy, was playing outside his home on a farm in Lawndale, Illinois.

Suddenly his mother and some other folks sitting on the farmer's porch saw two enormous birds dropping down out of the sky over their fields. The great birds were headed straight towards Marlon. One of the birds swooped in and seized the boy with its talons, picked him up, and carried him for a distance of between thirty and forty yards. The great bird then unceremoniously dropped him, and both of the birds flew off.

The family later did some research in an attempt to understand what had happened to Marlon, and stated that the birds had resembled California Condors. This incident was the start of a rash of sightings in Illinois involving a bird that was similarly described by several other witnesses.

The Marlon Lowe incident is curiously similar to the Piasa stories found in the Native American mythology of the Illinois area.

Documented modern reports of these creatures in Illinois run as far back as 1673. Based on these historical sightings, there even appears to be a migration of these birds in the spring and summer months, from the Ozarks down into the Appalachian Mountains.

There also seems to be a similar migration in the West. The creatures seem to be sighted mostly during these migrations. There is also an incredible number of historical sightings of these types of birds in the Black Forest area of Pennsylvania, which, in addition to Illinois, appears to be one of their main haunts. There are enough reports by credible witnesses regarding these Piasa-like creatures for us to at least consider the possibility of such a creature existing today in North America.

What might account for the existence of giant birds like the Thunderbird and the Piasa today? Nothing in any of the reports points to any known living bird. The birds with the largest wingspans on the planet today are the Wandering Albatross, with a wingspan of up to 12 feet, and the Andean Condor, with a wingspan of up to 10.5 feet. The California Condor, with a wingspan of up to 10 feet, has the largest wingspan of any bird in North America. None of these species frequent any of the other areas where Thunderbirds are typically witnessed. This lack of a good candidate among our existing bird species forces us to consider other explanations.

Few people are willing to speculate about the existence of a surviving dinosaur, such as the Pterosaur, a giant flying reptile with a wingspan of up to thirty-five feet, that was the biggest creature to ever take off. And so, much of the speculation today regarding a biological candidate for these "big birds" involves the possibility of a surviving bird species from the relatively recent past. This theory is based on the idea that there a few survivors of a race, currently believed to be extinct, holed up in remote wilderness areas like the Ozarks, the Black Forest of Pennsylvania, and just possibly, the Hockomock.

The best avian candidates for filling this role are the Teratorns, a species of giant, condor-like birds that lived from 8 million to 10,000 years ago. The Teratorns were supposed to have gone extinct at the end of the Pleistocene, presumably at the same time so many of the "mega mammals" they fed on did, hastened to their bloody end by the Paleo peoples.

Specifically, *Teratornis merriami*, or "Merriam's Teratorn," seems to best match modern descriptions of the Thunderbird. Merriam's Teratorn was a giant, vulture-like bird that had a wingspan of twelve to fifteen feet. When it stood up, it would have looked you straight in the eye. Merriam's was the first Teratorn of many eventually discovered (L. Miller, 1909), and one of the most intensely studied. Surprisingly, the species was actually one of the smallest representatives of its race. Its largest cousin, *Argentavis magnificens*, was the largest known flying bird, sporting a wingspan of eighteen to twenty-four feet.

Scientists today know a fair amount about Merriam's Teratorn because over a hundred of their skeletons have been found in a massive prehistoric tar pit in California, that is known as Rancho La Brea. The birds were believed to have been snared in oil seeps there, while feeding on dead and dying large mammals that had been similarly trapped.

The bones of Merriam's have led scientists to believe that the creature had fairly good locomotion, similar to a turkey's. It was able to walk, run, and leap into the air to take off under its own power, as opposed to relying on powerful winds. In contrast, "Argentavis," its huge cousin, was probably totally dependent on the incessant high winds of ancient Patagonia to fuel its movements, due to its enormous wingspan. Merriam's Teratorn may even have stalked its prey on the ground.

Merriam's wing bones, the upper part of which is as big as the leg bone of an elk, have led scientists to conclude that it flew in the manner of vultures, soaring and gliding on thermals caused by the heating of the Earth's surface, as well as on passing storm fronts such as thunderstorms. This theory resonates with both Native American and modern accounts of the Thunderbird, which often describe the creature as appearing in the midst of powerful storms.

Merriam's feet had long, curved toes that were blunt on the end, indicating that they were not used for "catching and carrying" like the feet of eagles and owls.

This would effectively rule it out as a candidate for the Piasa and similar creatures. It had a beak with a hinged jaw, built for catching and swallowing small prey. This means it was not, at least primarily, a scavenger. Although scientists don't know what Merriam's feathers looked like, some think it is possible that it had a white ruff around its neck, like the Andean Condor, which is also a feature often noted in modern Thunderbird sightings.

Scientists know that condors originally had a far wider range than they do today. California Condor remains from 9,000 B.C. have been found as far east as western New York. Based on fossil finds, they also know that the birds were capable of tolerating a wide range of both habitats and climates. The climate in New York 11,000 years ago was cold. The land was just emerging from the melting glaciers, and was characterized by boreal vegetation, such as spruce and jack pine. The California Condor remains there were found along with fossils of caribou, wapiti (*Cervus elaphus*), and mastodonts (*Mammut americanum*).

These fossil finds indicate that Merriam's Teratorn might have been right at home in the boreal forest that characterized the Hockomock region after the glacier of the last ice age departed. It is possible that Merriam's Teratorn could have been part of the landscape of the Hockomock in Paleolithic times. So, based on this tentative assumption, the question becomes whether this dark-winged creature of dreams could have survived in there until modern times.

It is certainly tempting to believe it. As mentioned, Merriam's Teratorn could walk, hop, and launch itself straight up into the sky, without the aid of the updrafts created by thunderstorms and other fronts. That's not to say that it would not hitch a ride on thermal updrafts; most of these creatures surely did so in their day. The point is that unlike many of its extinct cousins, Merriam's could get itself around under its own power, and do so in a manner far more difficult to detect than flying. Perhaps, somehow, a few Teratorns survived the last ice age, and are at the root of the "big bird" mystery in the Eastern part of America.

Other theories regarding these "big birds" involve the paranormal. One of these theories is that somehow we are witnessing apparitions of creatures from our prehistoric past. Defenders of this paranormal theory point out that if the Thunderbird and other "big birds" are biological creatures, then it's hard to understand why no physical evidence of them has ever been preserved. All we have in the way of hard evidence for them is only what is typically found in the cryptozoological, or mystery animal realm—the word of the witnesses themselves.

There was a farmer in Crawford County, Pennsylvania, who supposedly captured a Thunderbird in 1898. He said he caught it when it was feeding on a dead cow. Witnesses described this creature as three-to-six feet tall, with a wingspan of over fifteen feet. The farmer apparently assumed he had captured an Andean or Californian Condor, despite its much larger size. However, nobody today seems to have any idea what happened to it.

There is another paranormal aspect of the "big bird" mystery that truly threatens to turn any attempt at rational theorizing on its head. As charming as the mystery begins, with "Grandfather" Thunderbird, it just may end in a place of nightmares. According to a significant body of literature on the subject, it seems that the mystery tends to morph, somehow, into what is quite possibly the most bizarre and frightening of all paranormal phenomena: Mothman.

The Mothman phenomenon, presented in blood-chilling detail by John Keel in his book, *Mothman Prophecies*, is an apparition of intense Evil. It sometimes resembles a Thunderbird, minus its head, with a large pair of burning red eyes centered squarely in its chest. Other times, Mothman may resemble a giant moth, or even a hideous cross between a man and a moth. Mothman is said to carry with it calamity, death, and malignant curses. Although most of us probably wish Mothman would go away, it appears that whatever this bizarre aspect of the "big bird" mystery is, it is here with us to stay.

Tom Downey's a rational, laid-back guy. He says he doesn't know what it was, exactly, that erupted from that dark country road in front of him over forty years ago. For him, it remains a mystery. Some kind of giant, unknown bird, maybe. But he definitely doesn't buy the opinions of all those crazies that came to his doorstep after the sighting, raving about Mothman and similar nonsense. It's not that Tom isn't willing to entertain the idea that things outside the realm of science exist. He just doesn't feel, in his gut, that he saw something like that.

Today, Tom's stance on his sighting is remarkably similar to that of other credible witnesses of unexplained events in the Hockomock.

"I saw what I saw," Tom says firmly. "I stand behind what I saw."

And like the other credible witnesses, there's really no reason to doubt him. Why? Because by going public with his sighting, Officer Downey had nothing to gain by it, and everything to lose.

Like other credible witnesses of unexplained phenomena all around the world, Tom Downey spoke out simply because it was the right thing to do. We should applaud him, and all the others, for having the moral courage to do so.

It all started in Taunton, Massachusetts, at 9 Railroad Avenue, the site of the old Tony Rose Farm.

"He had been clawed to shreds," said Mrs. Johnson, who was referring to Irving, her goat.

Mrs. Johnson said she had once seen a large animal on her land that was black with a white mask, that she thought was a dog, and that had sometimes bothered her goat. But she didn't think that animal could have killed the goat.

"I thought at first some kind of wild cat had done it, but there couldn't be any animals of that sort in this area... [but] I can't imagine how a dog could have done such a job to the goat, who stood fairly high and had a good set of horns. Also, we were home the night the goat was killed, but we didn't hear any barking."

The family had found Iving the goat dead in their yard, along with four dead ducks.

They found some tracks, too. Big tracks.

The Johnsons' neighbor, Mrs. Dunham, who also found tracks in her yard, described them as being "as large as the top of a two pound coffee can," an estimate with which Mrs. Johnson concurred. Tracks were also found along the railroad tracks at the end of the street. Frank Dunham, Mrs. Dunham's son, said that he had glimpsed a "large animal" on those railroad tracks earlier that year.

Recalling that event, Frank said he had gone outside when he heard the family dog barking.

"The dog ran to the railroad tracks, where some kind of yellowish-black animal seemed to be walking. Then our dog reared up, made a fast turn, and ran back to the house." Frank added that the dog was intimately familiar with the native animals, so whatever it was that had caused it to run must have been a "strange" animal.

Both the Johnsons and the Dunhams mentioned that if the animal that had invaded their yards had been a dog, their own dogs would have challenged it, creating a ruckus they surely would have heard. But neither of them had heard a peep.

The Taunton Police and a representative from the Massachusetts Department of Natural Resources investigated this sighting, but they did not come to any definite conclusions.

"The man from the Department of Natural Resources was unable to identify the animal that left those prints," said Mrs. Dunham. "He implied that they were too large to be a dog's." The creature later came back to the area and killed another duck.

Then, on Sunday, July 9th, Douglas Horton of 18 Center Street looked over at the grounds of the Bristol County Agricultural School and saw an African lioness staring back at him. The school property was adjacent to his own, and just through the woods from the Railroad Avenue neighborhood where Mrs. Johnson and Mrs. Dunham lived.

Horton told the Dighton Police that the lioness was about 200 feet away from him, and that he could see her clearly. He said the animal looked right at him, then moved away to the north. The Dighton Police found large prints in a cornfield on the Aggie School property, and were able to photograph them. The prints were approximately ten inches long and four inches wide.

Horton told police that he knew what he was talking about because he had worked in Wild West shows and had learned to recognize many different animals. He apparently believed the animal he had seen was an African lion, because he told police he knew the animal was a lioness because it "had no mane" and it "had a ball of fur at the end of her tail." Later that week, William Clarke, owner of the Hidden Hollows Country Club in Rehoboth, reported seeing a lion.

By this time, reports of lion sightings were flowing in steadily to both the Dighton and Rehoboth Police Departments. The police had warned residents to use caution if they traveled, camped, or fished in wooded areas. In addition to the police, dog officers, game wardens, and other local officials were on high alert. As the frenzy mounted, the Department of Natural Resources made a supply of tranquilizer guns available to local police departments.

Rehoboth Police Chief Roger Bennett tried to make plaster casts of the tracks left in the yard of one Rehoboth woman who had called in a sighting, but the ground was too damp. The woman had complained that the animal had pulled down her badminton net. Rehoboth Police, accompanied by representatives from the Massachusetts Society for the Prevention of Cruelty to Animals, launched searches for the animal, but they couldn't find it.

On Friday, July 14th, two men from the Department of Natural Resources armed themselves with dart guns and together with the Rehoboth Police, went on safari. They searched the wooded areas in which the animal had been seen. The cops tried to track the animal with dogs, but later said it was too hot, and the ground was too damp, for the dogs to pick up the animal's scent. It is unclear whether they ended up scrambling a helicopter to the scene of the chase, which they had seriously considered doing.

In the meantime, to complicate the situation even further, a woman in Seekonk reported that her pet ocelot was missing. She described Sasha as being "about two feet long and about fourteen inches high," and looking "like a miniature leopard." The only other exotic animal that was reported as gone missing was a coyote from the Records Brothers Wild Animal Show in North Kingston, Rhode Island. Nothing was reported missing that remotely resembled a lion.

It seems that nobody, at this point, was really sure whether they were chasing a lion or a huge dog. On the day of the safari, the Dighton Police told the paper that a zoologist from the Franklin Park Zoo in Boston had identified the tracks at the Aggie School as those of a lion. But curiously, they also stated that they had not yet eliminated the possibility that the animal was a large dog. The Southwick Animal Farm in Boston had expressed interest in obtaining the animal if it was captured.

In the end, they didn't catch the elusive cat, or whatever it was. On Monday, July 17th, the Rehoboth cops announced that it was still on the loose. The cops were now, however, referring to the creature as a "mountain lion," apparently based on the fact that an unidentified woman, who had accompanied the police and described herself as a "chemist," had located some tracks in muddy ground near Hidden Hollows Country Club and identified them "as those of a lion or mountain lion." This assessment apparently left open the possibility that the animal was an African lion. The woman said that the tracks she and a male companion had found were headed towards Dighton.

After the safari, no new reports were called in. Both the Rehoboth Police and the Department of Natural Resources backed off from the case. Chief Bennett, perhaps tired of the public hysteria and endless phone calls, said that "the mystery may cause some residents to imagine that they have seen or heard a lion." He also said that the police weren't planning on investigating any more reports unless there was conclusive evidence, such as tracks. The DNC had been working straight out on the case for four days in a fruitless attempt to capture the animal. They too said that they would not be sending out any more representatives unless additional, conclusive evidence of the creature surfaced.

The coyote, described as looking like a small German Shepherd, and Sasha, the little spotted ocelot, were still on the lamb, but nobody seriously connected them with the case of the vanishing lion. It was over. The "lion" of Rehoboth, or whatever it was, was never seen again.

In 1972, the Hockomock region was a place defined by turbulence, confusion, and strife. The appearance of the mystery "lion" seemed to be just one more symptom of a pervasive madness that had inflicted the region and the world. In April, 100 long-haired Bridgewater State College students marched on the local National Guard Armory in protest of the Vietnam War. Forty-five of them were arrested. The unrest at Bridgewater spread to other area colleges. Seemingly unaffected, the war raged on; towards the end of the year, even as peace proposals were finally debated, the American bombing in Vietnam escalated significantly.

James Mosely, considered at the time to be one of America's foremost experts on flying saucers, spoke to the students at Bridgewater in their student union.

To their surprise, Mosely told his audience that based on the extremely high frequency and wide distribution of current UFO sightings, it was not probable that they were from another solar system. Instead, said Mosely, UFOs coexist with us here on Earth, and they may even be from another dimension that humans have not yet probed.

On the conservation front, John Ames III was upset because even though he had gotten the Wetlands Purchase Act of 1971 passed, the state was still not buying up land to preserve the Hockomock. Meanwhile, Cumberland Farms, a convenience store chain, had been very busy doing just that. They had purchased some 450 acres of prime Hockomock meadowland along Route 24 to graze their herd of dairy cattle.

To make matters worse for him, one year later, in 1973, the Massachusetts Bay Transportation Authority (MBTA) would purchase from the former railroad the rail bed that John's ancestor, Oliver Ames, Jr., had built back in the 1860s. The purchase of this rail bed, that runs straight through the Hockomock Swamp Area of Critical Environmental Concern (ACEC) that John's legislation helped establish, practically ensured that the route would remain a permanent option for any future development of the region's railways.

At the Massachusetts Correctional Institution at Bridgewater, two sex offenders escaped from the bakery and were pursued by 200 men and the usual pack of dogs.

By 1972, tensions between Native Americans and the general population in the Unites States in 1972 had reached a new peak. On November 24th, Indians boarded the *Mayflower* replica in Plymouth in a Thanksgiving Day protest.

On December 8, a suspicious fire, the cause of which was never determined, destroyed the reception center at Plymouth Plantation.

The "Rehoboth lion," though a shock to area residents, was hardly a unique occurrence. It was part of a well-known, universal phenomena known as "mystery cats." Today, mysterious large cats like the Rehoboth lion are routinely seen in Britain, Australia, the United States, and other parts of the world. These cats are typically described as resembling *Puma concolor*, the cat species commonly known to Americans as cougar, mountain lion, panther, or puma. Some of the reports describe smaller animals that are closer to the size of a lynx or bobcat. Thousands of these reports emanate from areas in which there are no big cats, or very few of them.

In the Eastern United States, mountain lions ranged from Maine to Florida until humans forced them into extinction in the late 1800s. These animals weighed approximately 105 pounds (females) to 140 pounds (males). Their main prey was white-tailed deer, the major game animal in the Hockomock. This mountain lion subspecies is known as the Eastern Cougar, *Puma concolor couguar*.

The last record of an Eastern Cougar in Massachusetts was in 1858. The U.S. Fish and Wildlife Service placed them on the List of Endangered and Threatened Wildlife in 1973, and they are still protected by the Endangered Species Act. Today, like black bears, the big cats are gradually starting to reappear in Southern New England, although scientists are not sure whether the cats popping up are the same subspecies that inhabited the area originally.

However, in the 20th century, the time frame in which the Rehoboth lion was sighted, the only surviving population of mountain lions was in the Florida Everglades. Despite this fact, however, reports of large, mysterious cats resembling mountain lions have been steadily received from most of the Eastern states throughout the 20th century to the present day.

Mystery cat sightings typically involve a muscular, mountain lion-like creature at least five or six feet long, two-and-a-half to four feet tall, and sporting a long tail at least two-and-a-half feet long. A few sightings even describe creatures that look like African lions, complete with a mane.

However, these sightings don't always involve a creature that looks exactly like a cat. Sometimes, people who get a good look at them aren't sure what they are looking at, and later describe the creature as "cat-like." And sometimes, witnesses cannot say for certain whether the creature they saw was a cat or a dog. No matter what they look like, however, mystery cats are routinely described as "ferocious," and sometimes even "evil looking." In general, mystery cats have a reputation as very, very bad characters.

A significant percentage, maybe a third, of mystery cat sightings in the Eastern U.S. involve a pure black animal. These sightings are particularly baffling to scientists, as black panthers are virtually unknown in Zoology. Leopards are sometimes black, but they live in Africa and Asia, not in the United States.

It seems reasonable to assume that the mountain lions that have started popping up in isolated parts of their old range in the Eastern United States have generated some of the overall mystery cat sightings. Some of the creatures that are spotted are probably escaped pets or circus animals. And many of the "mystery cats" that are seen are probably other animals, such as large dogs, feral cats, or possibly unknown species resulting from unions between feral and wild cat species.

But nonetheless, there remains a small core of sightings by credible witnesses in this arena that cannot be easily explained away. And at the very heart of the mystery cat enigma in America is the fact that nobody can reasonably account for the many mystery cat sightings that involve *black* animals. These animals simply don't exist.

Another aspect of the mystery cat phenomenon that puzzles wildlife experts is the boldness of these creatures. Mountain lions are by nature secretive animals. And mystery cats, apparently, are anything but. They regularly appear in the open, even in the daytime, and seem to have no fear of man. In fact, by most accounts these creatures appear to hate our species.

Mystery cats have a tendency to commit acts of ultra-violence against both us and our domestic livestock. Many of the encounters reported with them involve some sort of vicious physical attack.

Large mystery cats are commonly seen in areas where farmers have reported massive killings of farm animals. These creatures do things like destroy a herd of fifty sheep in a night. Some incidents involve the deaths of very large cattle such as 1,000-pound bulls.

Another rather frightening aspect of these attacks is that mystery cats don't always kill for food. Oftentimes, reports of farm animals killed in areas where mystery cat sightings have occurred clearly involve killing merely for killing's sake. Heads, legs, intestines scattered everywhere, with no body parts consumed, as if the unknown perpetrator had killed simply for the joy of it. These body parts often display very large claw marks on them.

Mystery cats are often witnessed in areas where other strange creatures and events abound, such as UFOs, Bigfoot, and black dogs. Many people who study the paranormal, in fact, believe that the black variety of mystery cats are a sort of "modern version" of the black dog, or hell hound, that in traditional folklore represents Death. These circumstances have led some observers to credit mystery cats with the "cattle mutilations" that sometimes accompany events involving UFOs and other paranormal phenomena. In the Hockomock, cattle mutilations have occurred historically in the Freetown State Forest. These mysterious and grisly incidents have been investigated but never solved.

Mystery cats are often described as having glowing yellow, green, or red eyes. They commonly leave very large, five-toed cat-like tracks, which trackers often associate with an animal of at least 300 pounds. These tracks typically are longer than they are broad, and show partial claw marks, which is very strange because panthers have retractable claws that don't show in their tracks. And sometimes, unaccountably, the prints of mystery cats are sunk deeply into hard ground.

No mystery cat in the United States has ever been shot dead, or captured for that matter, despite numerous attempts. This is quite strange, for hunters routinely run mountain lions up a tree with a pack of hunting dogs and then shoot them. In contrast, mystery cats typically disappear, seemingly into thin air, when chased. If they are treed, they are somehow able to jump into other, nearby trees and get away. Oftentimes, once the hunters get anywhere near the mystery cat, their otherwise courageous hunting dogs will cower, seemingly terrified, grow silent, and refuse to chase the creature at all. Dogs, when it comes to certain things, just seem to know better.

A significant percentage of the mystery cat accounts in the literature involve attacks on passengers in motor vehicles. It seems that if you encounter a mystery cat while you are driving, your car's engine may fail. The giant felines seem to share with UFOs this ability to stop engines. The enormous cat may then assault, as in crash into, your vehicle. Based on existing reports, at that point you definitely *do not* want to get out.

If you do get out of your vehicle, you will probably discover quite quickly that even if the cat hit your car, it is not hurt. Mystery cats typically fight while standing on their hind legs. The huge cat will most likely come at you that way, out of the darkness, screeching and making monster noises. It will seem as if it is consumed with rage at the mere fact that you exist.

Mystery cats are very strong and fast. After charging you, the cat will most likely begin to pummel you with powerful blows, using its two front paws like a boxer. At the same time, it will try to rip you with its claws and bite you with its sharp fangs. The cat will beat and claw you to within an inch of your life, assuming, that is, you are able to fight it off, which you can usually do if you give it your all.

And there is one more thing you should keep in mind, if you are unlucky enough to be involved in such an incident. If you manage to shoot the cat, don't expect it to die. History demonstrates clearly that not much, if anything, will happen to it when it is struck by your bullets.

Mystery cats have historically been reported in the Hockomock area, most notably in the Towns of Mansfield, Easton, Bridgewater, Norton, and Rehoboth.

By far the most dramatic and credible episode involving a mystery cat in the region was the terrifying and inexplicable appearance of the lion in the Rehoboth/Dighton area in the summer of 1972. This "lion" was a classic mystery cat of the very large variety. Another one of these elusive big cats, which is said to resemble a black puma, is so well known in the Hockomock today that locally it has earned the name "The Phantom."

Another well-publicized mystery cat episode that occurred in the Hockomock involved a cat of the smaller variety, closer to the size of a bobcat than a cougar. This curious feline was sighted on numerous occasions in both Norton and Stoughton in the spring of 1993. Stoughton Police Officers Robert Bohn and Michael Williams, responding to a call from a homeowner in early April of that year, reported observing a golden-colored cat weighing thirty to forty pounds, that was hunting birds in some reeds. The homeowner that had called them described it as "two-to-two-and-a-half feet tall, and eighteen inches high." The police said it looked like "Morris the Cat on Steroids."

When the mystery cat fled from the cops, it jumped four feet in the air and cleared a ten-foot-wide drainage ditch without even touching the banks. The officers said it was definitely not a cougar. Some members of the Stoughton Police Department, however, started calling this creature the "Commuter Rail Cougar" because it was seen so often near the railroad line. Nobody ever figured out exactly what this animal was, and like its larger cousin, the Rehoboth "lion," it was never caught.

Rehoboth, Massachusetts, lies directly to the north of Massasoit's former seat of power in Bristol and Mount Hope, Rhode Island. Historically it was, in a sense, the great chief's front yard.

Rehoboth is also where the intrepid Captain Benjamin Church repelled down the face of Annawon Rock and finally captured Annawon, Philip's wizened, battle-hardened war chief. It is the place where King Philip's War, at least in southeastern Massachusetts, ended, the place where the Wampanoags' dream of pushing the English colonists back into the sea died. Rehoboth is, for the Wampanoag Tribe, an extremely ancient place, one that today also symbolizes bitterness and defeat. Of all the places in the Hockomock, Rehoboth is one place that Hobbamock might still be expected to frequent.

Was Hobbamock summoned up by a modern-day Indian shaman, or perhaps by members of a local cult, in Rehoboth, Massachusetts, in June 1972? If an evil spirit was summoned, either intentionally or unintentionally, might it have chosen to manifest itself in the form of a *mountain lion*?

From accounts of Hobbamock from the 1600s, we know that these evil spirits are said to have manifested themselves in forms that were peculiarly frightening to those people to whom they appeared. The Rehoboth lion certainly conformed to that pattern. As a fellow inhabitant of the Hockomock region in the 1600s, the Eastern cougar would certainly have been a familiar, if not outright revered, animal to the local Wampanoags.

If summoned, would such an evil spirit have chosen to obtain vengeance on the inhabitants of its tribe's former lands by *slaughtering domestic animals in Rehoboth?* History tells us that the Wampanoags hated the colonists' domesticated animals, such as the cattle, horses, and goats that trampled their fields, as much or even more than the colonists themselves. We also know that Tispaquin, Philip's war chief, and his warriors made a regular practice of slaughtering these animals, and that they did so in the most brutal and offensive ways possible in order to get their point across.

"But the idea of an evil spirit manifesting itself as a lion is simply ridiculous!" you might say, and perhaps rightly so. And yet, we must ask ourselves: Is this possibility more ridiculous than that of an *actual lion* creating mayhem in *Rehoboth, Massachusetts,* in the summer of 1972?

BLACK SHUCK
APRIL 30, 1976 A.D.

It was a peaceful spring night. A huge form, blacker than the surrounding gloom, floated over the fence of the corral that lay behind the peaceful home. The two sleeping ponies inside the paddock stirred, and began to neigh and snort in fright. But no one ever heard their cries, for they died too quickly, their throats torn out of their bodies.

At 7 a.m. that morning, a Friday, 12-year-old Melissa went out, as she always did, to feed her beloved pets. As she approached the corral in the low morning light, the girl hurried forward in sudden confusion, for she had tethered her ponies to trees inside the fence the previous evening, and now she couldn't see their silhouettes. She knew that ponies don't sleep laying down.

"Sprinkles?! Tommy?! Where are you?!"

Instead of the welcoming whinnies the girl expected, her call was met with a long, low growl. And then she saw them.

Her ponies were clearly dead. They were both laying with legs splayed in the dirt, covered in blood. A lot of blood. And crouched over one of them was a very large, dark, and monstrous thing. Whatever it was, it had its head down, and appeared to be tearing at the flesh of one of the fallen ponies.

Then, slowly and deliberately, the creature brought its massive head up and regarded the girl. The creature that stood there in the low light of morning, looking straight at her, was coal black, with a gray chest. Its entire head, neck, and chest were dripping blood. The beast gazed at the little girl silently and intently, with large, glimmering eyes that sent terror straight into her soul. It looked like a dog, but it was bigger—far bigger—than any dog she had ever seen.

"DAAAADDYYYYYYY!!" the girl screamed, over and over again, as sheer terror coursed through her body.

Jimmy Beale, busy fixing breakfast inside the house, knew in his heart exactly what that cry meant. He reached the back of his home in seconds, took one look out the window, and then went for his gun.

"Run!!" he shouted at his daughter, then, as the creature turned to flee, Beale raised his rifle and fired at it. He must of missed. The creature fled into the woods behind the house, and got away.

Then Jimmy Beale did what any good father would do in that situation. He went to collect his distraught little girl, and began the long, painful process of picking up the pieces of her shattered world.

The disturbing event portrayed above occurred on April 30, 1976, in Abington, Massachusetts, at the home of Jimmy Beale. Jimmy, at the time an Abington Firefighter, reported it to the local police that morning. The police later reported that the dog weighed around 150 pounds, and that it looked like a cross between a German Shepherd and a Doberman Pinscher.

The cops asked around the neighborhood, trying to find out who owned it, but the locals told them they had never seen a dog like that one around. The cops, who had never heard of a dog that big single-handedly killing anything as big as a pony, put out the word that the dog was on the loose, and that since it had tasted blood it might attack humans. They warned everyone to take precautionary measures.

People panicked. Residents who owned horses locked them up inside. Kids were told they couldn't play outside that weekend. Then, terrified, the townspeople of Abington went for their guns.

The Abington cops fielded a ten-man unit to catch the huge black dog. They issued a "shoot to kill" order that even the MSPCA supported. Police Officer Frank Curran caught sight of the frightening monstrosity that afternoon, as it moved slowly along railroad tracks near the Abington/Whitman town line, off Route 58. Curran shot at it with a shotgun at a distance of approximately seventy-five yards, but apparently he missed, because the huge, black beast simply walked away and disappeared. There were no further attacks reported on Friday.

Meanwhile, the Abington cops were swamped with hundreds of phone calls from people that said they had seen the "Killer Dog." The police spokesman said that they discounted most of the reports, however, noting that: "Every time they see a big dog, we get a call."

On Saturday morning, a 9-year-old girl who lived on Centre Avenue in Abington was shot in the leg when a gun her brother was unloading accidentally discharged. The boy said he had armed himself in case the dog came into their yard.

That Monday, with the town on high alert, Jimmy Beale told the newspapers, "I'm concerned for the safety of other people's animals and children. I hope the police catch it soon and kill it." But Jimmy Beale's wish was not to be. Later that week, the cops were clearly coming up empty.

One officer said, "We think the dog has been taken in by somebody. We don't think it's still loose."

Another, perhaps more realistic member of the force said he thought the beast may have rejoined a pack of wild dogs that might be hiding on a small island "in the nearby swamp." At any rate, the huge, black beast that so mercilessly slaughtered Sprinkles and Tommy disappeared, and was never seen again.

There were plenty of crazed dogs running rampant around the Hockomock region in the 1970s. In 1976, most towns in the area, including Abington, were just implementing leash laws. Many of these dogs were loose domestic animals, some of them were semi-wild, and a few, for all practical purposes, were wild. In 1972, Benjamin Flynn, the dog officer in nearby Attleboro, reported that up to 250 dogs, most injured or underfed, had been dumped recently in the area. Flynn had once attempted to stop a man who was wildly unloading dogs from a pickup on an unfinished section of Route 295. He had to jump off the road when the man accelerated his truck towards him and made his getaway, running over several unfortunate dogs in the process.

There had also been numerous attacks on farm animals in the area in 1976.

In February, a pack of at least two dogs had attacked and killed three sheep and injured twelve more in East Bridgewater. The animals were being raised by children for a 4-H Club project. The local police said it was the third attack on farm animals by dogs in the last three years.

In areas such as Middleboro, there were large packs of wild dogs that were certainly strong enough, and bold enough, to take down large domesticated animals, and also pose a real threat to humans. But these dogs typically hunted in packs, and they killed animals smaller than ponies. A lone dog of such tremendous size killing two ponies on its own was considered to be a highly unusual event.

For at least 500 years, people the world over have witnessed ghostly black dogs. Today, so many ghostly black dogs are reported in England and other countries, including the United States and Canada, that dedicated web sites exist to track them. These creatures of the moors and marshlands are so well known in rural England today that their names are household words.

In the region of East Anglia, England, these mysterious creatures are still called by their traditional folklore name, "Black Shuck." "Shuck" is an ancient word, probably derived from the Old English "scucca," meaning "devil." Other names for the black dog in England, depending on the locality, include "Guytrash," or simply "Trash," "Padfoot," and "Skriker." In Scotland, black dogs are known as the "Muckle Black Tyke."

Sir Conan Doyle was so taken by local stories of Black Shuck he heard at the Royal Links Hotel in West Runton that he based aspects of one of his most famous Sherlock Holmes mysteries on them. *The Hound of the Baskervilles*, published in 1901-1902, is based on the legend of an actual 17th century English squire that is said to have sold his soul to the Devil. It relates a haunting tale of an ancient curse that doomed successive generations of the Baskerville family to death by hell hound.

Some say the legend of the black dog in England originated in the middle ages when that country, particularly East Anglia, was ravaged by the Vikings. The Vikings came very close to conquering all of England in the latter part of the 9th century before they were defeated by Alfred the Great, who was then King of Wessex.

The Norse Vikings arrived in the company of giant war dogs that they used to terrorize the English people. In Norse mythology, Thor, the god of thunder, had a dog named "Shukr." Odin, the Viking's reigning god at the time, was himself said to travel with a pack of hell hounds.

One of the earliest, and most famous accounts of the black dog phenomena was recorded in England in 1577. The original document recording the event, now held by the British Museum, describes it as follows:

> Tempest in Suffolk.—On Sundaie the fourth of August, between the hours of nine and ten of the clocke in the forenoone, whilest the Minister was reading of the second lesson in the Parish Churche of Bliborough, a Towne in Suffolk, a strange and terrible Tempest of Lightning and Thunder strake through the wall of the same Churche into the ground, almost a yard deepe, drave down all the people on that side above twentie persons, then renting the wall up to the Vestrie, clefte the doore, and returning to the Steeple, rent the timber, brake the Chimes, and fled towards Bongie, a Towne six miles off. The people that were stricken downe were found groveling more than half an houre after, wherof, one man more than fortie yeares, and a boi of fifteene yeares old were found starke dead: the others were scorched.

The document goes on to describe similar damage and serious injuries wrought during the same storm at the Parish Church of Bongay, which lay several miles off near the City of Norwich. This account was subsequently fictionalized to include graphic descriptions of a black dog killing churchgoers in the "Suffolk Literary Chronicle" by Abraham Fleming, an English rector and a prolific author who died in 1607. Fleming perceived this event, and framed it in his piece, as a direct warning from the Lord to mankind to abandon our sinful ways.

Fleming writes the following admonition in his Preface to the Reader:

> The occasion that I have wrote this warning, (which I would to God I had the grace to followe), was a wonder lately wrought in Norfolke, and so lately wrought, that the terrour of the same is at this instant freshe in memorie. A spectacle, no doubt, of God's judgement, which, as the fire of our iniquities hath kindled, so, by none other meanes then by the teares of repentance, it may bee quenched.

Fleming's story, which characterizes the murderous black dog as an incarnation of the Devil, may be based on more than just a fertile imagination considering the tragic events caused by a thunderstorm of seldom-seen magnitude. That is because in the title of the original document describing these tragic events is a crude drawing *of a black dog*.

It is questionable, to say the least, whether the churchgoers at Bliborough and Bongay actually saw a creature that resembled a black dog on that dark, confusing, and frightening day in 1577. Perhaps what is significant about this account is not whether the dog was actually present, but how the people at that time and in that place *perceived* the deadly events that transpired. Clearly, they perceived them as a function of God's wrath, and they *naturally associated these events with the black dog as an earthly manifestation of the Devil.*

Those people who are schooled in folklore and the ways of the hell hound fear it more than anything else in this world, or any other world, for that matter. This is not so much because of the frightening appearance of the beast, nor even its ability to inflict sudden, violent death when encountered. Those in the know fear it most because seeing the hell hound means that you are cursed, or damned. That is, if you are unfortunate enough to see Black Shuck, you, or someone else in your immediate family, is probably going to die quite soon. Folklore informs us that this is especially the case if you dared to meet the gaze of the creature's glowing red eyes.

It is somewhat of a relief to know that there are notable exceptions to this rule. It appears to matter which black dog you meet out there, in the darkness, in regards to what happens to you later. For example, some black dogs are not malevolent, but on the contrary, seem bent only on helping lost travelers find their way.

This version of Shuck, though still ghostly, is friendly in comparison to his brutal counterpart. He will patter up next to you, out of the gloom, and pace along beside you for a while before simply disappearing into thin air. That is, he will patter up to you, but you won't actually hear him coming. The black dog is sometimes known as "Padfoot" because his gait is always silent. He will howl terribly, though, at times, out there in the marshes, and disturb your sleep.

Shuck's ties with death go deeper than acting as the bearer of it to unfortunate witnesses. For centuries the black dog has been recognized in world folklore as the gatekeeper to the Afterworld, and the Protector of the Dead. He is usually encountered at night, and often near water. The black dog seems to favor abandoned routes of human travel, such as defunct roadways and paths.

He is often seen literally standing at the entrance to a gate, or where a gate used to be long ago. Shuck is also frequently found in cemeteries, especially ancient ones near churches, that were probably built on ley lines. Ley lines (pronounced "lay") are geophysical pathways of earth energy, along which ancient peoples in Britain and elsewhere regularly built roads and churches. Ley lines were, and sometimes still are, considered to be natural routes for the spirits. Some people speculate that the black dog frequents these lines, and the church cemeteries built along them, both as part of its role as Protector of the Dead and as a spirit in its own right.

Most cultures, in fact, believe that the black dog is not a dog at all, but a sort of demon, an apparition that chooses to takes the form of a dog. This belief is based on a long history of incidents during which unfortunate witnesses see the dog vanish, attempt to touch it but have their hand pass through it, or actually see through the creatures "physical" form.

Other characteristics of this creature that seem to place it in an otherworldly context are its glowing red eyes and its massive size. Witnesses often report this creature to be "as high as a table top," or sometimes even "the size of a calf." The "black dog" that is witnessed is not always black. In fact, among other shades, it may actually be white.

On a final note, it seems that the black dog, whether biological creature or spiritual being, is becoming increasingly rare in our world. Strange as it may seem, there is a general consensus among observers of these types of phenomena that in the places where the black dog roamed in eons past, it is being systematically displaced by black pumas. In fact, in recent times, these two distinct types of creatures have seemed, somehow, to merge. Witness are often unable to say, exactly, whether the large black creature they saw was of the cat or dog variety. This is yet another mysterious aspect of the creature that acts as fodder for those who believe that it is an apparition.

As they are elsewhere in the world, black dog encounters in the Hockomock are rare today. Somewhat more common there, however, are encounters with the mystery cat known as "The Phantom," a jet-black puma. Based on the universal trend described above, these encounters may well be, in some way, related to the much older black dog phenomenon.

How might Jimmy Beale's black dog incident fit into the universal mythology of the black dog? There are several aspects of it that bear note, the most obvious of which were the creature's size and color. A 150-plus-pound dog would match nicely both the "high as a table top" and "size of a calf" descriptions so routinely provided by black dog witnesses. And despite the fact that the dog in Abington may have had a gray chest, it was routinely described by witnesses as "black."

Other aspects of the "Abington Killer Dog" incident are also reminiscent of Black Shuck. The dog's appearance was accompanied by extreme violence, terror, and death.

Many reported encounters with black dogs involve bullets passing through them with no effect. Beale somehow missed a 150-pound target, in his backyard, with a rifle. And when Officer Frank Curran, a trained marksman, shot directly at the creature, he apparently missed as well. Curran's miss is more understandable, as the accuracy of a shotgun at seventy-five yards is questionable.

And finally, in keeping with all black dog sightings in history, Abington's black dog, despite rigorous and valiant attempts by police, was never caught.

If this strange event actually did represent a legitimate appearance of a ghostly black dog, then why did it appear in Abington in 1976? We know that dogs have historically played a major role in shamanism as guards of and guides to the Underworld. Today, black dogs are a staple of cult lore and ritual. Satanic cults regularly sacrifice dogs such as German Shepherds in their ritualistic ceremonies. Is it possible that the mysterious "Killer Dog" of Abington was really something evil, that was either summoned up by one of the satanic cults known to have been practicing in the Hockomock in the 1970s, or appeared on its own volition?

Did the Devil appear in Abington in the early morning hours of April 30, 1976? Or was it just an enormous black dog? In the end, the answers to these questions may be irrelevant. Because the reality is, to that poor little girl who stood there staring at her beloved dead pets on that tragic spring morning so long ago, the distinction between these two questions is meaningless.

Melissa Beale, like the terrorized churchgoers at the Churche of Bliborough four centuries before her, must have had no doubt that the Devil came to her that morning, bearing terror and death. And he came to her in the form of a great *black dog*.

CLAYBANKS
APRIL, 1978

Joe DeAndrade was very afraid that freezing April morning, so afraid that he couldn't think or move. For just 200 feet away, across tiny Claybanks Pond, lurched a giant, Frankenstein-like creature: Immense, thick-skulled, wide-shouldered, and covered with long, thick, brown hair.

"Wayne!!" he whispered urgently to the man by his side. "Wayne—TURN AROUND."

Despite his fear, Joe realized that he needed another witness. But fate was against him, for a man who is lighting his pipe is not easily distracted. In exasperation, Joe spun around, yanked Wayne's shoulder hard, and spun back only to see the creature's massive, hairy skull dropping out of sight behind the small ridge on the far side of the pond.

"WAYNE, PLEASE!"

His companion, hunched down against the cold in his plaid wool jacket, finally mumbled the classic pipe-mumble and turned to look. But it was too late—the creature had vanished. Joe was left only with his fear, his anger, and the numbing cold.

"Let's get out of here," he said, thoroughly disgusted.

It's a hard thing to see the unexplained. Joe DeAndrade didn't know it then, but this 25-year old underprivileged kid from Bridgewater, Massachusetts wasn't going anywhere, wasn't leaving anything behind. One brief interval in time had irrevocably altered the course of his existence. Joe would spend the rest of his life struggling to understand what he had seen that day on the other side of Claybanks Pond, and trying to convince others that whatever he had seen was real. Like others around the globe that witness unexplained phenomena each day, Joe had become, whether he liked it or not, part of a world that remains unsanctioned, even scorned, by both science and society.

For Joe, the events of that day had originated many months before with Miram, the local Wampanoag boy.

"He's in there," Miram had told Joe matter-of-factly, referring to the monster that was rumored to inhabit the Claybanks area of ponds and streams that lays close to the Town River in Bridgewater. "My people have always known about Sasquatch."

Over and again, Miram related the stories: How he and his Dad had hunted the Claybanks area when he was a kid, how they had once shot something they thought was a black bear, but it had screamed like a human when hit. How his grandfather, a seasoned hunter, had been unable to identify the long, brown hairs they later found plastered with blood to the leaves on the forest floor. And how once, while hunting, they had startled a large animal near the Town River that had fled into the woods. After descending to the spot by the river where it had crouched, they found several large fish floating, dead, in a quiet pool surrounded by Highbush blueberry.

And strangest of all, Miram told Joe how his Native American relations routinely explained the ephemeral capabilities of this beast by the existence of a hidden, subterranean tunnel that led to a "secret chamber" beneath the pond. On, and on, Miram's stories about Sasquatch continued.

Eventually, Joe's natural curiosity peaked, and he decided to investigate Miram's claims. So he called up his old friend Wayne, and convinced him to accompany him into the area. Together, they started to go "in there," slogging through the reedy marshes, around the little ponds, and across the connecting rivers, looking for signs. They called these trips "patrols" so they would sound more official. They didn't find anything right away. Miram got pretty defensive about their lack of success, so after some hard words, Joe and Wayne dumped him as an exploring partner. On the day of the fateful hairy monster sighting, Joe and Wayne had gone in there alone, after a fresh snowfall, searching for tracks.

Claybanks is a small body of water, only about an acre in size. It's sunk down right near a couple of main roads, so when you're "in there" you can almost always hear cars humming by. Occasionally, you hear the distant "Toot, TOOT!" of a train whistle from nobody-knows-where. In short, it's a small woods, just like all the small woods scattered across America. Definitely not the kind of place that you would expect to encounter a Bigfoot.

On the fateful day of the sighting, Joe and Wayne, since they both still lived at home, dutifully said good-bye to their moms. Then they slipped into their puffy, 1970s-style ski jackets and scratchy wool hats, and headed down the path that leads from Pleasant Street in Bridgewater down into Claybanks. They clapped their hands together and breathed on them as they strode along, and watched their steamy breath rise up through the cold air. Spent shotgun shells and beer cans peppered the sides of the path, along with the occasional abandoned car tire. The two joked and laughed, just typical, small-town American kids glad to be out of the house, away from their parents, away from the worry surrounding their futures, and happy to be doing something, anything, even if it was kind of screwed up.

Joe, with a wide smile on his face, told his friend that this was exactly what he should be doing—exploring, being an adventurer. Taking pictures of what he saw. Problem was, he couldn't get anyone to hire him to do it. Wayne laughed at that and told him that it wasn't easy getting a job you liked. He asked Joe if he remembered that lousy shoe factory job his father made him get when Joe dropped out of high school, and then he asked him if his father was still working there.

"Yep," said Joe. "He'll be over there until he retires. If they paid him a fair wage, he'd be a millionaire by now. I've never seen anyone work harder than he does. Thank God, I only worked there for a little while."

Wayne asked Joe what he had done at the factory. Joe told him that there were many different things you could do at a shoe factory; for example, you could work in the warehouse…but not him. He, unfortunately, had to work next to his father. He told Wayne that his father was an unpleasant person to work with. Joe had done different things at the shoe factory. He would sometimes fetch the lasts—plastic, and shaped like a shoe—then they would build the shoe around the last.

"You're lookin' around for double E, triple E, whatever, then you put 'em on these wooden racks. At least you don't get your fingers cut doin' that. If you operate a machine, you get a little more money, but it's more dangerous.

"There's leather cutters that go *BOOM*; they got this blade shaped with a certain format…you gotta make it bigger than the regular shoe. Upstairs in the cutting room they cut that—and they waste leather like crazy; they don't care, why should they care? And they rush people like crazy, and so people make mistakes… terrible mistakes."

Wayne asked him candidly if it had really been that bad.

"It was a nightmare," replied Joe. "Factories are like Hell. They work you to death, and they pay you crap. If I had to live on my own on that kind of money, I couldn't do it! It's just evil. I'll tell you somethin' right now—if I said 'roles are gonna change' to Management, they'd walk right out that door. I saw one guy work for an hour and leave!"

Wayne asked him how he had lasted there at all. Joe told him he had been taking night classes in photography, which helped him get through the thankless toil during the day.

Suddenly, Joe halted abruptly on the path that led down to the pond. Cursing, he explained to his friend that he had forgotten his camera. Wayne told him not to worry about it, to just keep moving, that he was starting to get cold and wanted to get back to the house. As the pair started walking again, Joe continued his rant.

See, he had been wasting his real talents there, at the shoe factory. He would get up early, go in there, take crap from the boss—it was boring, aggravating, you couldn't talk to anybody, it was so unfair. Then, when he got his check, and it was a joke! An insult! "If you ever saw it, Wayne, you'd say, 'Oh my God!' You got your hands dirty."

See, God had given him a talent—lots of people had complemented him on his pictures—but at the same time, they wouldn't hire him! They were a bunch of hypocrites—they told him how good he was, but they wouldn't hire him!

"Take it easy man," said Wayne, "you'll get there some day. You're only 26 years old." Then he asked Joe how his old man had put up with the place for so many years.

Joe thought about that for a while, then explained to Wayne that his father had grown up in Portugal. On San Miguel, in the Azores. Under that dictator, Salazar. It was a country for the rich. His father used to have to doff his hat to rich folks there. Could he even imagine? There was no opportunity for the regular guy in Portugal. So, his father had seen the shoe factory here in the States as a Godsend. But not Joe. He hated it. It was evil, just another way for the rich to oppress the poor.

The pair finally fell into contemplative silence, trudging softly through the wet snow on the path that was now beginning to circle the pond. It was then that Joe spotted a large impression in the snow, and the duo stopped to examine it. It looked as if a bear, or something else very large, had abruptly planted its hindquarters down. Then Wayne noticed something else, something quite strange.

"There's no footprints around it!" he announced, with a puzzled look, and he was right. The two sat there for a while, scratching their heads, wondering how an animal this big had gotten in and out of there leaving no trail whatsoever.

After examining the massive print, Joe and Wayne continued walking around the pond. Joe spotted something stuck in a hole in the ice, so they walked over to it and Joe wrenched it out. "Look at that, Wayne." It was a dead squirrel, with its jaw gnawed away. Wayne observed shrewdly that something was "probably saving it for later," which caused both of them to hastily take a look around them. Joe stuck the bloody carcass back in its hole, and the two returned to the path and kept walking until they ran up against some fallen trees and dense brush that forced them to turn back.

It was then that Joe got to thinking. They had only two small pocket knives between them with which to defend themselves. Joe knew that if anything big, such as a Sasquatch, did attack them out there, they were probably going to end up badly hurt, or worse. And neither of them had a camera. Even if they saw anything conclusive, he asked himself, how could they ever prove what they saw?

On their way back, Joe and Wayne decided to return to the giant body print. They made another search around it for footprints, but found none but their own. Wayne complained, louder this time, that his feet were freezing, and that he wanted to head back. Joe's feet were okay, but his hands were getting really cold, so he agreed and the two started towards the road. When they got to the front side of the pond, near the access path, they paused to rest. Joe jammed his now-numb hands in his pockets, and Wayne started to light his pipe.

It was there, standing with his back to the pond, that Joe had heard the voice from inside his head. "Turn around quickly!" it said. So he did, and that's when he saw it: the huge, hairy, lumbering brute, descending the ridge on the other side of the pond. Later, Joe estimated that the creature stood at least six feet tall, and weighed at least 400 pounds. He has often wished that he had seen its face, or legs, but he always stuck to his original story of the partial view. Joe even drew a sketch of the monster, a brown crayony-thing, depicting only its back and massive head.

When Joe got over the initial shock of the sighting and could think straight, his lasting impressions of the creature were the massive size of the upper body, bigger than any man's, and the hair, especially the hair. Lots and lots of long, dark brown hair. But there would be no photograph, no absolute proof. Joe would never forgive himself for forgetting his beloved camera that day, and he would never again hike anywhere without it.

That evening, in the warm parlor of the DeAndrades' white farmhouse near the Town River, the site of the original Bridgewater settlement, Joe sat with his family and described to them what he had seen.

His sister, always the difficult one, spoke up first. "Maybe you saw something else, Joe. Your story's hard to believe."

Joe, indignant, tried to convince her that he had no reason to lie, but his sister would not be persuaded. Joe told her that he knew what he saw, and that from what he had heard of Sasquatch, that was it. Furthermore, he said he believed that he was meant to see it.

At this, Joe's father stood up and starting walking out of the room. Then the hardworking Portuguese shoemaker turned, and warned his son that although he might be lazy, he still held the respect of the townspeople. But if he went telling this crazy story…. Joe acknowledged his father's implied statement, but held his ground. He knew what he had seen. His father, incredulous, stormed out in anger, and refused to ever again discuss the sighting. Joe's sister rose abruptly and followed him.

Joe was left there, then, with just his mother, in the Old World parlor with the elaborate red-patterned plates, glassware, and other keepsakes brought long ago from the Azores, the very same islands off Portugal that Miguel Corte-Real of Dighton Rock fame had once called home. "What do you think, Ma?" he pleaded, "Do you believe me?"

Joe's Mother replied very gently that Yes, it was possible he had seen something most out-of-the-ordinary. Then she told him, very seriously, to be careful if he went back in there. Very, very careful. After a long period of silence, his mother cleared her throat, and regarding her son with great kindness, continued talking. This time, she spoke in the sonorous, melodic language of Portugal. She asked her beloved son if he had ever heard the word "clarividência"?

Joe shook his head, no. His mother told him it was a Portuguese word, from the Old World. It meant "someone who can see things that others cannot." At this, Joe lifted his troubled gaze from the floor, and his eyes met hers with hope. His mother continued. When she was a girl—back on San Miguel—she had sometimes seen things. For example, once, in the house at night, she had seen a lantern coming down the stairs, with no one carrying it. She told Joe that she was a clarividência, and thus it was quite possible that he was one as well.

His mother went on to tell him that she knew that he was aware of the dreams that she and his sister had. She told him that she knew that he had them, too. Joe nodded, remembering the dream he had had recently in which his brother had crashed his car and gotten hurt, a few days before it had actually happened. There had been other dreams as well.

Then, looking very seriously at her son, Mrs. DeAndrade continued. She reinforced his father's view by warning him point blank that if he told his story to the people of Bridgewater, they would talk; they would say he was crazy. She added that she knew this from experience. Joe contemplated his mother's words a long time before responding.

"I know Mother," he said. "You're right. But I know what I saw. I have to tell the truth."

Seemingly unsurprised, his mother nodded in agreement. Then she told him to do what he thought was right—for that was the important thing in life. If he did that, the Lord Jesus Christ would always be with him. As a devout Christian, that statement made an impact on Joe, and helped him form his decision to talk.

In the end, some of the people of Bridgewater believed Joe's story about what happened at Claybanks, and some didn't. But the neighbors didn't talk to the family much after that. Joe just learned to live with it, is all—the hushed whispers, the guarded stares, even the occasional outright accusation of fraud. This became his new world, as the creature sighting slowly began to redefine his very existence. Joe never forget what he had seen that day at Claybanks. And of one thing in regards to his sighting he is completely certain. Whatever that thing was, it will never, for the rest of his life, let him forget.

At the time Joe saw what he believed to be Sasquatch, he had no idea that there were other people in the world just like him. As a small-town kid, he couldn't possibly have known that fleeting encounters with unexplained phenomena such as Bigfoot had altered countless human lives throughout history. After the sighting, he was just a typical victim, struggling in isolation to cope with his experience, and with the grave repercussions it held for his life.

Joe also didn't know, at the time, that his creature sighting had happened in the heart of one of America's infamous "hotspots" of paranormal activity, that area of Southeastern Massachusetts that just a few years later would gain international renown in paranormal circles as the Bridgewater Triangle.

Years later, as Joe desperately sought answers to his burning questions regarding what he had seen at Claybanks, he would learn much more about the place that the Wampanoags referred to as the "Place Where the Spirits Dwell." DeAndrade would ultimately even explore its mysteries with his own paramilitary expedition team, which he modeled loosely after the dashing style of Miguel Corte Real and the other brave Portuguese explorers of old. But unfortunately for this young, troubled soul seeking answers, all of that lay years in the future.

After the sighting, Joe, a person of above-average intelligence, rationally worked his way through all possible explanations. Had it been a prank? Was somebody—perhaps Miram—pulling his leg? Joe couldn't say why, exactly, but he felt strongly that whatever he had seen was real, at least "real" in the sense that it hadn't been someone dressed up in a Sasquatch suit attempting to make a fool of him. Joe did briefly consider the fact that at the time of his sighting, a homeless black man was rumored to be living in the woods at Claybanks. But he quickly dismissed the idea that he had somehow mistaken this man for the creature as ridiculous. Nobody was as big as that thing was, he reasoned.

So, if it was not a hoax, then what was it? The obvious answer was that it was an animal of some kind—maybe a bear? But Joe had gotten a good enough look at the creature to know it was no bear, that it had to be something else. So was it, as Miram said, a Sasquatch? A Bigfoot?

In Bridgewater?! Joe didn't know a whole lot about Bigfoot at the time, but he had enough sense to know that his little New England town was not the ideal habitat for such a creature.

Modern Bridgewater was essentially a suburb, albeit one that included part of the Hockomock Swamp, but even this trackless wetland was minuscule compared to the vast natural environments in the West, such as the Cascades, where Bigfoot are typically reported.

And if what he had seen was a living, flesh-and-blood animal, then there was one question in particular that Joe could not answer to his satisfaction, and that was how it could possibly find enough to eat. For that matter, how could any creature that large—even a bear—survive for long around Claybanks? In a similar vein, Joe also questioned how such a large creature could stay hidden for so long in such a heavily populated environment. Both of these were valid questions that others, upon hearing his tale, would ask as well.

Later on, Joe's initial concerns about food and habitat availability posed less of a dilemma for him. Through his research, he learned that the Hockomock, at 17,000 acres, is one of the largest wetlands in New England. With its vast supply of cattails, berries, and other prime food sources, it acts as a veritable supermarket for wildlife. That meant that tribes of Bigfoot could probably survive in there just off the edible water plants, not to mention the immense deer herd. Joe also learned, from others who knew the Hock's complex geography of wetlands and woods intimately, the local maxim: "Anything could hide in there."

Sometimes Joe thought that the creature was real, but not an animal, at least not in the traditional sense of that word. He wondered if these creatures might be the unfortunate progeny of human-animal sexual unions. He speculated that perhaps these "half-breeds" had been abandoned, perhaps out of shame, and left to forage along with their wild relations. Joe considered this idea seriously because somehow, the creature he saw didn't strike him as all animal, but partly human as well.

Then there was the possibility, which had seemed plausible after speaking with his mother, that the creature he had witnessed was not flesh-and-blood at all, but something entirely different. Some kind of vision, maybe, of a creature from somewhere else. Maybe, Joe reasoned, it had been something that had lived in the area long ago. Something prehistoric. Or maybe, it was something that lived there, in the Hockomock, but it was something that other people couldn't see. Like, in a different dimension kind of thing.

Joe knew that the dreams he sometimes had were not of the normal variety, that they contained elements of prophecy. As time went on, after the sighting, Joe would become significantly more cognizant of this aspect of his character, through the manifestation of multiple psychic and religious experiences. Once, in his weekly Catholic prayer group, Joe would even lay his hands on a person possessed, and successfully cast out their demons.

But if this were the case, Joe pondered, if the creature was some sort of supernatural apparition…then *why* did he see it? Or rather, *why had he been allowed* to see it? What did it mean? There were just too many questions, though, and Joe, just a young man struggling daily with his dilemma, had no answers for them.

Joe DeAndrade was a good kid, who undoubtedly saw something very strange in his little neighborhood woods. He has this in common with thousands of other credible witnesses of unexplained phenomena across the world. These witnesses are good, honest people, who just happened to see something weird. But all too frequently, these witnesses are victimized by a society that has become wrongly convinced that those things that science cannot explain simply do not exist.

There are several aspects of the Claybanks sighting that conform to traditional Bigfoot sightings.

One thing that Joe didn't know at the time, but those schooled in the ways of these furry denizens of the forest do, is that the defining characteristic of the Claybanks area—its intricate network of ponds and rivers—would make it an attractive habitat for any Bigfoot. There is a common refrain about this creature that permeates Bigfoot literature: "It follows the creeks."

Another aspect of Joe's Bigfoot sighting that has strong universal parallels is the mysterious body print. People everywhere have grappled with similar conundrums in regard to Bigfoot prints. For example, in remote snowfields large footprints are often found that appear out of nowhere, and lead to nowhere. They just stop. Butt and other body prints are found dropped onto wide mud flats, seemingly out of the sky. Trails lead straight into bushes, and do not come out. This lack of context associated with trails is one of the elements of Bigfoot literature that appears over and over again. It is undoubtedly one of the most baffling aspects of this creature, and also one that has led many serious students of the unexplained to the conclusion that another kind of phenomenon exists, in addition to, or perhaps even to the exclusion of, Bigfoot.

This Bigfoot-like creature is of the paranormal variety, and is sometimes referred to as a "BHM" ("Big Hairy Monster"). Its red, glowing eyes are its primary characteristic, and the main physical feature that sets it apart from its biological cousin. This frightening apparition, though physically resembling its biological counterpart, is given to appearing and disappearing at will, among many other ultra-disturbing behaviors.

BHMs have been observed on countless occasions moving across muddy riverbanks and over snow, but searchers later find no tracks. None. As a matter of fact, no conclusive *physical* evidence of Bigfoot's existence, whether biological, BHM, or other, has ever been found, anywhere. No bodies, no bones, no hair, nothing. So the question becomes, what is it, exactly, that so many decent, credible people around the world are seeing? The answer, say supporters of the BHM theory, is obviously that Bigfoot *is not of this world.*

Although Joe initially believed that he had seen the elusive animal the Native Americans call Sasquatch, he would later wrestle endlessly with this idea that the creature was some sort of paranormal manifestation. Unfortunately, even his willingness to seriously entertain such an idea as this one would ultimately bring him no closer to discovering what it was he had seen that freezing April afternoon.

Joe DeAndrade will probably struggle with his personal dilemma for the rest of his days. And ironically, in the end his only solace may be that countless other Bigfoot witnesses around the world will continue to similarly struggle, and fail, to penetrate the enigma that we know as Bigfoot.

The Hockomock region has a reputation for unusually high numbers of brutal murders, suicides, and disappearances. One of the most tragic and heavily publicized of these cases was the murder of Mary Lou Arruda. On September 8, 1978, Mary Lou, a petite, fun-loving high-school cheerleader who had turned 15 just two days earlier, was kidnapped. She was taken to the Freetown State Forest, raped, and killed. Her decomposed body was found two months later, tied to a scrub oak, with her head laying next to her left foot. Investigators later said that Mary Lou was "either strangled or died of fright."

James Kater, a local man with former, similar convictions, was arrested for the crime, sent to jail, and never let out. Kater was tried four times. The court system named his trials "Kater I," "Kater II," "Kater III," and "Kater IV," just like horror movie sequels. Unbelievably, although Mary Lou was killed in 1978, James Kater was not locked up for good until 2007, when the U.S. Supreme Court rejected his final appeal, twenty-nine years after her death. To this day, both Kater and his attorney maintain that he is innocent of the crime. This is the perplexing, and oftentimes terrifying, story of the longest-running criminal case in the State of Massachusetts.

There are some things about what happened to Mary Lou Arruda that we know for sure. For example, on the day she was taken, the girl decided, on her way home from school, to get off the bus early at a friend's house to pick up her bike that she had left there the prior day, before going home. Mary Lou asked her brother, who was on the bus with her, to carry her books. She then got off the bus on Hill Street in Raynham, Massachusetts, went to her friend's house, picked up her orange ten-speed, and rode down rural Dean Street towards her house on Church Street. Meeting a friend, Helena McCoy, she stopped to chat briefly before continuing on alone. Shortly after that, she was snatched. Nobody saw it.

At the time that Mary Lou was taken, Joanne Arruda, Mary Lou's mother, felt a sick feeling in her stomach in the basement of her Dean Street home, where she was busy doing laundry.

She was the mother of two girls and two boys. Later that afternoon, the neighborhood paperboy, Patrick McCoy, Helena's brother, stopped by. The neighborhood where Mary Lou grew up is small, rural, and close-knit. The boy told Joanne Arruda that he had found Mary Lou's bike about a half-mile away, laying abandoned on the side of Dean Street. The kid had taken the bike and used it to complete his route.

Sensing that something was wrong, Joanne Arruda called the Raynham Police. Raynham Police Sergeant Louis Pacheco would become the lead investigator in the case. The officer who arrived at the Arruda home, a rookie named David Bonaparte, took her seriously and immediately launched a search. Bonaparte found tire tracks at the site where Patrick McCoy had found the bike, and as a result of his timeliness, was able to preserve them. These tracks were later used as a key piece of evidence to convict James Kater.

Although the Raynham Police started searching for Mary Lou Arruda almost immediately after she was snatched, and ultimately conducted a massive, intense search, they didn't find her. Her body was found by two boys dirt biking in the Freetown State Forest on November 11th, more than two months later.

On September 9, 1978, the day after Mary Lou Arruda was raped and killed, James Kater of Brockton, 32, married his 19-year-old girlfriend, and left for Canada to celebrate their honeymoon. By leaving Massachusetts without court approval, Kater violated his probation, as he had two previous convictions. He had met his teenaged wife in the Brockton donut shop that he managed.

On September 19, when he got back from his honeymoon, Kater heard that the cops were looking for him, so he went down to the Raynham station. A couple of months later, on November 28, seventeen days after they found Mary Lou's body, Kater was arrested for the crime, and charged with murder and kidnapping. The Raynham cops said they had their man. But in fact, the long, sordid, and mysterious case of James Kater was only just beginning.

The Raynham cops had no witnesses to the crime. So, they had to gather enough circumstantial evidence to convince a jury that someone was responsible. They had the tire track, which had a peculiar wear pattern, that they had found near the abandoned bike. And after they interviewed the locals, the cops found at least four people who would testify that they had seen a car like Kater's on Dean Street around the time that the girl was abducted. Kater owned a somewhat unique car at the time, a lime-green, foreign Opel with black racing stripes on the side.

Some of these witnesses stated that they remembered a partial plate number, the number "5," from the car. And some of them even said they saw a man who looked like Kater in the car. But that was mostly it. The cops continued to collect more bits and pieces of circumstantial evidence, but the accounts of the car witnesses were the best evidence they had.

The other half of the equation that led them to Kater, according to the Raynham police, was James Kater himself. He had two prior convictions, one of which was an admitted assault that had been carried out in a fashion similar to Mary Lou's. But in accordance with Massachusett's law, these prior convictions would not be allowed as evidence in a new case. So it came down to an alibi. Where had Kater been when Mary Lou was taken?

He had been working that day, Kater said, at the donut shop in Brockton, from the early morning to the afternoon. Later that afternoon, at around the time Mary Lou was snatched in nearby Raynham, he said he was out shopping for a blouse for his fiancé, whom he was preparing to join in holy wedlock the next day. Kater even produced a receipt from the local store where he said he bought the item. But there was no timestamp on the receipt. Kater also claimed there were several people who could testify to his whereabouts on the afternoon of September 8. But in the end, his alibi was far from air-tight, and the police knew it. They felt they had enough. They arrested James Kater for Mary Lou Arruda's kidnapping, rape, and murder.

KATER I

Although the Raynham cops had enough evidence to arrest Kater, they knew that convicting him would be a different story. Down at the station, there was an officer who had taken a mail-order hypnosis class, of the variety generally used to help smokers quit the habit. At some point, before Kater's first trial, he and the other Raynham cops decided to get all the car witnesses together, in one room, and hypnotize them, in an attempt to get them to remember more about what they had seen on the afternoon of September 8.

They were especially hoping, they later testified, of retrieving a full license plate number, or a better recollection of a man they said looked like Kater, from the memories of the witnesses. All that the witnesses collectively offered before the hypnosis was that the car they said they saw was green, and the numbers "5" and "3" were on the plate. Kater's license plate on the Opel was "563 AGQ."

Kater was put on trial in Bristol County Superior Court in New Bedford. He was represented by Attorney Edward L. Reservitz, a talented young defense attorney from Brockton, who would later become a prominent member of the legal community. During the trial, Judge James P. McGuire allowed the prosecution, Bristol County Assistant District Attorney Lance J. Garth, to put several of the witnesses that had been hypnotized on the stand. They testified to observations from the afternoon of September 8, including those they had remembered only after the hypnosis session.

Three women and one man testified that they saw a man who looked like Kater, driving a car that looked liked Kater's green Opel, on Dean Street just after the time Arruda stopped and spoke to her friend, Helena McCoy. Helena McCoy said she saw the Opel pass by her on Dean Street shortly after she had talked to her classmate. Albert Santos, a woodcutter from Lakeville, and originally a suspect himself, said he saw Kater's car as he drove down Dean Street.

Barbara Lizzotte of Raynham said she got a quick view of the driver of the Opel. Sheila Berry of Lakeville said she almost crashed into the Opel as it sped around a corner and passed her at high speed. Berry also said that when she looked in the rear-view mirror, she saw the number "5" on the license plate. Berry also testified to additional numbers of the plate, that she had remembered only after hypnosis.

Garth introduced evidence, including a nine-inch gash on Kater's Opel that he said was caused by the car hitting the girl's handlebar, and an unevenly worn tire on the car that an automotive expert said matched the track they had found near where the bike was located. Garth said this proved that Mary Lou Arruda, riding her bike, had collided with Kater's car, and he had then offered her a ride home. But instead of bringing her home, maintained Garth, Kater had taken her to the Freetown State Forest and raped and murdered her. Attorney Reservitz, however, introduced five witnesses, including Kater's teenaged wife, who testified on Kater's behalf that he had been somewhere else on the afternoon Mary Lou was taken. But it wasn't good enough.

On June 22, 1979, Judge James P. McGuire found James Kater guilty of first-degree murder and kidnapping, and sentenced him to life in prison without parole for the murder, and ten additional years for the kidnapping. Kater was convicted on circumstantial evidence only. Nobody had seen him and Arruda together. After his conviction, Kater tried to convince Judge McGuire that he deserved a retrial, to no avail.

Reservitz had his own ideas on how best to appeal the case, but Kater, who is an intelligent man, strongly disagreed with his approach, and abruptly severed relations with his attorney. Boston Attorney Jonathan Shapiro was subsequently appointed to represent him.

There was intense post-trial publicity in Bristol County. Kater was widely reviled for the horrendous brutality of the crime for which he had been convicted. He was sent to the Massachusetts Correctional Facility at Norfolk to serve his sentence. In 1980, after just around a year, he was abruptly moved to a nameless prison in California.

Lance Garth, when interviewed, declined to cite the reason for Kater's move, but he did mention that the new jail was "a very secure facility."

On March 23, 1983, the Massachusetts Supreme Judicial Court, reacting to an appeal by Shapiro, ruled that some of the evidence obtained under hypnosis that had been used to convict Kater should not have been admitted. The high court overturned the verdict and ordered a retrial. They said that no witness in Massachusetts may give testimony that was obtained through hypnosis, which was a landmark decision for the state. Shapiro was very concerned about all the publicity the case had received, so he asked for a change of venue for the retrial, based on his belief that his client could not receive a fair trial in Bristol County. His request was granted.

KATER II

Kater went back to court for his second trial on November 6, 1985, in Middlesex Superior Court in Cambridge, Massachusetts. Judge Robert S. Prince had heard motions for six months about which parts of the witness's testimony would now be admitted, largely based on Shapiro's requests to suppress certain evidence. It was sticky business. Prince ultimately ruled that in the new trial, the four main witnesses for the prosecution could testify to things they remembered before the hypnosis, but they could not be asked about or testify to anything they remembered from after it.

Prince impaneled a jury, and sent them to see several sites that would be discussed in the coming trial, including Dean Street in Raynham, the donut shop in Brockton where Kater had worked, and the Freetown State Forest. Garth told the jury they wouldn't see the scrub oak the girl had been tied to with two kinds of twine because they had cut it down and impounded it as evidence.

When the trial started, it was understood by all that the witness's recollections of things they remembered after the hypnosis session, like Berry's extra license plate digits, would not be allowed in court. But in his opening argument, which was repeatedly interrupted by Garth, Shapiro claimed that he would show, with the help of a psychiatrist who was an expert in hypnosis, that no memories obtained from a hypnotized person were reliable, and thus none of the prosecution's witness testimony should be taken into account. It's all about "confabulation," and suggestion, said Shapiro. It's safe to say that at this point, at least some of the members of the jury were becoming confused. What were they to believe, and not believe?

The problem with hypnosis, as it turns out, is that the results evoked by the seemingly magical process are, in reality, riddled with uncertainty. The hypnotism process has to be completed within strict guidelines if the results have any hope of being valid or believable. People who have been hypnotized are known to fill in gaps in their memories by making stuff up. This is what Shapiro meant by "confabulation," a ridiculous piece of jargon the use of which, in hindsight, he would probably have been better off avoiding. The other problem with using testimony from hypnotized witnesses, which is more widely understood, is that thoughts can easily be planted in a person's mind during the session. This "power of suggestion" can later cause the hypnotized person to accept these suggestions as their own thoughts.

Shapiro basically claimed in court that the Raynham cops had suggested things to the four car witnesses that they later had "remembered." Shapiro's expert witness, Dr. Martin Orne, who was the head of a Philadelphia research lab, testified that hypnotizing witnesses in a group setting was especially known to create the confusion caused by the power of suggestion. Orne said that nobody else should be in the room during the hypnosis, either, and the Raynham police had apparently treated the event like some sort of party. All in all, it didn't look good for the prosecution's key evidence. And Kater's two previous convictions were also still inadmissible, so the jurors who had been selected for Kater II knew nothing of them.

On November 8, 1985, two days after the trial began, the *Boston Globe*, who followed the case closely, printed an article by Mike Barnicle called "A Mother's Lament..." It included a letter to Barnicle from Joanne Arruda, Mary Lou's mother.

Arruda's letter included this:

> The scum responsible for this brutal act, James Kater, was arrested, tried, and convicted of Murder 1 on June 22, 1979. This person had a long record of being sexually dangerous.

Arruda's letter went on to question the need for the trial, and said that the judiciary was concerned more about the rights of criminals than the rights of victims. Shapiro was critical of the column, citing concerns that members of the jury may have read it, and on November 8th, Judge Prince delayed testimony to question all fifteen of the jurors. All of them stated that they had not read the piece.

By all appearances, the jury was under enormous stress. In the middle of Helena McCoy's testimony, the last person known to have seen Mary Lou Arruda, during which she strode over to Kater, pointed at him, and dramatically announced, "I saw you," the trial had to be adjourned when one of the jurors became ill. McCoy testified she had seen Kater and his green Opel, but Shapiro was quick to point out that at the last trial, Kater I, she had said she thought a yellow VW Rabbit resembled the car she had seen.

Sheila Berry testified that she had almost hit the green car with the black stripe and had seen Kater up close. At Garth's cue, Berry walked over to Kater, pointed at his chest, and identified him as the man she had seen. Then she raised her voice and said, "You are the man." Shapiro objected to the dramatics, and Prince had her statement stricken from the record. Berry also testified that her brother, who at the time was a part-time Raynham police officer, had taken her to Kater's donut shop and she had identified him there. She said that when he saw her looking at him, he ran into the back and didn't come out.

Joanne Arruda then took the stand, and crying, examined Mary Lou's purse and identified her orange bike. Arruda also testified that she had seen a green Opel with a black stripe pass her house, as she waited for her daughter to get home.

In the end, the jury heard more than three months of testimony. Shapiro delivered a four-and-a-half hour closing argument, one of the longest anyone involved had ever heard, during which he asked the jurors to "end the injustice and nightmare (Kater) has endured." He also focused on the unreliability of the witnesses due to the hypnosis, and Kater's alibis, which amounted to getting ready to be married and go on his honeymoon the next day.

Garth, in a two-hour argument, told the jury they had enough facts to convict Kater for the crime. On February 6, after both the Defense and the Prosecution rested their cases, the jury was sequestered to a hotel. On the 12th, they began their deliberations. On Saturday, the 15th, the jury asked Prince to let them see some handwritten notes that Helena McCoy had testified she had made the night of the day Mary Lou Arruda disappeared. Prince said they couldn't see them because they were not in the evidence as an exhibit.

On Tuesday, February 18, the jury told Prince they were at an impasse, and needed some guidance. They emphasized, however, that they wanted to continue. Prince essentially told them that another jury would be no better off than they, with no better evidence, so they should go listen to each other some more.

On Wednesday, one of them, Steven B. Martin, got sick of an unspecified illness, and they were delayed. Later that day, they announced they had finally reached a verdict. They had deliberated for forty-two hours over eight days. They had heard seventy-two witnesses over seventy days of testimony, and seen 109 exhibits. The Arrudas and their supporters prayed out loud as the exhausted jurors entered the courtroom.

Then jury foreman Linda J. Gunn, who had a picture of Mary Lou Arruda in her breast pocket, stood up and pronounced Kater guilty as charged. The Arruda clan broke into cheers.

Kater collapsed, and said, "Don't take my life from me. I've lost my life because I owned a green car."

Prince immediately sentenced Kater to life without parole, with more to come for the kidnapping conviction.

Lance Garth said it had been seven years of work, and that the verdict was just. Shapiro agreed with Kater. The man, he said, had been convicted based on the fact that he owned a green car.

A few members of the jury, including Martin, spoke to the press later. Martin said the long deliberations, one of the longest in Massachusetts history, had been very heated, so much so that he had gotten sick from the stress. They had spent an awful amount of time going over a large diagram of Dean Street, that had been heavily marked up by the witnesses to show where they had been and when. Many of the jurors seem to have been scared. Scared by the horrendous crime, scared of Kater, but mostly scared of the chance that he would go free, back to the street, possibly to hurt someone else.

Martin said that:

> the majority [of the jurors] were for guilty from the start of deliberations…but there were some people who were not really convinced because there were gaps in the [Prosecution's] story. You must remember, it was all circumstantial evidence, so there were some gaps. But we hung in there.

The group decided that, no matter what, they would not emerge from that room as a hung jury. It was like a long nightmare for them, but in the end, with tears, and joined hands, the jury came together and convicted the Monster.

KATER III

March, 1991. The Massachusetts Supreme Judicial Court overturned the guilty verdict in Kater II. They ruled that hypnotized witnesses could testify only about information they had remembered *before hypnosis.* This was stricter than their first ruling that had overturned Kater I, which said only that no evidence obtained *during* hypnosis could be used. To make things worse for the Prosecution, Judge Peter M. Lauriat, who would preside over the next trial, placed even greater restrictions on the case's evidence. In early January 1992, Lauriat reiterated that only the evidence the four witnesses had recollected before hypnosis would be admitted, and also *only that evidence obtained prior to hypnosis that the Raynham police had documented at the time.* Lauriat justified his documentation restriction on the fact that fourteen years had passed since the witnesses had provided their initial testimony, which he said meant that the cops' memories would now be unreliable.

Lauriat went still further. He restricted the testimony of four Raynham police officers and two other witnesses who had testified in the last trial that the witnesses had added practically nothing to their stories after hypnosis. In essence, Lauriat and the Massachusetts SJC were barring almost all of the evidence from the witnesses who had formerly claimed to have seen Kater and his green Opel. And Kater's past convictions would still not be admitted; the jury would be oblivious to them.

Joanne Arruda was furious. "I don't like any of the rulings. They make no sense," she said, from the liquor store next to her house where she worked. She went on to say, among other things, that, "The law's only on the side of someone who breaks it."

The prosecution appealed Lauriat's additional restrictions on evidence to the Massachusetts SJC, asking them to overturn the lower court's decision. Shapiro argued that limiting the cops' testimony to information they had recorded during the investigation was warranted because in prior trials, "police have testified with more detail than they were able to provide at earlier court hearings."

On June 9, 1992, the SJC said they would let Lauriat's decision stand. There would be no undocumented evidence obtained before hypnotism allowed in court. Garth maintained that despite the SJC's decision, they still had enough evidence to convict Kater.

The trial began on Monday, November 2, 1992. The district attorney in Kater III was Paul Walsh. He was assisted by Lance Garth as a special prosecutor. Shapiro, who had filed all the motions and appeals that had successfully barred the hypnotically-obtained evidence, once again defended Kater.

The attorneys and Lauriat spent an hour, without the jury, questioning Helena McCoy, who had by then moved to California. Lauriat was trying to determine what evidence she had given before hypnosis, and if that information had been documented by the cops. They had her look at the Opel, which they had down in the basement of the court building, sitting there with its paint fading.

McCoy, 30, who had been sixteen when Mary Lou Arruda disappeared, said she had seen a bright green car and a light blue car pass down the street after she had stopped to talk to her friend that afternoon. She later testified that in addition to seeing a man who looked like Kater in the green car that passed her, she had also seen a younger, heavier man driving the blue car.

The four witnesses took the stand, for the third time, and began testifying to events from fourteen years earlier. Some had trouble remembering, often saying, "It happened so long ago." Some lost their tempers with Shapiro as he questioned them persistently, trying to discredit them. McCoy acknowledged to him that in 1985, she had said that the green car she had seen looked like a VW Rabbit, and that she once had told the cops it looked like a Honda. Shapiro also presented a series of witnesses that testified to Kater's alibis.

With the strict restrictions on evidence, there wasn't a whole lot the witnesses could say. Three of the four witnesses who had been hypnotized were barred from presenting certain parts of their story. They couldn't say they had seen Kater's car, or that they had seen Kater. They couldn't identify him in court, because the SJC didn't believe the prosecution had proven the IDs were based on prehypnotic memory. All they could attest to was that they had seen a car that was similar to Kater's, and seen a man who looked like Kater, at the time Mary Lou Arruda was kidnapped.

In addition to the witnesses' testimony, an FBI agent testified that a tire track found near Mary Lou's body was "consistent" with the wear on one of the Opel's tires. And somebody else testified they had seen Kater's car near the Freetown State Forest on the day Mary Lou was snatched.

The trial ran for almost two months, and sixty-five witnesses were called. Finally, the jury was sequestered, and went into deliberations. On Tuesday, December 22nd, they reported they were deadlocked. They asked the judge to define for them the legal terms "beyond reasonable doubt" and "circumstantial evidence." Judge Lauriat advised them and told them to keep at it, just as Judge Prince had told their forerunners in Kater II.

Then something went badly wrong. On December 24th, Christmas Eve, after deliberating for fifty hours and entering their seventh day, Lauriat suddenly declared a mistrial. Kater III was over. Nobody really seems to know, exactly, what happened to cause Lauriat to end the trial. But it surely had something to do with Christmas. Shapiro, the defense attorney, made the motion for the mistrial. Garth, strangely, didn't object. Apparently, the jurors had asked some questions, questions about being sequestered, about being away from their families for the holiday. They may have been trying to figure out the best way to get out of there for Christmas. And that worried both attorneys and the judge. They probably figured the jurors were going to ignore evidence and the law, coerce the minority into giving in, and go home for Christmas. They had to call the trial.

Garth maintained they still had enough evidence against Kater to have another trial. Shapiro said that the Prosecution's case amounted to witnesses who saw a guy with curly brown hair and glasses, driving a green car near where Mary Lou had disappeared. He couldn't believe the jury had not decided the evidence against Kater was "all very circumstantial." Interestingly enough, subsequent interviews with two of the jurors, in January, 1993, indicated that at the time the mistrial was called, the twelve-member jury favored Kater's acquittal. They had believed, these jurors said, that the prosecution's case was not strong enough.

One of the jurors, Richard MacDonald, later said he was deeply troubled when, after the trial, he learned that Kater had twice before been convicted of killing Mary Lou, and that Kater had prior, similar convictions. Kater had previously done seven years in the Treatment Center for the Sexually Dangerous in Bridgewater, for the kidnapping and attempted murder of a 13-year-old girl in Boxford, Massachusetts, for which he had been convicted in 1969. The girl had been badly beaten, tied to a tree, and left to die, but she had slipped her bonds and gotten away. She had not been raped. Kater had been released from Bridgewater a few years before Arruda was killed.

When Lauriat declared the mistrial, members of the jury bowed their heads and started crying. Joanne Arruda sobbed in anguish. DA Paul Walsh blamed the Massachusett's SJC, and said he felt like sending them the enormous bill for the upcoming, fourth trial. There was a highly emotional press conference after the trial. Joanne Arruda also blasted the SJC, saying the "laws are too damn protective" of defendants.

Apparently referring to Kater's previous conviction in the Boxford incident, she also wanted to know "where the law was when he kidnapped a 15-year-old girl way back when, when he was supposed to be serving a sentence in prison and instead they sent him to Bridgewater to slap his wrists and let him back out on the street." According to Joanne Arruda, Kater "should have gotten the chair way back when."

As for Kater, he was "relieved, but disappointed over the outcome" of Kater III. Shapiro said the whole process had taken a great toll on Kater, because he had spent "fourteen years of his life hanging in the balance, swaying back and forth." Lauriat set a conference to schedule a fourth trial.

The Arruda's did not give up hope that Kater would once again be convicted. Her brother, Antone, 28, said of Mary Lou, "If there was a purpose for her to die, it was to save somebody else." For the Arrudas, it would be a very difficult Christmas.

KATER IV

The chances of gaining Kater's conviction were fading as quickly as the paint on his lime-green Opel, and the Prosecution knew it. DA Walsh, interviewed by the *Boston Globe* before the trial in February, 1993, said:

> After 14 years it is almost impossible for the Commonwealth to bring a successful prosecution. Memories are fading, evidence has deteriorated, some witnesses are just getting old…

There were high levels of public emotion throughout Bristol County. Shapiro alone spoke up for Kater, stating:

> I think the system fails when a person who has not been proven guilty spends fourteen years in prison and remains there today waiting for a fourth trial.

The Arrudas were extremely bitter from the mistrial in Kater III. Joanne Arruda, interviewed at the same time as the others, said, "It was a bright green car, an unusually colored car, and people noticed it." As she said this to the *Globe* reporter, she slid two cigarette butts, representing Kater's Opel and her daughter, towards each other across the red plastic tablecloth that covered her dining room table.

Sheila Berry was particularly upset that she had been barred from identifying Kater in the courtroom. She told the reporter that as she drove past Kater's car, "(Kater's) arm was on the steering wheel, and I saw a bulky object on the seat beside him."

Kater IV was scheduled to start in September of 1993. But then something significant happened. For some reason, after the mistrial, Shapiro withdrew from the case. Maybe Kater let him go. Perhaps Shapiro felt that Kater couldn't win. Maybe, he had just had enough of it all. Whatever the reason, Kater was assigned a new defense attorney, Public Defender Stephanie Page, and in August, 1993, the trial was pushed back to January, 1994 to give her time to come up to speed on the case.

Kater apparently wasn't happy with Page's appointment. In May, he had taken out the following, somewhat shocking ad in *Lawyers Weekly*:

> Seeking a new Court appointed representation. Criminal trial/post-conviction lawyers. 15 years at bar. High profile case, four SJC decisions. 1994, 4th trial. Will last 2-1/2 months…Must work cooperatively with clients. Reply ASAP to James Kater.

On January 11, 1994, Kater's sister posted his $35,000 bail, that had been set by Lauriat in December, but he was kept in jail. The Massachusetts Parole Board held him on an old parole violation. As it turned out, Kater had made a big mistake by breaking his parole on the Boxford conviction by leaving the state for his honeymoon. By this time, he had a new attorney, Joseph Krowski of Brockton.

On Monday, January 24, SJC Justice John Greaney ordered Lauriat to raise Kater's bail to $100,000 cash, which he did. Kater IV was set for April, and they weren't taking any chances.

On Tuesday, January 25, 1994, the *Boston Globe* published another article by Mike Barnicle that was related to the case, entitled "Dropping Our Eyes at True Evil." In the article, which in general deplores the fact that our society's concept of "fairness to all" has gone too far, Barnicle wrote:

> As he sits, undergoing mental tests, the Commonwealth of Massachusetts is about to grant a fourth murder trial to James Kater, who has twice been found guilty of torturing and murdering 15-year-old Mary Lou Arruda in 1978. Why there are only a few groups left that people feel bold enough to make judgments about: The obscenely rich, the chronically poor, Catholics, politicians and the police…we apply the false label of victim to all those who are killing us.

More than two-and-a-half years passed as the legal machine churned. Kater was now 50. He had been held in jail for almost eighteen years. Kater's attorney, Joe Krowski, maintained that Kater was innocent of the crime. He had filed a seventy-two-page brief that charged the Raynham police had "contrived evidence and botched the investigation." And he had told the press he was going to file new motions with Lauriat, but he didn't say what they were. Krowski revealed his cards on the eve of the fourth trial.

On October 15, 1996, at an evidentiary hearing in Middlesex Superior Court, Krowski asked Lauriat to outright dismiss the murder charge against Kater. There had been a cover-up, he said. Krowski's claims were disturbing. He told the judge that prosecutors had withheld evidence that implied that Mary Lou Arruda had been killed as part of a Satanic cult ritual, and by somebody other than Kater. "There was some egregious conduct here," the attorney stated firmly.

Krowski had discovered negatives of photos taken by Freetown Police Officer Alan Alves at the time Mary Lou Arruda had been killed, that had been stashed away in the case's evidence files. When Krowski asked authorities to develop them, he saw with great surprise that the photos were of a wooden cross, ten feet high, with a seven-foot crossbar. The cross had been found less than a mile from the site where Mary Lou Arruda had been tied by her neck with twine to the scrub oak. Krowski was claiming that the presence of the cross cast doubt on the entire case against his client. At the hearing, Alves said that he had never told the murder investigators about the cross, but later turned over the negatives to them. His rationale for not turning over the negatives immediately, he said, was that "it wasn't a crime scene."

There was more, said Krowski. In addition to the cross, Alves had found a pair of yellow shorts near the cross. And they were stained with blood. Alves was one of the two officers to see Arruda's body after it was discovered by the dirt bikers on November 11, 1978. He had been led to the cross by the hunter who found it, about a week after the body was found. When interviewed, Alves said the cross may have been used as part of cult rituals.

At the hearing, Alves stated that he did not believe the cross and shorts had anything to do with Mary Lou Arruda's murder. He said that although there was blood on the yellow shorts, there wasn't "the volume of blood" that would have linked them to the girl's death.

And he also said that the materials he found near the cross were about a week old, which would have placed whatever events that took place at the site at about the same time Mary Lou Arruda was found, or long after her death in early September.

At subsequent pretrial hearings, Raynham police testified that they attached "no importance" to the "many cases of people, mostly teenagers, practicing satanic rites." Krowski, however, continued to insist that the evidence meant the girl could have been sacrificed as part of a satanic ritual. At the time that Krowski brought up the cross, Judge Peter Lauriat was also considering another important issue with great bearing on the case. He was trying to decide whether he should admit evidence of Kater's former convictions into the upcoming trial.

The next day, on October 16, 1996, Lauriat ruled that he would not dismiss the case against Kater, which cleared the way for jury selection. The judge said that he thought the failure of prosecutors to turn over the photographs to the defense may have been only an oversight. But he did say he would admit the photos as new evidence in the upcoming trial, which encouraged Krowski and Kater.

Lauriat said he was still trying to decide whether to admit evidence from Kater's killing of the girl in Boxford. That girl's head had also been tied to a tree. Krowski argued that the cases were sufficiently different that the evidence from Boxford should not be admitted. In the end, despite Krowski's strenuous objections, Lauriat made a fateful decision. He decided to let jurors know about Kater's past conviction during the upcoming trial.

Kater IV began on November 4th, 1996, in Cambridge, a safe distance from the emotional furor that infused the case in Bristol County. Bristol Assistant DA Walter Shea told jurors he would produce evidence that Kater had abducted Mary Lou Arruda in 1978 and killed her in the Freetown State Forest, including the fact that many people had seen a car resembling his Opel, and that Kater's alibis for that afternoon just did not stand up. Ellie Cypher was also a prominent player in the case for the DA's office.

Krowski promised to reveal to the jury a dramatic cover-up that police had perpetrated for the last eighteen years in order to railroad his client, James Kater, who was innocent of the crime. He referred to the prosecution's case as "a suspicion set in concrete."

One of the main reasons Kater had been convicted twice previously for Arruda's murder was that he didn't have a good alibi. Prosecutors had proven that Kater had lied when he had testified he had been at a department store in Braintree that afternoon, buying a blouse for his soon-to-be-wife. Detectives had hunted down the checkout clerk, and proven that Kater could not have been at the store before 6:45 p.m. This would have given him plenty of time after knocking off work at the donut shop in Brockton at 3 p.m. to travel to Raynham, then Freetown, and back to Brockton by 7:30.

On Monday, December 16, Kater took the stand. He said he was "absolutely not responsible" for Mary Lou Arruda's death. Then, under questioning from Krowski, he proceeded to change his alibi story, the one he had told police eighteen years prior, the one that nobody had bought and caused him to be convicted twice. In his new story, Kater claimed that on the afternoon Mary Lou Arruda was killed, he had actually never left Brockton. He said he went home, then to a post office, then to an optical shop, and finally to a carwash. However, none of this new information could be corroborated. Shea hammered away hard at Kater, but he held up and stayed true to his new assertions. In fact, in an apparent attempt to appear folksy, Kater even cracked a few jokes.

Under Krowski's guidance, Kater also attempted to refute the prosecution's evidence of the unevenly-worn tire track found next to Mary Lou's abandoned bike that matched the Opel's, by stating that he had damaged the wheel bearing on his car when he ran off a paved road onto a dirt one on his honeymoon in Canada. And then he tackled the big one. The Boxford conviction.

Kater admitted to the jury that in 1968 he had kidnapped a 13-year-old Andover girl, assaulted her, and then left her tied to a tree in Boxford.

That girl got away, and later identified him to police. This looked very bad for Kater, especially since on November 22nd, veteran pathologist Dr. George Katsas had testified in court that in his opinion, Mary Lou Arruda had died of strangulation from twine that had been used to tie her to the scrub oak. Neither Katsas nor other pathologists had been able to establish the date that Mary Lou died.

"I took responsibility for it," said Kater on the stand, referring to the Boxford incident. "I took the punishment…I went into therapy to make sure it would never happen again."

Then Kater actually told Shea that the girl in Boxford had been tied to the tree differently than had Mary Lou. Shea insinuated that only the killer of both would know that. Kater was noncommittal.

Krowski focused on trying to use the cult evidence to convince the jurors of reasonable doubt. He described the huge wooden cross to them. He told them that at the base of the cross was a flat stone. On the flat stone had lain the blood-smeared yellow shorts, as well as leather thongs. And what's more, related Krowski to the transfixed jurors, the seven-foot crossbar of the cross had been decorated with twine. The same type of twine that had been used to tie Mary Lou Arruda's neck to the scrub oak.

Krowski produced a witness who testified that one night, the week before the girl had been taken, he and his girlfriend had witnessed some sort of strange ritual near the site of her death. He said they had seen twenty-to-thirty people filing into the Freetown State Forest, in the darkness, bearing torches.

The testimony in Kater IV took eight weeks. The jurors viewed 178 different pieces of evidence. The prosecution gave their closing arguments the week before Christmas. They mentioned Kater's prior conviction several times. Krowski objected to this and moved for a mistrial, but Lauriat denied it.

The jury went into deliberations, and after three days they were reportedly close to reaching a verdict. Then one juror came down with the flu, and was replaced with an alternate.

They started again from scratch. Five hours later, they reached a verdict. Late in the day on December 23rd, two days before Christmas, they announced that they had found James Kater guilty as charged.

The verdict was met with cries and cheers by spectators, all of whom had been thoroughly frisked for weapons before entering the courtroom. Kater slumped forward against a table, covered his mouth with a handkerchief, and shook his head in disbelief and denial. Shea later said he was satisfied that the jury had done the right thing.

"The family finally has some closure to their pain and suffering," he added.

Krowski reacted by saying he would file another appeal, based on Judge Lauriat's decision to admit "prior bad acts" evidence. He noted that the jury had been "instructed, instructed, and instructed on that prior bad act to only use it for a limited purpose. I just don't think they were capable of doing it."

On Christmas Eve, 1996, four years to the day after the jury in Kater III declared itself deadlocked, Judge Lauriat sentenced James Kater, again, to life in prison without parole for abducting, raping, and killing Mary Lou Arruda. He rejected Krowski's motion to delay the sentencing pending appeal, then allowed Joseph Arruda, Mary Lou's brother, to read the family's statement. Afterwards, Lauriat said:

> It was a long and difficult road this case has taken, a total of 175 trial days and five full appeals to the SJC. This was a particularly horrible and vicious crime. For the Arrudas this has been a long, gruesome ordeal. May their daughter rest in peace.

Krowski had some choice words for the jury.

> Most jurors came to this court prepared to support the family. Once that (the Boxford) evidence came in, it was a downhill slide. Reasonable doubt never came in because it was overwhelmed by emotion.

The defense attorney also reiterated that he would appeal the case, to the United States Supreme Court if necessary, because Kater was innocent.

Joanne Arruda, when asked about her thoughts on the chances of another reversal, responded this way: "I cannot believe the SJC could again be so stupid." Then, crying, she said, "There will always be an empty chair at the table, but it will be a better Christmas this year." Joanne had said earlier that she would have preferred Kater had got "the chair, but this will have to do."

Joseph Arruda affirmed again his belief that Kater would have killed again if he had been freed, and then offered, "I feel a lot better now, but there is a little girl out there who feels much better." In a final, parting shot at Kater, he concluded:

> We have had to read your name in the papers and look at your face on television. We
> hope that if we hear your name again, it will be on the obituary page so Mary Lou's spirit
> will finally rest in peace.

At his sentencing, James Kater was allowed to read a few words that he had prepared. They included the following:

> I will always be ashamed of that act (Boxford)—but I did not have anything to do with
> Mary Lou Arruda's murder. I am sorry for your loss, Mrs. Arruda, but it was not me...I
> am innocent.

And with those words, on Christmas Eve, 1996, James Kater was led away to prison.

On August 30, 2000, James Kater's conviction was upheld by the Massachusetts Supreme Judicial Court. It was not until April 16, 2007, however, that the U.S. Supreme Court rejected his final appeal. It had been twenty-nine years since Mary Lou Arruda was abducted. Stolen when she was 15, she would have been forty-four years old when Kater lost his last possible appeal. The case had proven to be one of the longest criminal cases in United States history.

"Certiorari" is the legalese term that means "the appeal process to the United States Supreme Court." The Court has the right to consider, or not to consider, any appeal they receive. Kater's decision came down in just two written words from the High Court. "Certiorari denied."

So now we must pose the obvious question. Did Kater do it? Did he abduct, rape, and kill Mary Lou Arruda in 1978? But why, you ask, should we even address this question?

Death row is full of people who didn't do it. DNA tests now prove that fact on a regular basis. Kater was convicted solely on circumstantial evidence. Contrary to some statements made by the press at the time, this is not typical of murder convictions. There is usually more evidence against the suspect; reports by family members of suspicious behavior, a prior bad relationship with the victim, *something*.

Not so in Kater's case. The tire track evidence was sketchy. There was no evidence found by the technician who searched the Opel. No hairs from Mary Lou Arruda, nothing. There was no relationship between the Katers and the Arrudas. It was what is known in crime circles as a "random pickup," and there were other random pickups in the Hockomock area around that time as well. And there was more than one person in the area at the time, known to police, that was capable of carrying out such an act.

Perhaps chief among them were the cult members active in the Freetown State Forest, the ones that Krowski described as carrying torches, that he pointed out could be responsible for sacrificing Mary Lou in a ritualistic killing. But in the end, what mattered was that people said they saw Kater's car. And he had a weak alibi. And the man had done some bad things in the past, and the decision was ultimately made to inform the jury of those things. So it is possible, at least, that James Kater didn't do it.

But there is, perhaps, an even better reason for posing our question than concern over whether a man lost his freedom because he was wrongly convicted of a crime. Joseph Krowski, his last defense attorney, said it after Kater IV: "…the real tragedy is that the real killer, or killers, is still out there."

If they are still out there, how many others have paid, and will pay, the price for convicting the wrong person? If they are still out there, did Mary Lou Arruda die to save somebody else, as her brother reasoned, or did she in fact die in vain?

Witches are people who actively contact spirits in the hope of gaining magical powers. Magic is the power of the spirits. Examples of magic include the ability to see events that will transpire in the future, shape-shifting, and healing. The ancient tradition of Western Ceremonial Magic, formerly known as Witchcraft, says that there are at least three dimensions in our world: the Physical, the Etheric, and the Astral. We are said to inhabit the Physical, the "lowest" level of existence, as does pretty much everything we see about us.

The Etheric layer in Western Ceremonial Magic is said to be the home of most beings we might, for our purposes, refer to as spirits. In this regard, it corresponds to the underground spirit world alluded to in other world mythologies. The Etheric borders on the Physical layer of existence in that concentrated Etheric energy can marginally impact the Physical, *such as in the form of footprints*, or thrown objects. We, as part of the Physical layer, can typically not see the creatures of the Etheric, unless they choose to make themselves visible to us, or we invoke them using certain obscure Magical methods, such as the ones used by shamans and cult members.

In addition to being granted powers directly from spirits, it seems that the act of simply encountering a spirit being can result in these powers being "brushed off" on the person that encounters it. Heightened intelligence is a common example of this phenomenon.

The two great enemies of magic are the Church and Science. When Christianity and the other monotheistic religions began to gain traction, around 2,000 years ago, they swept away the local religions like a flood. "There is only one God," the new priests told the Pagans, "not many. You must give up your lesser Gods."

Christianity also forbid its followers contact with spirits and the spirit world in general, warning that spirits are both deceitful and dangerous to Mankind.

Christianity's assault on magic and spirits, however, was ultimately unsuccessful. In places such as the remote fens of Ireland, Scotland, Norway, and other parts of the Old World, the people retained their beliefs in magic and their folklore. They may have been Christians, but like most of the indigenous cultures around the world today, they did not adopt Christianity to the letter. Instead, they blended Christianity with their traditional beliefs in lesser gods to create a hybrid faith that more practically addressed their world. Magic and folklore survived.

Ironically, although they forbid their followers from seeking magic, the stance of the Christian Church on it has always been that these powers from the spirit realm exist. Except for the fact that they don't call it "magic." The Christian Church says that if God bestows special powers on someone, such as Prophecy, He does so at a particular time and place, through the Holy Spirit, to be used for a special purpose, in order to glorify Him and benefit mankind.

The Church refers to these special gifts as "charisms," from which is derived the word "charisma," a word used to refer to lesser personality gifts. However, if someone seeks out, and obtains special gifts such as Prophecy on their own, *to further their own ends*, then this is not a charism, says the Church, but rather something Evil. Magic. Thus all "magic," is technically classified by the Christian Church as bad.

But although the new monotheistic religions failed to eradicate popular beliefs in magic, it had a potent new enemy: Science. The Scientific Revolution that arose around 1550 was ultimately successful in suppressing popular beliefs in magic. While Christianity had offered the spirits of the Etheric some quarter, Science did not. "These spirits simply do not exist," said the new order. "There is no proof."

During the core years of the Scientific Revolution, from about 1550 to 1750, skeptics of the new way were silenced, and those who held on to the old knowledge of magic and folklore hung on only in the most remote of areas. They were labeled "backward," and afraid of ridicule, effectively silenced. This trend is still very much alive today, manifesting itself in the similar treatments received by the thousands of credible witnesses of events that cannot be explained by the scientific establishment.

Witchcraft exists today in several versions. These versions seem to exist mostly so that witches can set themselves apart from other witches. The White witches, or Wiccans, believe that magic is part of Nature, and profess to use the magic imparted to them by spirits for only good deeds, such as healing or protection. Next on the sliding scale from Light to Darkness are the Black Witches, who use the magic they are given from the spirit world to do harm. At the far end of the Black Witch spectrum are the Satanists.

Satanists are the people that no one wants to talk about. After millennia of hiding in the darkness, they finally stepped into public view in 1966, with the official establishment of the Church of Satan. The goal of Satanists is to offend God. To achieve this goal, they do things such as torturing and sacrificing innocent people in ritual ceremonies. By offending God in such ways, these witches seek to gain magical powers from God's arch-enemy, Satan, previously known as Lucifer, and from the evil spirits of his realm.

Satanists worship the carnal, or the flesh. Their symbol is the pentagram, which is a five-pointed, upside-down star with a circle drawn around it. In other words, two points of the star face up, like horns, instead of the typical one point. As the sworn enemy of God, Satanists are the enemy of all Christians.

The Hockomock, "the Place Where the Spirits Dwell," is recognized as a special place by all those people who seek magic, such as Shamans and Witches, because the spirits, primarily evil spirits, seem to be readily available to them there. Psychics who profess to use magic for good purposes typically become terrified when taken into the Hockomock, demand to leave immediately, and refuse to ever go back. Satanists are drawn to the Hockomock like flies.

When you enter into the territory of Satanists in the Hockomock, you are typically aware of it, because they mark their boundaries well. The cult members don't want anybody there, and they let you know it. Sometimes, you see pentagrams spray-painted on boulders. Other times, you see dead, bloody chickens hanging from tree branches around their perimeter. And in some cases, you may come upon their actual ritual sites, complete with ritual objects, pentagrams on which they torture people, and God only knows what else. In any case, according to the local people around the Hock, who seem to know a fair amount about these things, if you are smart you get the message and leave well enough alone.

The Freetown State Forest, where Mary Lou Arruda's body was found, is composed of 6,000 acres of open forest and ponds. It lays in the southwestern corner of the Bridgewater Triangle, on the eastern border of the City of Fall River, Massachusetts. The forest, sandwiched between Massachusetts Routes 24 and 140, is just a ten-to-twenty minute drive from the cities of New Bedford, Taunton, and Fall River, which are collectively home to several hundred thousand people.

The Forest lays to the east of Mount Hope Bay and Mount Hope, which was formerly Massasoit's capitol. It spreads itself just to the east of the Pocasset Swamp, through which Philip, Weetamoo, and their warriors fled in the summer of 1675 to reach the vicinity of Dighton Rock, where they crossed the Taunton and headed for Nipmuc territory.

It lays in the former tribal territory of Weetamoo, the Wampanoag female sachem of the Pocassets. Weetamoo was originally married to Wamsutta, Massasoit's oldest son, who died in the hands of Josiah Winslow, whose father was Edward Winslow, the Pilgrim who first learned of the Indian's worship of Hobbamock. Weetamoo was Wampanoag royalty. Her younger sister was Philip's wife and the mother of his son, who was sold into slavery after the war. Weetamoo, as the later wife of the Narragansett Sachem Quinnapen, fought side-by-side with Philip and Tispaquin in the war, and was also the cruel mistress of Mary Rowlandson.

In 1658, the same year that the settlers of Bridgewater petitioned the Plymouth court for the Hockomock, Massasoit, Wamsutta, and Weetamoo sold thirty-six square miles of territory to twenty-six English colonists in what was known as the "Freeman's Purchase." This land became Freetown, Massachusetts. After the war, and after Weetamoo had drowned in the Taunton River and had her head cut off and sent to Plymouth, an Indian reservation composed of several hundred acres was established in Freetown for surviving, friendly Indians.

Ironically, the Indians awarded this grant of Weetamoo's ancestral land were those that had served so successfully under Benjamin Church against Philip and Weetamoo's forces. Church's friendly Indians were joined by remnants of the Assonets, the Indians who lived in the vicinity of Dighton Rock, and by other Indian survivors of the war.

This Indian reservation, which now lays within the boundaries of the Freetown State Forest, is called Watuppa, after the Wampanoag name for the two big ponds in the Forest. In the 1800s, a famous Wampanoag shaman named P.P. Perry lived on the reservation.

The Watuppa Reservation sits sandwiched on a small sliver of land in the far, southwestern corner of the Forest, between Route 24 and North Watuppa Pond, which now acts as the City of Fall River's water supply. The reservation is situated directly next to Fall River, which lays just to the west across Route 24.

In 1907, the City of Fall River took away most of the Indian's reservation land by Eminent Domain, in an ongoing attempt to set aside land to protect their water supply, North Watuppa Pond. Although the Indians were fairly compensated for this seizure, it bred bad feelings among them, some of which have endured to the present day. The Indians were left with 227 acres.

In the late 1800s and early 1900s, like Bridgewater's fictional Samuel Nash, the Freetown farmers gave up on their New England farms in favor of work in the city. In their case, the work available to them was in the burgeoning textile mills of New Bedford, Fall River, and Taunton that had been spawned by the collapse of the New England whaling industry. In the early 20th century, the state began buying up these abandoned farms, that were giving away to woodland, and eventually assembled the massive tract that would extend north and east from the Watuppa Reservation to become the Freetown State Forest. This state-owned land has been open to the public since the mid-1930s.

From 1935 to 1937, the 105th and 110th Companies of the Civil Conservation Core (CCC) worked in the Freetown State Forest. The crews built a network of dirt fire access roads and deep, round cement pools to hold water to put out forest fires, and stone bridges. They also built a fine longhouse building for the Wampanoags on the Watuppa Reservation.

Today, the Sate Forest is criss-crossed by fifteen miles of trails, and the old fire access roads and the cement pools, now moss-covered, murky, and seemingly bottomless, are still there. There's also an old rock quarry there, that was in use from the late 1800s to the 1930s, and a fine statue of a CCC worker, shirt off, shovel in hand, commemorating the work the group did there. The Forest is frequented by hikers, hunters, fishermen, environmentalists, and other outdoorsmen.

The longhouse is still there, too, on the Watuppa Reservation. Today, Watuppa, like Mashpee on Cape Cod and Aquinnah on Marthas Vineyard, is one of the centers of Wampanoag life. It is the last remaining sliver, the last stronghold, which Massasoit's people have retained in the Hockomock.

There is even a rock ledge there called Profile Rock that the Indians say looks like Massasoit. Watuppa is used for gatherings of the Wampanoag Tribe. It is also known nationally as a general meeting spot for Indians of all tribes, not just the Wampanoags. Watuppa is used by the Wampanoags for traditional ceremonial activities. Some of these tribal ceremonies are open to Massachusetts state officials, and others are not.

The Freetown State Forest, particularly the southern part, is another place in the Hockomock region, in addition to the Hockomock Swamp, where you can feel an extremely strong presence, a palpable sense of evil. In addition to being a beautiful natural resource and a spiritual center for the last of Massasoit's people in the Hockomock, the Forest is a place of extremely high numbers of violent crimes. It's a place where, after dark, at least, really bad things can happen to you. Murders, physical and sexual assaults, suicides, car burnings, and even animal mutilations occur in the Forest on a fairly regular basis. There is also a long history of fires there. One blaze in 1980 raged for two weeks, burning up 250 acres of land before it was finally put out.

The local police, among other groups, maintain that the geographical placement of the park, set as it is near three major cities, is the reason for the violent crime. In this sense, the Forest is similar to the Pine Barrens in New

Jersey, which have traditionally acted as an isolated natural "dumping ground" for nearby New York City criminals.

The southwest part, near Fall River, historically seems to be the Forest's most dangerous part. Mary Lou Arruda's body was found in that area. The cult site found by the Freetown Police investigating Mary Lou Arruda's murder less than a mile from her body, the one with the cross, the bloody yellow shorts, and other ritualistic objects, also lays in this area. This area has an established history of Satanic cult activity.

Why is it that the Raynham police attributed "no importance" to the known proximity of occult activity in the area where Mary Lou Arruda was found?

At the time, it was no secret to anyone that the Freetown State Forest was a primary base of Satanic cult activity in the Hockomock area. Could it be because they didn't take the activities of the cults seriously enough? Were these activities, as the police seemed to insinuate in court, truly just the relatively harmless actions of teenage kids?

Just over a year after Mary Lou Arruda was abducted and killed, in the period from late 1979 to early 1980, three young prostitutes from Fall River were brutally murdered in Manson-like cult slayings. These girls were tortured, raped, and killed by Satanists in ways that are hard for a normal person to even understand. Some parts of their dismembered skeletons were later found; other parts were not.

Three of the cult members were later convicted of the crimes and sent to jail. Witnesses in the murder trials testified that the leader of the cult regularly held Black Masses in the Freetown State Forest. Satan was summoned at these séances, and they sometimes demanded ritual sacrifice.

Many of the events exposed by the trials, and the people involved in them, were directly linked in numerous ways to the same area of the Freetown State Forest where Mary Lou Arruda's body, the cross, and the other paraphernalia were found, the area recognized for Satanic activity.

One of the three cult members convicted of these grisly slayings died in prison. Another is now free, as the result of cutting a plea deal with prosecutors. Some of the people involved in the killings, for various legal reasons, were never convicted. Nobody was ever even tried for the rape and murder of one of the girls. They're still out there. And so is Hobbamock.

HOME PLATE
MARCH 23, 1979 A.D.

Jerry Lopes is the consummate newsman. So much so, that he was once even involved in a major news story himself. On March 23rd, 1979, along with Steve Sbraccia, a fellow newsman, Lopes saw a UFO. And it wasn't just any ordinary UFO. They saw the mothership.

It all began when Jerry and his friend, Steve, decided to get out of town after a hard day's work on the reporting beat. They headed down to the Raynham Dog Track to blow off some steam. Both of them were young guys then, working as radio newsmen at WHDH Radio in Boston, Massachusetts. Jerry was covering City Hall and Boston Mayor Kevin White, as well as Beacon Hill, home to Governor Michael Dukakis. He also did the evening news, and was the anchor during the *David Brudnoy Show*.

Lopes had made himself available to WHDH twenty-four hours a day, seven days a week, to cover stories. Sbraccia worked as a morning drive reporter for the radio station, specializing in spot news. Steve was known as "the Everywhere Guy," because he seemed to show up at every story in Boston, day or night. At the time, it would have been impossible to find two people more in tune with the pulse of Boston news than Jerry and Steve.

That evening, after work, the two newsmen escaped the city and drove south down Route 24. Jerry was driving his black, two-seater sports car. As they were about to exit onto Route 106 west, Steve saw a bright light in the sky. He pointed it out to Jerry.

"Probably just a street light," commented Lopes.

But Steve wasn't so sure. They had been to the dog track that way a number of times, and he knew there was no bright light there. In 1979, Route 106, now festooned with gas stations, convenience stores, and stoplights, was rural and dark. The pair planned to take Route 106, which runs directly along the northern border of the Hockomock Swamp, a short distance west to Route 138, which they would then follow south a few miles to the track.

Lopes exited off Route 24 at Route 106. The pair drove right onto that tract of "valuable swamp and meadow lands" that the Plymouth court had granted to the settlers of Bridgewater back in 1662. Just a few miles to the east lay the spot where, in 1908, Prophett and Flynn had seen the mysterious "balloon" descend over the Stanley Ironworks. Unbeknownst to them, they were in the very heart of the "Place Where the Spirits Dwell."

"Hey, look, it's still there," said Sbraccia, as they halted at a stoplight on 106.

As the two sat at the light, they looked up into the sky intently. The light was positioned at about 10 o'clock. It looked to be about a mile or two away, and it was moving towards them.

"I'm getting out," said Sbraccia, with a hurried look at the traffic behind them.

Steve opened his door and leaned against it while looking up. Lopes, behind the wheel, was hanging halfway out his window trying to get a better view. Behind them was a whole line of cars, sitting stationary on 106, with their occupants staring curiously skyward. All of them watched as the lighted craft approached them. It was a perfectly clear night, and their view could not have been any better.

The giant ship came down and passed right over them. It was low, low enough, as Lopes remembers, that he could have hit it with a rock. Sbraccia's first impression was of the stars in a very large, arrow-shaped area of the sky overhead being blotted out by something that was obviously solid. At first the two thought it must be a plane. But then they saw that it wasn't shaped like a plane at all. It looked just like the home plate on a baseball diamond; five-sided, pointed in front, with a squared-off back.

The point was tipped slightly downward towards them, and there was a powerful white searchlight shining down from it in a triangular beam. There were rows of bright red lights along both sides of the ship, and a row of white lights dotted the back. "Holy Cow, Jerry," shouted Sbraccia, "look at how big it is; it's blocking the sky!"

Oddly enough, there was no noise, even when the craft was directly overhead, "low enough," as Jerry puts it, "when there should have been."

Lopes estimates that the craft was roughly the size of a C-130 cargo plane, the ones that look as big as a football field when they appear in the sky. He thinks it was flying at a low elevation, maybe "helicopter height," or even lower. Steve, on the other hand, struggles to this day with the size and height question.

"The problem was perception," he says. "I didn't know what altitude it was at. It was pitch black, there were no lights around there, and there were no reference points. But it *was huge*. I think that at the point where it was a rectangle, you could put four, maybe five 747s wingtip-to-wingtip across the width of the thing."

Steve recalls most vividly its bright white searchlight.

Interestingly, although Steve perceived the craft to be significantly larger than did Jerry, he also thinks its altitude was much higher—maybe 1,000-2,000 feet.

"But again," reiterated Steve, "*perception* was the big problem. We were looking, literally, straight up into the dark, and all we had (to judge by) was the stars being blotted out, and the shape of this thing as it went silently overhead."

Viewing the huge ship, Jerry didn't feel scared, but he did feel concerned. Very concerned. His first thought, after thinking he could hit it with a rock, was that this ship was like no plane he had ever seen.

"*That's not one of ours,*" he said to Sbraccia, as the craft passed directly overhead.

Sbraccia glanced at his friend with surprise, because he knew Lopes had served in the Air Force.

It wasn't so much the odd shape of the ship that was puzzling Jerry. It was the way it was moving. The thing had clearly demonstrated to him that it could fly like both a plane and a helicopter. It could zoom around fast, and then drop down and hover. Jerry knew damn well from his experience in the Air Force that there was nothing, at least in the U-S-of-A, that could fly like that.

As the immense ship passed silently over them, the two friends turned to each other and exclaimed in stereo: "What *the Hell* was that?!" It was, as Sbraccia now puts it, "sort of a life-changing moment."

Despite the excitement they had felt during the sighting, Lopes and Sbraccia were anything but elated as they drove away afterwards. The main problem both of them struggled with initially was that each of them were big-time UFO skeptics. They had heard all the whackos in the '60s, talking about how they had been to Venus. Both of the newsmen honestly believed that the people who saw UFOs were nuts, or perhaps drinking too much gin.

And there was another problem, as well. What on earth were they going to tell people? As reporters, they, better than anybody, knew how people who reported these things were perceived. As nuts. So, that night, barely paying attention to the dogs racing at the track, they talked the subject over at length, and finally decided that it would be best to keep their mouths shut.

But for Lopes, at least, there was more to it than that. He was genuinely concerned for the safety of the public, and he just couldn't let that part of it go. Sbraccia remembers that Lopes was still worried about that part six months later. That's because in his past life, Jerry had scrambled fighter jets against incoming enemy aircraft. Lopes was legitimately concerned because he had been professionally trained by the military to recognize and respond to airborne threats.

Jerry Lopes was an enlisted Sergeant in the United States Air Force for four-and-a-half years during the Vietnam War. He was what they called a "292 Ditty Bopper" in the Air Force Security Service. This means that he was trained to intercept enemy communications, and then call in F-4s or B-52s, depending on who they were copying, to blow up the enemy planes. He flew his 100-plus combat missions as a backend crewmember of a C-47 "Goony Bird."

Lopes became intimate with many planes in the Air Force. One of his favorites was the Lockheed SR-71 "Blackbird" spy plane that flew over major Chinese cities, taking great pictures, completely unbeknownst to the public. He watched the Chinese scramble their big jets after it, but it was no contest.

"That thing would go up and down the Chinese coast *so quick*," he remembers, the thrill he felt at the time still evident in his voice.

Jerry remembers other things, too, besides the planes. Like Nixon telling the American people that we had stopped the bombings, when Jerry knew we hadn't.

He knew because he was sitting there looking at them, every day. And so in 'Nam, Lopes also learned never to put anything past our government.

"So you see, I've witnessed all kinds of aircraft," says Lopes. Remembering that clear evening back in the spring of '79, he says, his voice breaking ever so slightly, "*That one* is not....*That one*...heh-heh...you know, it was very clear to me, that aircraft was *not in the U.S.A. fleet*, that I was aware of."

And so, after the pair's initial sighting, despite the fact that they decided the word was mum, Jerry didn't forget about it. Far from it. He actually started paying more attention, started going out at night, to try and see the mysterious thing again.

"I wasn't afraid," says Jerry, looking back on the incident, "I was curious."

And then, on the 26th, came the call from Sbraccia. He had seen the ship again. Out over the Mass Turnpike, in Newton. And then, almost unbelievably, Jerry saw it again too. On April 7th, two weeks after the initial sighting. He had been over Vin Maloney's house in Braintree, talking most of the night. Vin, whom Jerry describes as one of the finest radio broadcasters ever to work in Massachusetts, was his mentor. Jerry was the youngest guy on the 'HDH staff, and Vin was probably the oldest. The old master and the rising star had formed a strong relationship.

Jerry finally left Vin's at about 4:20 that Saturday morning. He looked up into the sky, and saw a light.

"It was a perfectly clear night and I knew immediately what it was. There was nothing else in the sky," said Lopes at the time.

It was the giant ship. Jerry rushed down to the Braintree Police Station, and dragged the three officers on duty outside.

"They all saw it," Jerry was quoted as saying at the time, "but when I suggested we drive over that way, they didn't want any part of it."

This time, the craft shot a puff of black smoke out the back as it zoomed silently away.

The officers gave Lopes the toll-free number to the National UFO Reporting Center (NUFORC). It was the same hotline number that the police have given out to everyone that sees a UFO since the mid-1970s, after the government officially gave up on tracking UFOs by ending Project Blue Book in 1969. Jerry, calm and collected, called in his report to the hotline. About a week or two later somebody, he recalls now, gave him a call back to ask a few questions. And that was it.

"Unfortunately," says Jerry, "there is no procedure for handling these cases. You report them to the police, but all they can do is give you the toll free number to make a report."

Now Jerry was even more concerned about the safety of the public. After all, Braintree lays just south of the City of Boston. He suggested that the police look out for the ship.

Jerry had called Steve immediately after his second sighting, and the pair discussed the situation once again. It was different now, because by this time, several other people had seen UFOs in the area as well. Randolph Police Sergeant Richard Mahan called in that Saturday morning from the neighboring town to report sightings of a UFO that he said shot sparks out the back, and was traveling in a southeasterly direction. It disappeared after it had been observed for five-to-ten minutes.

The Randolph Police had also received many calls late that Thursday night and early Friday morning about UFO sightings. As a result of these sightings, the two newsmen finally decided to come forward.

"It was because of the stigma," recalled Jerry, "you know, that people who see these things are nuts, that we felt it was our obligation to come forward and lend credibility to the whole thing."

Jerry talked about their sighting on Route 106 to the newspapers, on the radio, and around WHDH. The artist at the *Brockton Enterprise* made a drawing of the ship, based on his account, that Sbraccia says depicts it perfectly.

Lopes wasn't exactly thrilled with the reactions to the press coverage. "People do act differently," said Jerry. "I almost got a sense here…like, oh yeah, you saw something, what are you going to see next…Pink Elephants? It's funny how people react to that. It's almost like your credibility takes a hit."

But Jerry was a successful, up-and-coming guy. Nobody at the radio station hassled him, or tried to demote him back to being a general assignment reporter. And he didn't dwell on the situation personally, not for long, anyway. He just moved on. It was pretty much the same with Sbraccia.

"You know…I saw what I saw, I reported what I saw, I made the information, and myself, available to the officials, and I moved on. Deal with it, try and resolve it, or, you know, shuffle it under the rug. I saw what I saw, I stand by what I saw, some thirty-odd years later," Lopes says, with confidence and resolve in his voice. "I had nothing to gain by any of that. I had all to lose. You know, people could have said, this guy's a news guy…I'm not listening to him anymore, he's a kook!"

But even though the personal treatment he received after reporting the incident didn't bother Jerry too much, thirty years later it's obvious that the security issue associated with it still does. The first thing he asked when I called him about the sighting was: "What ever happened with that, anyway?" Meaning, "How were the reports of those UFO sightings resolved?"

Lopes still describes the presence of the giant ship as "very, very troubling."

"It's *no joke,*" he says with emphasis, as he recalls the reactions of those who scoffed at his sighting.

Lopes knew that the UFO Hotline was not a government organization, just a private group documenting the events that were called in. And no government official has ever approached him.

"It's almost like our government could care less," Lopes argues. "You could conclude from the seriousness with which the government handles this that *there is* something here. *They know it*—but they just don't want the American people to panic."

I never asked Lopes directly whether he eventually concluded that the UFO was from outer space. But I did ask him whether he thought it might be an aircraft from another country, perhaps something experimental. His reply was incredulous, and perhaps telling.

"What 'enemy experimental craft' would be over damn *Massachusetts*?!"

Steve Sbraccia, to whom I did pose the question directly, told me straight out that he had concluded that what he saw was from outer space. Steve reasons that nothing with that odd shape—like home plate—could have flown in 1979. Yes, he concedes, today there are some planes, such as the Stealth Bomber, that can maintain non-aerodynamic shapes and still stay in the sky. But they can't do it alone, without the aid of computers. There was just no technology like that available on Earth back in 1979.

The other thing that convinced Steve that the UFO was not-of-this-world is that apparently, it did not show up on radar. Within a day or two of the initial sighting over the Hockomock, Steve checked with the FAA and was told that nothing had been reported. This puzzled Sbraccia, because the ship should have been seen by Logan Airport's Air Traffic Control. The radar problem was also baffling to Lopes.

Today, Sbraccia is inclined to believe that the airship they saw in 1979 possessed stealth technology, similar to what we have today, which enables planes built using a special physical design and materials to display little or no radar image. He speculates that whoever built the advanced craft was surely years, perhaps centuries ahead of us, so it is quite probable that they would have had stealth technology, or something better, even back then.

Steve Sbraccia was at WHDH from 1978 until 1983. He went on to win an SDX National Award there for his courageous coverage of the Somerville Chemical Disaster, a dangerous event during which a wrecked tanker truck hemorrhaged toxic chemicals into the city.

He also followed the Massachusetts delegation to the 1980 Republican National Convention in Detroit, where he reported on the nomination of Ronald Reagan. As the lead reporter for Channel 5 (WCVB-TV), Sbraccia finished his successful career in Boston as one of the most recognizable faces on Boston TV, and one of the most prominent reporters in the Boston metro area.

Steve is still very much in tune with the pulse of news today. He now works as a reporter for NBC-17 (WNCN-TV) in Raleigh, North Carolina. When he called me to discuss these events, he was very noticeably working a police chase during which the suspect drove over the median strip. I could hear Steve calmly guiding the actions of the excited news crew around him when he politely broke away from our call. When the man being chased finally stopped the car and "bailed," Steve apologized and said he had to call me back. He later contacted me to say that the suspect had been apprehended, and thankfully, no one involved had been injured.

In regards to what he saw over the Hockomock, he says, somehow still in stereo with his old friend Jerry Lopes, "I stand by what I saw." Then he quickly adds, "That is something that will always stay with me."

For his part, after the sightings, Jerry Lopes proceeded to move straight to the very top of the American News scene. But before he did, he experienced three failed attempts to become Director of News at WHDH. The first time he tried, he wasn't ready to become Director, after just a year-and-a half at the station, but he wanted to send a signal to the management that he had higher aspirations than just being a reporter, running down politicians. They hired a guy that was inexperienced, and canned him after just a year. The next time around, they hired a big-name guy from KHJ in Los Angeles, a big-time city.

The local guys at the station, who knew where the bodies were buried, who knew one side of Boston from the other, didn't appreciate being passed over. The management ended up going into this guy's office not long after, on a Friday night, and told him to clean out his desk, "tonight."

The third time around, Jerry was really ready for the promotion. He was even running the News Department, as the Interim News Director. But they hired Ed Bell instead, from WHDH's biggest competitor, WBZ. But Jerry liked Ed, now Bureau Chief for the Associated Press, liked him a lot, so he couldn't get too bent out of shape. Lopes felt he had made a valiant run to become director, and in the end at least he had got the management to focus on hiring a quality local guy.

"Given the circumstances," recalls Jerry, "if it were Lopes making the determination, I might have made the same decision." Jerry finally realized that running WHDH just wasn't in the cards for him.

Fortunately, the folks at Sheridan Broadcasting in Washington, D.C. had attempted to recruit Lopes about six months prior, but he had politely put them off, citing the potential news director opportunity in Boston. Sheridan saw the news on Bell's hire in the trade publications, and called Jerry immediately with a job offer. Jerry left WHDH, where he had worked since 1976, in April of 1980 to become News Director of Sheridan Broadcasting Network in Washington.

He wasn't the only talent who left the Boston station. Over that six-month period, WHDH had three newsmen leave to become News Directors of major networks in the country, and Jerry was the last of the three. Dave Cook left to go to the RKO Radio Network, and Jim Cameron left for NBC.

When Jerry left Boston to run Sheridan Broadcasting Network in Washington, they were operating out of Mutual Broadcasting in Crystal City, Virginia, just across the bridge. It was before satellite technology, so they were operating off Telco telephone lines to disseminate their signal to radio stations across the country. The two networks shared this same line of distribution.

When satellite technology came in, Sheridan knew they had to get their own satellite distribution system. So in January of 1983, Sheridan Broadcasting moved their network from D.C. to Cocoa Florida, to become the first commercial radio network to be completely distributed by satellite.

The only other network using it at the time was National Public Radio (NPR). Sheridan had their own 15 Kilohertz, 24-hour satellite channel, so they could distribute their signal, uninterrupted, to radio stations across the country. The corporate headquarters for Sheridan was still in Pittsburgh, however, so they had made the Florida move planning to be there for only two to five years. In July 1985, two-and-a-half years later, they consolidated with their corporate headquarters back in Pittsburgh. Lopes has been in Pittsburgh ever since.

In 1992, Sheridan Broadcasting merged with National Black Network to become American Urban Radio Networks. Jerry stuck with them through all those years, and rose from Director of News there to President in 1997. He's been President at American Urban Radio Networks since then, though he has to pause to count them.

In the end, Lopes, who is still only in his 60s, went from being a morning news announcer to running the network. When asked about the talent 'HDH lost way back then, Jerry's not the least bitter.

"Well…an awful lot of talented people pass through the doors of 'HDH," he reflects. "And not just 'HDH, but a number of stations in Boston. Boston, for many years, has launched the careers of lots of [news] folks. It's got a great history of feeding the nation with very talented people."

One regret Lopes does have is that back when he saw the massive ship, we didn't have the technology that we do today.

"Back then it was just I-said-he-said-she said," he remembers. "Now, we can commit these kinds of sightings to video, to cell phones…you can lend greater credence to some of this stuff, back it up with video." He wonders whether the number of reports for UFO and other types of similar sightings will drop as a result of these technologies.

Jerry also wonders, sometimes, whether whatever it is that is at the source of such sightings realizes that we now have these kinds of technologies, and whether that realization would have any effect on the numbers of sightings.

The 1979 UFO sighting by Jerry Lopes and Steve Sbraccia, two highly credible witnesses, raises many important questions. Was it simply by chance that this object appeared to two such active newsmen, and that it appeared to each of them *twice*? Why, in the initial sighting, was the perception of the craft's size and altitude so different for both men? And why didn't the object appear on radar? Could it have been because the "ship" was never there at all, at least physically, but was instead some sort of illusion?

Perhaps the most troubling of all the questions raised is in regards to Jerry Lopes' central, lingering concern. What about public safety, our government's accountability, and any subsequent attempts to ultimately reconcile the strange sightings that he "officially" reported back in 1979? *Whatever happened with that, anyway?*

PHONE CALL TO THE NATIONAL UFO REPORTING CENTER (NUFORC)

JANUARY 2010

"Hello, I'm looking for an account of a sighting that was called in by Jerry Lopes in early April of 1979."

"Who are you, and why do you want to know?"

(Answered).

"I'm sorry, I don't have access to those records. I can only go back to 1993."

"Then where would I get them?"

"The only one that could provide that information is my predecessor, Director Gribbles."

"You are the Director?"

"Yes. There is only one person that picks up the phone here."

"And how might I get in touch with Mr. Gribbles?"

"Gribbles is in his 80s. Gribbles doesn't answer his phone. Gribbles doesn't use a computer."

"The man responsible for a database of almost twenty years of public UFO records doesn't use a computer?"

"That's correct. The only ones that can reach Gribbles are the State Directors. I'll give you their number. They might be able to reach him. But Mr. Gribbles doesn't answer his phone. Gribbles has left UFOs behind him. And I don't know what his motivation was, but I believe he destroyed all the records."

"Destroyed all the records?"

"I believe Mr. Gribbles either destroyed all the records or sent them to Mexico."

It was a dark winter's night in "the Place Where the Spirits Dwell." John Baker was alone in his canoe, drifting southward through the blackness, on the stretch of the Hockomock River that runs south across the heart of the swamp. Suddenly, the trapper became aware that something, somewhere, was watching him. And he noticed something else, something very odd. The familiar animal noises of the night-time swamp, the squeaks, the rustles, the hoots, had all stopped. Everything was deathly quiet. As an experienced woodsman, Baker knew damn well what that meant. Something was wrong out there.

Baker felt a strong presence. Then he heard something walking heavily on the bank, paralleling him as he drifted slowly down the river. With its every step, it was crashing loudly through the thick layer of ice that covered the pools of the frozen swamp around him. John could clearly tell from its gait that whatever it was, it was moving on two legs.

"Something was following me and I knew it was big," Baker later recalled. "So I took the boat down a small creek to a dry hill and kept it moving."

Then, still watching him, the thing came right down the bank of the narrow creek, came in very close, and passed right by him. Then it was gone. John never got a good look at it. But he knew nonetheless that it was huge, and he felt very afraid.

"My heart was up in my throat," recalled the veteran trapper. "You know what I mean. I knew it wasn't a human because when it passed by me I could smell it. It smelled like skunk—musty and dirty. Like it lived in the dirt."

In 1998, Ed Haywood, a *Boston Herald* reporter, had some rare free time, so his boss sent him down to the Hockomock for a few days to investigate recent rumors of a "Hockomock Swamp Creature."

"It was one of the *funner* stories I did at the paper," recalls Ed with pleasure. Banging on random doors asking about the Swamp Creature, Ed was told by the locals to "go talk to John Baker." Ed found John at home, at the little house on the bend in the river, and they talked, out in the yard, about the trapper's strange experience fifteen years prior.

The account above is derived from Ed's article that resulted from that conversation.

Ed got the sense from the locals that John was a reputable member of the community. He also learned that Baker hadn't talked about his experience much over the years. At any rate, he sure wasn't a guy looking for publicity. But John did talk to Ed that day, and the trapper stuck by his original story.

"To this day, I don't know what it was," he told Ed, "but I know I saw it and it was out there."

Ed believed him. He told me that in his professional estimation, Baker "was a solid, credible witness."

After speaking with Ed, I decided the incident was credible enough to warrant an investigation of my own.

"It looked like *Battlestar Galactica!*" said Mrs. Baker, still shaking her head in wonder after all these years. That thing was *big*, with the lights and everything. It came right down, over there," she continued, pointing south directly over the roof of her house and into the Hockomock Swamp. Swiveling northwest, she pointed to a spot diagonally across the road. "The Easton cops were sitting *right there*, watching it. *They* saw it. And there was *no noise. None.*"

Incredibly, Mrs. Baker was talking about the UFO that Lopes and Sbraccia had seen in 1979. Her house sits about a hundred yards to the west of the traffic light on Route 106 where the newsmen sat and observed the craft.

"Nice place you have here," I commented lamely, mostly because Baker had caught me by surprise and I had no idea what else to say. That's because I hadn't come here expecting to hear about a UFO, never mind the same one witnessed by the newsmen. I was hoping to speak with her about the other mystery that her husband John Baker, now passed away, had experienced many years ago deep in the swamp. But I shouldn't have been surprised, because that's how things work in the Hockomock. The mysterious events that routinely occur there are somehow all intertwined together.

In one sense the Baker home is nicely situated. It is set on the banks of the Hockomock River in West Bridgewater, right where the river crosses under Route 106 and continues on its winding course through the Area of Critical Environmental Concern established by John Ames III's legislation in 1971. The Baker home, originally intended to be a general store, sits across the river from Wayne Legge's old white farmhouse, the neighbor who paddled downstream with Ames and Governor Sargent in a bid to raise awareness for the proposed legislation.

The Hockomock River sweeps around the Baker's modest old home in a pretty S-curve. The scene would be a peaceful, pastoral scene from New England's past, if only it wasn't for the road.

"It didn't used to be like that," commented Mrs. Baker drily, nodding at the busy traffic whizzing by on Route 106 just a few feet away.

It certainly hadn't been like that back in 1979, when Steve Sbraccia had guessed correctly that it wasn't a streetlight that he and Lopes saw as they exited off Route 24. Back then, when the mothership descended, the busy road out front of the house was just a quiet country road.

Mrs. Baker's late husband, John, had come from a long line of woodsmen. He had made his living as a muskrat trapper in the Hockomock Swamp. John had bought the little house on the river, that had originally been his grandfather's, because he wanted to follow in the footsteps of his father and grandfather, both of whom were trappers named John Baker. He could launch his canoe, loaded with his traps and equipment, right from the back yard of the house.

Baker ran his trap lines on the Hockomock River both to the north and the south of Route 106. To the south, Baker worked the stretch of river that crosses through the heart of the swamp under Montaup Electric's power lines on its winding, southerly course towards the Town River. It was the same stretch that Ames and Sargent paddled in 1971, pursued by the buzzing white helicopter loaded with newsmen.

In the 1970s and '80s, John worked the river every day from his canoe. He set the leg-hold muskrat traps on the runs in the undergrowth that led into the river, each trap set partly in, partly out of the water. The aquatic rodents would be trapped as they scrambled out of the water. "He knew right where they came out" recalls his wife with admiration. On most days, John would return to the house with seventy to eighty muskrats. There was money to be made trapping in Massachusetts, back then.

"When times were tough, you could make a living at it," recalled Mrs. Baker matter-of-factly. She now works in the medical industry.

Baker would skin the muskrats and sell their pelts. He would clean them, too, and put their guts outside in a barrel. Then a big luxury car would show up from Roxbury, in Boston, and the city folks in it would exclaim appreciatively over the entrails, and subsequently eat them with relish. John originally started cleaning the rats in the basement of the house, but his wife quickly put an end to that.

"John, you've got to *go outside* and do this," she told him, in her warm, laid-back manner, before booting him out of the house.

Back then Mrs. Baker used to work the trap line with her husband. She remembers fondly the wild beauty of the Hockomock River, and the mysterious animal noises that the two of them, working as a team, would hear around them at night in the swamp. She also recalls other things, that weren't nearly so pleasant. For example, Mrs. Baker still closes her eyes, squirms, and shakes her head vigorously when she remembers the death shrieks the trapped rodents let out in the darkness. John would dispatch the muskrats by knocking them over the head, with whatever it was he was using at the time to accomplish the task.

And Mrs. Baker also recalls, with unconcealed disgust, the backwoods camps that her husband would point out to her on the banks of the river, deep in the swamp.

"People were living out there, back then," she says, echoing Wayne Legge's recollection of the "kids" that had inhabited seasonal camps on the high pine island near his farmhouse during the same time period.

It wasn't so much the fact that people were living in such abject squalor that bothered Mrs. Baker. It was the kind of people they were. These people hung stuff up in the trees, evil stuff, around their makeshift camps, stuff that freaked Mrs. Baker out.

"You know, the dead…." she said, her voice trailing off, her hands floundering, her head shaking in denial of what she had seen. Whatever they were, they were too grim to discuss, those hung things, swaying in the river breezes on the tree limbs, back then in the 1970s.

And then there was the swamp itself. Mrs. Baker is a brave woman, and one who quickly shrugs off the idea of evil spirits. But in the midst of recalling those countless days spent in the canoe with her husband in the early morning darkness, her gaze turned towards the Hockomock and she suddenly went quiet.

"There are some places out there—*cold spots*—where you can feel something," she murmured at last.

John Baker, in addition to being a successful trapper, was highly respected as an outdoorsman in West Bridgewater and the region. He had a reputation as an accomplished hunter, having spent time pursuing big game out West, and also in Canada, mostly in British Columbia.

John probably knew the Hockomock Swamp, the guts of it, better than anyone living or dead, with the possible exception of a 17th century Wampanoag shaman. After all, he had been in there a long time. John's dad used to take him along into the swamp in the basket of his four-wheeler, recalls his son-in-law, Ed, *when he was just a baby*. John Baker was a modest, private guy, though, and he never bragged to anyone about knowledge of the area or his skill as a woodsman.

But he had a reputation nonetheless. Whenever the cops were chasing a suspect who fled into the Hockomock hoping to lose them, they would go to John's house. The cops went there because they knew John could find the fleeing suspect, no matter where they were, no matter how deep into that frightening dark morass they had ventured. And Baker never let them down. He always got his man. It would be interesting to know how many of those fleeing suspects actually thanked John for getting them out of there.

Thirty years is a long time to trap muskrats in a swamp. You get to know the place after that long. After the work of catching and killing the muskrats becomes second nature, you become intimate with the river, the highbush blueberry and swaying yellow reeds along its banks, the high pine islands, the deer, the coyotes, the fish, the birds, the bats, all the critters, big and small, that call the Hockomock wetland home. You even know what's moving down the riverbank towards you, as you drift along silently through the pitch blackness in your canoe, before it realizes you are there.

But John Baker didn't know what it was he ran up against that winter's night in the swamp in the early 1980s. That's because Baker, despite all his experience, had never seen anything remotely like it in the swamp, or anywhere else in the world, before. And as it turned out, he would never experience anything like it again. But that was just fine with John. After it happened, he hoped and prayed that he never would.

John Baker's chosen way of life came to an end in 1997, when Massachusetts voters passed the Wildlife Protection Act which banned the underwater use of leg-hold traps in the state. The use of leg-hold traps on land had been banned since 1975. John, and his fellow trappers in the state were out of a job, just like that. The days of trapping muskrat on the Hockomock River, an industry that had gainfully employed generations of the Bakers, were gone, probably forever.

Muskrats are large, wetland rodents, about two feet long including their long scaly tail, that typically weigh about three pounds. They love nothing more than to build vast tunnel systems in peaty marshlands like the Hockomock. They have dark, glossy fur, that until the decline of the fur industry was highly prized for both its durability and water repellency. About ten million muskrats a year were trapped for their pelts in the 1980s.

Muskrats are very good at making more muskrats. Females typically produce one-to-five litters per year, with as many as 11 young per litter. They tend to survive despite the ongoing destruction of their wetland habitats. Needless to say, the muskrat population exploded in Massachusetts after the 1997 trap ban put the local trappers out of business.

Ed, John's son-in-law recalls the passage of the Wildlife Protection Act with undisguised disdain.

"And they wonder why we have a coyote problem now," he quipped.

When I gave him a puzzled look, he added: "*They've got plenty to eat.* You can't trap any small animals in Massachusetts now."

The Massachusetts beaver population has experienced a similar population boom since the trap ban, resulting in serious destructive consequences to some developed landscapes.

John gave most of his muskrat trapping equipment to a friend, who moved out-of-state to Vermont to make a living. He successfully traps muskrats there today. Ed and Mrs. Baker later sold off John's remaining traps at a yard sale. His son-in-law, who knew John well, remembers with mixed feelings how they were purchased by folks who valued them simply as a historical curiosity.

When Ed Haywood interviewed John Baker in 1998, it was about a year after the referendum on leg-hold traps had been passed, the vote that took away his livelihood. Baker was just 48 years old. "But he was an old 48," recalled Ed thoughtfully. "He had a lot of miles on him."

Three years later, John Baker was dead. He died in the swamp, near his home on the Hockomock River. It was a tragic hunting accident, the details of which are somewhat murky. Wayne Legge, John's closest neighbor, still vividly remembers seeing all the police going in there, at night, to pull John out.

We will never know what it was that John Baker encountered on that dark winter's night deep in the swamp. If he believed he saw Bigfoot, he never came out and said it, at least not publicly.

He just wasn't that kind of guy.

FEBRUARY 2007

Fear. I had been searching for it in the Hockomock, and now, finally, I had found it. I had hiked in that morning well before dawn, alone, as I had several times before. It was the middle of a cold winter. I had chosen the winter to investigate the swamp because I knew there would be no disease-carrying mosquitoes there, and because I would be sure to find tracks. I was moving south over fresh snow, retracing my route back down the abandoned rail bed built so long ago by Oliver Ames, Jr., after following it north to Route 106. It was very cold that morning, and pitch dark. I moved quietly, with no light, attentive to the winter environment around me. I was within a mile of where John Baker had had his frightening experience some twenty-five years earlier.

The crashing started off in the frozen woods to my west, somewhere between me and Black's Creek, a stream that crosses under Route 106 and winds southward down into the swamp. Something deep in the woods was paralleling my progress. It sounded about 300 feet away. I kept moving at a steady walk, trying to see what it was, but the pre-dawn darkness was still too deep.

It was clearly moving on two feet, slowly and deliberately: *Crash!, Crash!, Crash!, Crash!* It didn't sound as if it was in a hurry, but nonetheless it managed to stay directly to my right despite the fact that I had quickened my pace and had the significant advantage of moving along an open trail.

At first I thought it might be a man, but then I realized, based on how loudly the ice was smashing, that it had to be something heavier. At that point I became confused, because I couldn't think of anything in the woods that big that moved on two legs.

I moved faster along the path, and managed to control my fear, refusing to break into a run.

It kept pace alongside me. At one point, becoming desperate, I stopped and squatted down, making myself small. I peered into the swamp, trying to make it out though the shadowy, dense stands of tupelo and swamp maple. But it was still too dark.

Then I resumed walking, not sure what else to do, expecting the worst. Finally, I reached the point where the path turned east, and the smashing receded into the distance, continuing along the path of the creek towards the south.

I paused for a moment, then, beside the old rail bed, staring at the large pockets of ice in the swamp beside it. I had to know. Walking over, I jumped onto a patch of ice. It was solid. Then I jumped higher, and purposely slammed both booted feet down hard as I hit. Despite weighing more than 200 pounds, I had no affect on the ice. I hadn't made the slightest crack. It was like hitting cement. In the rising light of dawn, I could see endless pockets of that same ice off to the west. It was then that I became truly afraid. I knew that whatever it was that had been paralleling me had to weight at least 400-600 pounds, perhaps much more. There was simply no way anything lighter than that could have broken through that thick ice with only its walking tread.

Later, safe at home, I did some research and discovered with some surprise that "Black's Creek" was a name traditionally given by the New England colonists to streams that were recognized areas of supernatural activity. There is one on Martha's Vineyard, for example, that has a long history of paranormal activity associated with it.

I don't know what I experienced that early morning in the winter woods, or whether it was the same phenomenon experienced by John Baker. But I am confident that it was no man.

Whatever was moving through the frozen swamp along that creek was massive. And I have no doubt that it was following me as I walked alone, through the darkness, in "the Place Where the Spirits Dwell."

REVELATION

The *Little Chief* ran next to *Hobbamock, his small legs churning hard to keep up with the loping dog. Hobbamock had manifested himself in the form of a black lab mix, a mutt with red eyes. His long pink tongue lolled out with thirst as the two unlikely allies made their way along the dirt access road beneath the power lines, each step kicking up dust. It was a hot, stifling July day in the Hockomock, and the pair was being harassed by a swarm of biting deer flies. They were moving too fast for the mosquitoes.*

The *Little Chief, clothed in toddler-sized blue jeans, t-shirt, and tennis shoes, saw the humans up ahead first.*

"Look there!" he shrilled. "In the river!"

The *black dog slowed to a walk, panted, and eyed with malice the small group that stood waist-deep in the Hockomock River, about 200 yards ahead. They were in West Bridgewater, just north of where the Hockomock River meets the Town.*

As the pair approached, they came to a green pickup that was parked haphazardly off to the side of the access road, near the banks of the river. On the back window of the cab was splashed an oversized sticker of a lunging, large-mouth bass, next to another that advertised "Harley Davidson Motorcycles." A bumper sticker proclaimed: "Don't Knock the Hock." There was a red table saw set in the bed of the truck, an orange plastic tackle box, and some freshwater fishing rods with red-and-white bobbers attached. A large blue cooler rested on the open tailgate, and beside the truck on the ground flamed a freshly-lit charcoal grill.

The *Little Chief glanced over as Hobbamock, still eying the people standing in the water, emitted a long growl, and then dropped into a low crouch.*

"Isn't it supposed to be the other way around?" the Little Chief remarked slyly, unable to resist a jibe at his cowering companion. The sweating cur's only response was a whimper before he leaped off the dusty road, horsed his way through a dense stand of waving reeds into the gray swamp maples, and disappeared. The Little Chief glanced nervously around before continuing on tentatively towards the river. In his experience, the only thing Hobbamock ran from was demons.

The *people in the river weren't fishing. His curiosity getting the best of him, the wizened little figure tucked his hands into the pockets of his blue jeans, and meandered unobtrusively down the bank towards the rushing water. It had been long before the Great Campaign had begun, since he had spoken to a Man, or at least a Man who was in a state other than sheer terror. The humans, five of them, were standing in a semi-circle in coursing, waist-deep water. They were grouped around the large, central figure of a man.*

The *man was huge, barrel-chested, with long, curly brown hair and an untamed beard. He wore waders with just a white t-shirt underneath, which was stretched tightly over bulging biceps. A handsome man with simple, likable features, he was speaking to one of the people, a heavy-set blonde woman. She was smiling broadly, as were the others, even as she lost her footing and splashed down awkwardly into the river. The woman was quickly lifted back to her feet by the happy giant.*

It was then that the Little Chief felt it, apparently much later than his evil companion had. An overwhelming feeling of Joy and Love. An inner warmth, a Goodness, such as he had experienced only once, in his childhood, which was so long ago now that he scarcely recalled it.

At this exact moment the big man looked up at him from the river and caught his eye.

"Well, hello there!" he roared, in a deep baritone voice. "Would you like to join us?" A broad grin split his tanned features as he added, "We could move closer to the bank!"

The Little Chief remained silent, still trying to come to terms with the memories from his youth that were now washing over him.

"Don't be shy now…it's a big river!" The heavyset blonde woman, and the younger boy and two girls with her smiled curiously at him. They were shifting about unsteadily in the current, trying to maintain their balance on the riverbed. One of the girls beckoned encouragingly for him to join them.

The Little Chief eyed their jocular leader steadily with his beady black eyes. The overwhelming tide of Joy seemed to emanate from him alone.

The Little Chief realized now, despite appearances, that this was no Man that stood before him.

"Are you Michael?" he ventured finally, with great trepidation.

"Speak up there, Little One!" roared the big man lustily from the river. "Don't be shy now!" The giant apparently did not possess the ability to speak in normal tones.

"I SAID," shrilled the Little Chief, more loudly now, "ARE YOU MICHAEL?!" The name had come to him from very deep in the past, from his childhood, when his father had been Chief, from just after the time the Others had come here to Earth, after they had fallen from Cautantowwit's Sky Kingdom.

"I am one not nearly so wise as he," replied the big man, suddenly sober. He eyed the Little Chief with renewed, kindly interest. "Say," he continued, "Don't I know you? Yes…yes…the last time I saw you, you were wearing buckskin, and wampum…but I recognize you just the same. You are the Little Chief, are you not?"

The wizened little figure expressed no surprise, and did not reply, only nodded cautiously in acknowledgement. For he was not at all sure with what he was dealing. And in the spirit world, ignorance is always a very dangerous thing. "Are you the Light?"

"I am not the Light. But I AM sent by the Light."

The Little Chief stared at him intently, his concern now turned to curiosity. "Then who are you?" he asked.

"I am the one that Men call the Baptist." Stepping forward and reaching the bank in just three huge strides, the man offered the Little Chief his soaking right hand, which was as big as a baseball mitt. *"I am John,"* he said, smiling.

Stunned, the Little Chief gazed up and attempted to shake the looming hand that enveloped his own. He was filled with awe as waves of Light coursed over and through his body. He felt simply wonderful.

"Now come, with us, for I have work to do."

Seemingly against his will, the Little Chief haltingly followed the Baptist into the river. The rest of the small group waded slowly in, nearer to the bank this time, to accommodate his stature. The humans smiled and laughed, and the Little Chief felt his tiny hands grasped by theirs as they formed once again a half-circle around John. The Baptist gestured at the boy, a teenager, who waded awkwardly forward. He wore a black concert t-shirt with "Kiss" emblazoned on the front, and his dirty-blonde hair was cut in a mullet. John, facing the current, held the boy about the waist, cupped his other mitt-like hand behind his neck, and gently dipped him backwards into the flow. Then, spluttering and drenched, the boy emerged. He was beaming with joy.

The Little Chief watched closely as John, after asking the small group to leave the river, turned away and made his way purposefully out into the middle of the flow. Standing with his massive arms draped out, palms facing up, he looked skyward and began to pray. Suddenly, the group heard a loud whistling, and a mourning dove descended straight down over the treetops in its chaotic landing pattern, and landed squarely on the Baptist's shoulder.

As the huddled group of onlookers watched from the bank, the water around John began to surge and well upward, as if boiling. Downstream, from the direction of Lake Nippenicket, great shrouds of mist and thick clouds began to rise off the surface of the river. And the onlookers could see that in those clouds were forms: writhing forms, tortured forms, sick, shivering, and wretched forms. They were the forms of demons. Some of them had no face, some of them had black faces, and some had faces with nothing but jagged teeth. Low moans came from the vapors, and terrifying screams accompanied the mists as they rose over the treetops.

The Baptist was wielding the Heat of Heaven to cleanse the hells that lay far beneath the Hockomock. His prayers ran deep, down into the underground springs where the shamans had dived, where those who seek to offend God are still diving, into the Spirit World, and down, further still, into those Hells that lay beneath it. And the Creator had opened those Hells.

The demons were driven back, far back, out of the Spirit World and deep into their Hells.

Freezing and blinded, as demons are wont to be when confronted with the Light, dragging themselves desperately away from the Light and the Heat wielded by the

Baptist, they were at last stripped of their evil power. The Great Campaign against Man was over.

By now, the Little Chief was staring in the direction of Nippenicket with a very frightened look on his wizened face.

"Do not be afraid," said the Baptist reassuringly to the group, as he strode back to the bank when the thing was done. "For you are all of the Light, and thus have nothing to fear." Even as he spoke, he gave the Little Chief a meaningful look, as if reinforcing his assertion.

Then the blonde woman, shaking with fear, grabbed John's arm. "John," she stammered, "tell us, please, why are you here with us now? Here, in this place?"

"I was sent by the Father to drive back the Darkness," replied the Baptist.

"But why here?" asked the Little Chief. "Why the Hockomock?"

"Because the Father is very angry," replied John, "with you and with Hobbamock. He is upset by your campaign against his chosen ones."

The Little Chief bristled at this reference to the special status of humans, even as he felt his blood run cold with fear.

"He will not have his children tortured in his brief absence," continued John.

"Brief?" thought the Little Chief, in wonder. In all his long years on Earth, he had not once heard of Cautantowwit's presence. Could it be that was going to change?

Then John laid hands on the members of the group, filling each of them with the Holy Spirit. The boy's eyes shone with wonder as he thanked the Baptist, over and again, while the other onlookers, filled with the Spirit, cried silently with Joy. The Little Chief was overwhelmed. He had never been this close to the Light, not since that day he had remembered from long, long ago, when God had sent Michael the Archangel to shepherd his fallen race to their purgatory on Earth.

The blonde woman turned to the Little Chief, and with tears in her eyes blurted out: "I have never, in all my life, been this happy!" Then, after retrieving a pack of cigarettes and staring at them thoughtfully for a moment, she tossed them into the river, and watched as they floated slowly downstream.

Her son gave her a look of shock.

"Don't need them anymore, Jimmy," she said. "Twenty years it's been, and now, I just don't need 'em."

The teenager smiled broadly. "That's great Mom," he said. "I'm happy for you."

John had been busy unloading Italian sausages and hamburgers from the blue cooler on the tailgate of the truck as they spoke. "LET'S EAT!" he declared, as unceremoniously as if they were tailgating at a football game.

As the sausages, accompanied by green peppers and onions, began to sizzle on the grill, the Little Chief rose unsteadily from a small tree stump beside the pickup, where he had been quietly sitting.

"Can't stay for dinner?!" the Baptist roared at him. "Well, I suppose you must be getting home…but be sure to tell your Little Ones to take it easy with their scary lights, won't you?! And for your sake, you had better chain those bounding beasties!"

The Little Chief just stared, and then nodded wordlessly at the grinning giant. "You will be leaving us?" he asked, after a bit, with sadness evident in his small voice.

"Ahh—YES," replied the Baptist, with apparent regret. "For this is not the only place that I must visit. As you know only too well, yours is not the only front in this uprising."

"And what will you tell the others?" asked the Little Chief curiously.

Rising up to his full height now, towering above them all, the Baptist replied solemnly: "I will tell them what I tell you now. I baptize you with water, but One who is far more powerful than me is coming. I am not worthy to untie the thong of His sandals. He will baptize you with the Holy Spirit and with Fire. He will judge the Living and the Dead. THE LIGHT IS COMING."

And then, the Little Chief ran away, his heart pounding, towards Lake Nippenicket. As he ran, he could hear the sounds of Christian rock and peals of laughter coming from the little group on the river. And he could feel something, too, as he ran, something new.

It was a sense of peace, and an absence of evil. Fear, destruction, and death had been washed away, at least for now. And all was quiet in "the Place Where the Spirits Dwell."

BIBLIOGRAPHY

GENESIS

Appenzeller, Tim. "The Big Thaw." *National Geographic* magazine, June 2007.

Braun, Esther K. and David P. *The First Peoples of the Northeast.* Bedford, Massachusetts: Moccasin Hill Press, Supported by Massachusetts Archeological Society, 1994.

Eliade, Mircea. *Shamanism: Archaic techniques of ecstasy.* Princeton, New Jersey: Princeton University Press, 1972.

Harner, Michael J. *The Way of the Shaman.* New York: Harper and Row, 1990.

Hartshorn, Joseph H. *Geology of the Taunton Quadrangle, Bristol and Plymouth Counties Massachusetts. Geological Survey Bulletin 1163-D.* Washington, D.C.: United States Government Printing Office, 1967.

Hoffman, Dr. Curtis and museum staff, personal conversation. Robbins Museum of Archaeology, Headquarters of the Massachusetts Archaeological Society, February 14, 2009.

Lindholdt, Paul J., edited and introduced by. *John Josselyn, Colonial Traveler: A Critical Edition of Two Voyages to New-England.* Hanover and London: University Press of New England, 1988.

Mitchell, Nahum. *History of the Early Settlement of Bridgewater.* Boston: Kidder and Wright, 1840.

Oldale, Robert N. *Cape Cod, Martha's Vineyard & Nantucket, the Geologic Story.* Dennis, Massachusetts: On Cape Publications, 2001.

Raymo, Chet. *The Path: A One-Mile Walk Through the Universe.* New York, New York: Walker and Company, 2003.

Raymo, Chet and Maureen E. *Written in Stone: A Geological History of the Northeastern United States.* New York: Black Dome Press Corporation, 2001.

Simmons, William S. *Spirit of the New England Tribes: Indian History and Folklore.* Hanover and London: University of New England Press, 1986.

DIGHTON ROCK

Brecher, Edward and Ruth. "The Enigma of Dighton Rock." *American Heritage* magazine, Volume 9, Issue 4, June 1958.

da Silva, Manuel Luciano. *Portuguese Pilgrims and Dighton Rock: The First Chapter in American History.* Bristol, Rhode Island: privately published, 1971.

Danforth, John. "The Legend of the Wooden House" (collected in the vicinity of Dighton Rock in 1680). As quoted in a letter by Greenwood in 1730. Also, Baxter, James Phinney, ("killed sachem" reference), New England Historical and Genealogical Register xli 414, 1887.

Delabarre, Edmund Burke. "Early Interest in Dighton Rock." Paper read by Mr. Albert Matthews, The Colonial Society of Massachusetts, 1916.

"Middle Period of Dighton Rock History." Paper read by Mr. E. B. Delabarre, The Colonial Society of Massachusetts, January 1917.

Recent History of Dighton Rock. Cambridge, Massachusetts: Reprinted from the Publications of the Colonial Society of Massachusetts, John Wilson and Son, 1919.

Haugen, Einar (translated and interpreted by). Voyages to Vinland: The first American Saga. New York: Alfred A. Knopf, 1942.

Jones, Gwyn. A History of the Vikings. New York, Toronto, and London: Oxford University Press, 1968.

Kendall, Edward A. "The Legend of the White Bird" (collected in the vicinity of Dighton Rock). Travels through the Northeast Parts of the U.S. in the Years 1807 and 1808.

Young, George F.W. Miguel Corte-Real and the Dighton Writing-Rock. Taunton, Massachusetts: Old Colony Historical Society, 1970.

COSMIC WAR

Forbes, Allan (compiled by). Other Indian Events of New England. Boston, State Street Trust Company, 1941.

Lepore, Jill. The Name of War: King Philip's War and the Origins of American Identity. New York: Alfred A. Knopf, 1998.

Mandell, Daniel R. King Philip's War: The Conflict Over New England. New York: Chelsea House, 2007.

Old Bridgewater Historical Society. Massacquoetnecut—the Original Settlement of Old Bridgewater. 162 Howard Street, PO Box 17, West Bridgewater, MA.

Old Bridgewater Historical Society. Indian Place Names in Bridgewater. Native American Documents Collection. 162 Howard Street, PO Box 17, West Bridgewater, MA.

Philbrick, Nathaniel. Mayflower: A Story of Courage, Community, and War. New York: Viking, 2006.

Salisbury, Neal. Manitou and Providence: Indians, Europeans, and the Making of New England 1500-1643. New York, NY, Oxford University Press, 1984.

Vanderbeets, Richard (editor). Held Captive by Indians: Selected Narratives 1642-1836. Knoxville, Tennessee: The University of Tennessee Press, 1973.

Weeks, Alvin G. Massasoit of the Wampanoags. Fall River, Massachusetts: privately printed, 1919.

Weston, Thomas. History of the Town of Middleboro, Massachusetts 1669-1905. Cambridge, Massachusetts: Houghton, Mifflin, and Company, The Riverside Press, 1906.

FRIGHT NIGHT

"A Mysterious Airship." The Bridgewater Independent, Friday, November 6, 1908, page 1.

"Balloon for Milwaukee." "For Those Who Cannot Afford Land Motoring There Is a Neat Little Motor That Flies Through the Air and is Ridiculously Cheap." "Duchess Aboard Airship."

"Wright Leaves for Dayton." "Farman Wins Height Prize." The *New York Times*, Sunday, November 1, 1908.

Forte, Charles. *The Book of the Dammed: The Collected Works of Charles Fort.* New York: The Penguin Group, 2008; first published 1919.

"Hovered Over Town." *The Brockton Enterprise*, Saturday, October 31, 1908, page 1.

"Mysterious Balloon Over Bridgewater." *The Brockton Times*, Saturday, October 31, 1908, page 1.

"Refutes Hot-Air Report" (Letter to the Editor). *The Brockton Times*, Tuesday, November 10, 1908.

Wells, H.G. *The War of the Worlds.* Boston: Paperview with Association with the *Boston Globe*, 2005.

GRASSY ISLAND

Delabarre, Edmund Burke. "A Prehistoric Skeleton from Grassy Island." *American Anthropologist*, New Series, Vol. 30, No. 3 [July-September, 1928] pages 476-480.

Johnson, Frederick and Hugh M. Raup. *Grassy Island: Archaeological and Botanical Investigations of an Indian Site in the Taunton River, Massachusetts.* Andover, Massachusetts: Phillips Academy, Published by the Foundation, 1947.

THE BRIDGEWATER BEAR

"Bridgewater Bear Eludes Searchers." *The Brockton Daily Enterprise*, Thursday, April 9, 1970.

"Dog Pack is Cornered after Wild Chase Through Streets." *The Brockton Enterprise and Brockton Times*, Thursday, February 12, 1970, second section.

"Indians' Attempt at Ellis Island Takeover Is Failure." *The Brockton Enterprise and Brockton Times*, Monday, March 6, 1970.

Nicolas, William K. Personal conversation. February 16, 2010.

"Tate Murder Witness Fears Black magic Spell May Be Cast on Her for Testifying." *The Brockton Enterprise and Brockton Times*, Saturday, December 6, 1969.

"West Bridgewater: Pack of Dogs Kill Angus Cow." *The Brockton Daily Enterprise*, Wednesday, April 8, 1970.

WONDER WETLAND

Ames, Oliver, Jr. "Personal Diary." Private collection. Used by express permission of the Ames Family, 2010.

Anderson, Kathleen S. *The HOCKOMOCK: Place Where Spirits Dwell.* Personal Notes, April 1988.

McEntee, Margaret M., Edmund C. Hands, Jeffrey E. Nystrom, Duncan B. Oliver, and Hazel L. Varella. *History of Easton, Massachusetts*: Volume II 1886-1974. Easton, Massachusetts: Published by the Lorell Press, Inc. for the Easton Historical Society, Inc., 1975.

Moore, Henry, Kathleen S. Anderson, Ted Williams, Paul T. Anderson, George Wood, and Russell

W. Buzzell (illustrator). *Hockomock: Wonder Wetland*. Publication made possible by a grant from The Fund for Preservation of Wildlife and Natural Areas and by donations from the Friends of the Hockomock, 1971.

Personal conversations with Wayne Legge, March 2010; Wayne Southworth Sr., April 17, 2010; and John Ames III and Sarah Ames, May 18, 2010.

"Water: Our Thirsty World." *National Geographic* magazine, Special Issue, April, 2010.

THUNDERBIRD

Downey, Tom. Personal conversation. May 12, 2010.

Ferguson, Diana. "Native American Myths." *Thunderbird and the Water Monster*. London, England: Collins & Brown, 2001.

SAFARI

Bloom, Jonathan. "SIGHTED: Morris the Cat on steroids." *The Brockton Enterprise*, April 4, 1993, pages 1 and 19.

"Lion Seen on Grounds of Bristol Aggie School." *The Taunton Daily Gazette*, Monday, July 10, 1972, page 9.

Polikoff, Shari. "No Sign of a Lion Despite 'Safari'." *The Taunton Daily Gazette*, Monday, July 17, 1972.

"Residents of Railroad Avenue Fear a Lion Loose in the Area." *The Taunton Daily Gazette*, Friday, June 16, 1972, page 10.

"Tracks in Dighton Those of a Lion." *The Taunton Daily Gazette*, Friday, July 14, 1972.

BLACK SHUCK

"Abington Killer Dog Still Loose." *The Brockton Enterprise*, Monday, May 3, 1976, page 1.

Bord, Janet and Colin. *Unexplained Mysteries of the 20ᵗʰ Century*. Chicago: Contemporary Books, 1989.

Clark, Jerome. *Unexplained!: 347 Strange Sightings, Incredible Occurrences, and Puzzling Physical Phenomena*. Detroit: Visible Ink Press, 1993.

Clark, Jerome and Loren Coleman. *The Unidentified & Creatures of the Outer Edge: The Early Works of Jerome Clark and Loren Coleman*. San Antonio and New York: Anomalist Books, 2006.

"Huge Dog Attacks and Kills 2 Corralled Ponies in Abington." *The Brockton Enterprise*, Friday, April 30, 1976, page 1.

"'Shoot to Kill' Is Order in Dog Hunt." *The Brockton Enterprise*, Saturday, May 1, 1976, page 1.

The Suffolk Literary Chronicle: A Collection of Miscellaneous Literature, and of Original and Selected Papers Relating to the County. Volume the First, 1838. *Suffolcisms. No. 7*. page 169, and *The*

Reporte of a Straunge and Wonderful Spectacle. Ipswich, England: Printed and Published by John King, County Press.

CLAYBANKS

DeAndrade, Joseph M. Personal conversations. 2006-2009.

KATER IV

Curtis, Mary Jo. *"Can't see the forest for the deeds."* The *New Bedford Standard-Times*, November 1, 1998.

Kandarian, Paul E., Paul Langner, Patricia Nealon, Ray Richard, Bella English, Zachary R. Dowdy, Sally Jacobs, and Richard Chacon. *Associated Press* and *The Boston Globe*: James Kater case coverage from January 25, 1980 to December 25, 1996 (90 articles, source—Newsbank, ProQuest LLC).

Krowski, Joseph. Personal conversations. December 22, 2009; Edward Reservitz, January 11, 2010; and Father Robert Edson, February 2010.

Myers, Andrew. "Justice Sometimes Slow to Arrive." Derry, New Hampshire: *The Derry News*, November 27, 2007.

Peck, M. Scott. *People of the Lie: The Hope for Healing Human Evil.* New York, New York: Simon and Schuster, Inc., 1983.

HOME PLATE

NUFORC personnel. Personal conversations. January 6, 2010; Jerry Lopes, January 9, 2010; and Steve Sbraccia, January 15, 2010.

"UFOs over Randolph? Some persons say yes!" *The Brockton Enterprise*, Monday, April 9, 1979.

IN THE DIRT

Hayward, Ed. "The Bigfoot of Bridgewater; Is it a man-beast or Hockomock crock?; Legend grows to monster proportions." *The Boston Herald*, April 6, 1998.

Hayward, Ed. Personal conversations. January 22, 2010, and John Baker family members, March 2010.

Pyle, Robert Michael. *Where Bigfoot Walks: Crossing the Dark Divide.* New York: Houghton Mifflin Company, 1985.

REVELATION

Proceedings of the 250th Anniversary of Old Bridgewater Mass at West Bridgewater Massachusetts.

Coleman, Loren. *Mysterious America: The Revised Edition.* New York: Paraview Press, 2001.

Greer, John Michael. *Monsters: An Investigator's Guide to Magical Beings.* St. Paul, Minnesota: Llewellyn Publications, 2001.

Kingslake, Brian. *Aqueduct Papers: Twenty Interviews with an Angel Concerning Life after Death.* North Quincy, Massachusetts: The Christopher Publishing House, 1970.

Moore, David R. *Images of America: Bridgewater.* Charleston, South Carolina: Arcadia, 2003.

Muscato, Ross A. "Tales from the Swamp: From Ape-like Creatures to Glowing Lights, Hockomock has Kept its Secrets for Centuries." *The Boston Globe,* October 30, 2005, page 1.

Rodman, Peter and Loren Coleman. "The Bridgewater Triangle." *Boston Magazine,* April 1980, v.72 #4.

Swedenborg, Emanuel. *Arcana Coelestia (The Heavenly Mysteries).* (1749-1756).

Swedenborg, Emanuel. *Heaven and Its Wonders and Hell: From Things Heard and Seen.* New York, New York: Swedenborg Foundation, Inc., Standard Edition, 1949. First published in London, in Latin, 1758.

Trobridge, George. *Swedenborg: Life and Teaching.* New York: Swedenborg Foundation, Inc., 1949.

The Bridgewater Book: Illustrated. Taunton, Massachusetts: William S. Sullwold Publishing, Inc., for the Old Bridgewater Historical Society, 1985). From two original books: *The Bridgewater Book* (published 1899) and *Bridgewater Illustrated* (published 1908).

"The Bridgewater Triangle file." Newspaper article collection of the Bridgewater Public Library, Bridgewater, Massachusetts 02324.

The Holy Bible. Revised Standard Version, Second Edition.

INDEX